Matplotlib for Python Developers
Developers
Second Edition

Effective techniques for data visualization with Python

Aldrin Yim
Claire Chung
Allen Yu

BIRMINGHAM - MUMBAI

Matplotlib for Python Developers
Second Edition

Commissioning Editor: Amey Varangaonkar
Acquisition Editor: Varsha Shetty
Content Development Editor: Mayur Pawanikar
Technical Editor: Prasad Ramesh
Copy Editor: Vikrant Phadke
Project Coordinator: Nidhi Joshi
Proofreader: Safis Editing
Indexer: Mariammal Chettiyar
Graphics: Tania Dutta
Production Coordinator: Shantanu Zagade

First published: November 2009
Second edition: April 2018

Production reference: 1200418

Published by Packt Publishing Ltd.
Livery Place
35 Livery Street
Birmingham
B3 2PB, UK.

ISBN 978-1-78862-517-3

www.packtpub.com

Cancer has taken away my grandfather, my aunt, and my friend, I hate cancer. This book is dedicated to the memory of my grandfather, ChiuKhan Chan, who thought I shouldn't study that much. May he rest in peace.

– Aldrin Yim

`mapt.io`

Mapt is an online digital library that gives you full access to over 5,000 books and videos, as well as industry leading tools to help you plan your personal development and advance your career. For more information, please visit our website.

Why subscribe?

- Spend less time learning and more time coding with practical eBooks and Videos from over 4,000 industry professionals

- Improve your learning with Skill Plans built especially for you

- Get a free eBook or video every month

- Mapt is fully searchable

- Copy and paste, print, and bookmark content

PacktPub.com

Did you know that Packt offers eBook versions of every book published, with PDF and ePub files available? You can upgrade to the eBook version at `www.PacktPub.com` and as a print book customer, you are entitled to a discount on the eBook copy. Get in touch with us at `service@packtpub.com` for more details.

At `www.PacktPub.com`, you can also read a collection of free technical articles, sign up for a range of free newsletters, and receive exclusive discounts and offers on Packt books and eBooks.

Contributors

About the authors

Aldrin Yim is a PhD candidate and Markey Scholar in the Computation and System Biology program at Washington University, School of Medicine. His research focuses on applying big data analytics and machine learning approaches in studying neurological diseases and cancer. He is also the founding CEO of Codex Genetics Limited, which provides precision medicine solutions to patients and hospitals in Asia.

Great pleasure to work with Allen and Claire. Also special thanks to Mayur and his team for making the writing process comfortable to us.

Claire Chung is pursuing her PhD degree as a Bioinformatician at the Chinese University of Hong Kong. She enjoys using Python daily for work and lifehack. While passionate in science, her challenge-loving character motivates her to go beyond data analytics. She has participated in web development projects, as well as developed skills in graphic design and multilingual translation. She led the Campus Network Support Team in college, and shared her experience in data visualization in PyCon HK 2017.

Allen Yu, PhD, is a Chevening Scholar, 2017-18, and an MSC student in computer science at the University of Oxford. He holds a PhD degree in Biochemistry from the Chinese University of Hong Kong, and he has used Python and Matplotlib extensively during his 10 years of bioinformatics experience.

Apart from academic research, Allen is the co-founder of Codex Genetics Limited, which aims to provide a personalized medicine service in Asia through the use of the latest genomics technology.

I feel honored to take part in this fantastic project. Special thanks to Mayur and Aldrin for leading the production process. Besides, I wish to thank my fiancée for her love and support. I am also grateful to be sponsored by the Chevening Scholarship, which is funded by the UK Foreign and Commonwealth Office (FCO) and partner organizations.

About the reviewer

Nikhil Borkar has also worked as a contributing author. He holds the CQF designation and a PG degree in Quantitative Finance from the University of Mumbai. He works as an independent fintech and legal consultant. Prior to this, he was with Morgan Stanley Capital International as a Global RFP Project Manager. He has worked on Quantitative Finance and Economic Research projects using R, Python, and Excel VBA. He loves to approach problems in a multidisciplinary, holistic way. He is actively working on Machine Learning, AI, and Deep Learning projects.

Packt is searching for authors like you

If you're interested in becoming an author for Packt, please visit authors.packtpub.com and apply today. We have worked with thousands of developers and tech professionals, just like you, to help them share their insight with the global tech community. You can make a general application, apply for a specific hot topic that we are recruiting an author for, or submit your own idea.

Table of Contents

Preface

Python is a general-purpose programming language that's increasingly being used for data analysis and visualization. Matplotlib is a popular data visualization package in Python that's used to design effective plots and graphs. This book is a practical, hands-on resource to help you visualize data with Python using the Matplotlib library.

This book shows you how to create attractive graphs, charts, and plots using Matplotlib. You will also get a quick introduction to the third-party packages Seaborn, pandas, Basemap, and Geopandas, and learn how to use them with Matplotlib. After that, you'll embed and customize your plots in third-party tools such as GTK+, Qt 5, and WXWIDGETS.

You'll also be able to tweak the look and feel of your visualization with the help of the practical examples provided in this book. Further on, you'll explore Matplotlib 2.1.x on the web from a cloud-based platform using third-party packages such as Flask and Django. Finally, you will integrate interactive, real-time visualization techniques into your current workflow with the help of practical real-world examples.

By the end of this book, you'll be thoroughly comfortable with using the popular Python data visualization library Matplotlib 2.1.x, and leverage its power to build attractive, insightful, and powerful visualizations.

Who this book is for

This book is essentially for anyone who wants to create intuitive data visualizations using the Matplotlib library. If you're a data scientist or analyst and wish to create attractive visualizations using Python, you'll find this book useful. Some knowledge of Python programming is all you need to get started.

What this book covers

Chapter 1, *Introduction to Matplotlib*, gets you familiar with the capabilities and functionalities of Matplotlib.

Chapter 2, *Getting Started with Matplotlib*, gets you started with basic plotting techniques using Matplotlib syntax.

Chapter 3, *Decorating Graphs with Plot Styles and Types*, shows how to beautify your plots and select the right kind of plot that communicates your data effectively.

Chapter 4, *Advanced Matplotlib*, teaches you how to group multiple relevant plots into subplots in one figure using nonlinear scales, axis scales, plotting images, and advanced plots with the help of some popular third-party packages.

Chapter 5, *Embedding Matplotlib in GTK+3*, shows examples of embeding Matplotlib in applications using GTK+3.

Chapter 6, *Embedding Matplotlib in Qt 5*, explains how to embed a figure in a QWidget, use layout manager to pack a figure in a QWidget, create a timer, react to events, and update a Matplotlib graph accordingly. We use QT Designer to draw a simple GUI for Matplotlib embedding.

Chapter 7, *Embedding Matplotlib in wxWidgets Using wxPython*, shows how you can use Matplotlib in the wxWidgets framework, particularly using wxPython bindings.

Chapter 8, *Integrating Matplotlib with Web Applications*, teaches you how to develop a simple site that displays the price of Bitcoin.

Chapter 9, *Matplotlib in the Real World*, begins our journey of understanding more advanced Matplotlib usage through real-world examples.

Chapter 10, *Integrating Data Visualization into the Workflow*, covers a mini-project combining the skills of data analytics with the visualization techniques you have learned.

To get the most out of this book

A working installation of Python 3.4 or later is required. The default Python distribution can be obtained from https://www.python.org/download/. The installation of packages is covered in the chapters, but you can refer to the official documentation pages for more details. A Windows 7+, macOS 10.10+, or Linux-based computer with 4 GB RAM or above is recommended.

Download the example code files

You can download the example code files for this book from your account at www.packtpub.com. If you purchased this book elsewhere, you can visit www.packtpub.com/support and register to have the files emailed directly to you.

You can download the code files by following these steps:

1. Log in or register at `www.packtpub.com`.
2. Select the **SUPPORT** tab.
3. Click on **Code Downloads & Errata**.
4. Enter the name of the book in the **Search** box and follow the onscreen instructions.

Once the file is downloaded, please make sure that you unzip or extract the folder using the latest version of:

- WinRAR/7-Zip for Windows
- Zipeg/iZip/UnRarX for Mac
- 7-Zip/PeaZip for Linux

The code bundle for the book is also hosted on GitHub at `https://github.com/PacktPublishing/Matplotlib-for-Python-Developers-Second-Edition/`. In case there's an update to the code, it will be updated on the existing GitHub repository.

We also have other code bundles from our rich catalog of books and videos available at `https://github.com/PacktPublishing/`. Check them out!

Download the color images

We also provide a PDF file that has color images of the screenshots/diagrams used in this book. You can download it here: `http://www.packtpub.com/sites/default/files/downloads/MatplotlibforPythonDevelopersSecondEdition_ColorImages.pdf`.

Conventions used

There are a number of text conventions used throughout this book.

`CodeInText`: Indicates code words in text, database table names, folder names, filenames, file extensions, pathnames, dummy URLs, user input, and Twitter handles. Here is an example: "Another parameter for tuning is `dash_capstyle`."

A block of code is set as follows:

```
import matplotlib.pyplot as plt
plt.figure(figsize=(4,4))
x = [0.1,0.3]
plt.pie(x)
plt.show()
```

When we wish to draw your attention to a particular part of a code block, the relevant lines or items are set in bold:

```
        self.SetSize((500, 550))
        self.button_1 = wx.Button(self, wx.ID_ANY, "button_1")
##Code being added***
        self.Bind(wx.EVT_BUTTON, self.__updat_fun, self.button_1)
        #Setting up the figure, canvas and axes
```

Any command-line input or output is written as follows:

```
python3 first_gtk_example.py
```

Bold: Indicates a new term, an important word, or words that you see onscreen. For example, words in menus or dialog boxes appear in the text like this. Here is an example: "Select **Qt** in **Files and Classes** and **Qt Designer Form** in the middle panel."

Warnings or important notes appear like this.

Tips and tricks appear like this.

Get in touch

Feedback from our readers is always welcome.

General feedback: Email feedback@packtpub.com and mention the book title in the subject of your message. If you have questions about any aspect of this book, please email us at questions@packtpub.com.

Errata: Although we have taken every care to ensure the accuracy of our content, mistakes do happen. If you have found a mistake in this book, we would be grateful if you would report this to us. Please visit www.packtpub.com/submit-errata, selecting your book, clicking on the Errata Submission Form link, and entering the details.

Piracy: If you come across any illegal copies of our works in any form on the Internet, we would be grateful if you would provide us with the location address or website name. Please contact us at copyright@packtpub.com with a link to the material.

If you are interested in becoming an author: If there is a topic that you have expertise in and you are interested in either writing or contributing to a book, please visit authors.packtpub.com.

Reviews

Please leave a review. Once you have read and used this book, why not leave a review on the site that you purchased it from? Potential readers can then see and use your unbiased opinion to make purchase decisions, we at Packt can understand what you think about our products, and our authors can see your feedback on their book. Thank you!

For more information about Packt, please visit packtpub.com.

Introduction to Matplotlib

1

"A picture is worth a thousand words." - Fred R Barnard

Welcome aboard to the journey of creating good data visuals. In this era of exploding big data, we are probably well aware of the importance of data analytics. Developers are keen to join the data mining game, and build tools to collect and model all kinds of data. Even for non-data analysts, information such as performance test results and user feedback is often paramount in improving the software being developed. While strong statistical skills surely set the foundation of successful software development and data analysis, good storytelling is crucial even for the best data crunching results. The quality of graphical data representation often determines whether or not you can extract useful information during exploratory data analysis and get the message across during the presentation.

Matplotlib is a versatile and robust Python plotting package; it provides clean and easy ways to produce various quality data graphics and offers huge flexibility for customization.

In this chapter, we will introduce Matplotlib as follows: what it does, why you would want to use it, and how to get started. Here are the topics we will cover:

- What is Matplotlib?
- Merits of Matplotlib
- What's new in Matplotlib?
- Matplotlib websites and online documentation.
- Output formats and backends.
- Setting up Matplotlib.

What is Matplotlib?

Matplotlib is a Python package for data visualization. It allows easy creation of various plots, including line, scattered, bar, box, and radial plots, with high flexibility for refined styling and customized annotation. The versatile `artist` module allows developers to define basically any kind of visualization. For regular usage, Matplotlib offers a simplistic object-oriented interface, the `pyplot` module, for easy plotting.

Besides generating static graphics, Matplotlib also supports an interactive interface which not only aids in creating a wide variety of plots but is also very useful in creating web-based applications.

Matplotlib is readily integrated into popular development environments, such as Jupyter Notebook, and it supports many more advanced data visualization packages.

Merits of Matplotlib

There are many advantages in creating data visualization with code so that the visualization streamlines into part of the result generation pipeline. Let's have a look at some of the key advantages of the Matplotlib library.

Easy to use

The Matplotlib plotting library is easy to use in several ways:

- Firstly, the object-oriented module structures simplify the plotting process. More often than not, we're only required to call `import maplotlib.pyplot as plt` to import the plotting API to create and customize many basic plots.
- Matplotlib is highly integrated with two common data analytics packages, pandas and NumPy. For example, we can simply append `.plot()` to a pandas DataFrame such as by `df.plot()` to create a simple plot, and customize its styling with Matplotlib syntax.
- For styling, Matplotlib offers functions to alter the appearance of each feature, and ready-made default style sheets are also available to avoid these extra steps when refined aesthetics is not required.

Diverse plot types

Often in data analytics, we need sophisticated plots to express our data. Matplotlib offers numerous plotting APIs natively, and is also the basis for a collection of third-party packages for additional functionalities, including:

- **Seaborn**: Provides simple plotting APIs, including some advanced plot types, with aesthetically appealing default styling
- **HoloViews**: Creates interactive plots with metadata annotation from bundled data
- **Basemap/GeoPandas/Canopy**: Maps data values to colors on geographical maps

We would learn some of the applications of these third-party packages in later chapters on advanced plotting.

Hackable to the core (only when you want)

When we want to go beyond the default settings to ensure that the resultant figure meets our specific purpose, we can customize the appearance and behaviors of each plot feature:

- Per-element styling is possible
- The ability to plot data values as colors and draw any shape of patches allows the creation of almost any kind of visualization
- Useful in customizing plots created by extensions such as Seaborn

Open source and community support

As Matplotlib is open source, it enables developers and data analysts to use it for free. The users also have the freedom to improve and contribute to the Matplotlib library. As part of the open source experience, the users get prompt online support from the members of the global community on various platforms and forums.

What's new in Matplotlib 2.x?

Matplotlib supports Python 3 since version 1.2, released in 2013. The Matplotlib 2.0 release introduced a number of changes and upgrades to improve data visualization projects. Let us look at some of the key improvements and upgrades.

Improved functionality and performance

Matplotlib 2.0 presents new features that improve user experience, including speed, and output quality, as well as resource usage.

Improved color conversion API and RGBA support

The alpha channel that specifies the transparency level is fully supported in Matplotlib 2.0.

Improved image support

Matplotlib 2.0 now resamples images with less memory and less data type conversion.

Faster text rendering

Community developers claim that the speed of text rendering by the `Agg` backend has improved by 20%.

Change in the default animation codec

A very efficient codec, H.264, is now used as the default, which replaces MPEG-4, to generate video output for animated plots. With H.264, we can now have longer video record time and lesser data traffic and loading time thanks to the higher compression rate and smaller output file size. It is also noted that real-time playback of H.264 videos is better than those encoded in MPEG-4.

Changes in default styles

There are a number of style changes for improved visualization, such as more intuitive colors by default. We will discuss more in the chapter on figure aesthetics.

For details on all Matplotlib updates, you may visit `http://matplotlib.org/devdocs/users/whats_new.html`.

Matplotlib website and online documentation

As developers, you probably recognize the importance of reading documentation and manuals to get acquainted with syntax and functionality. We would like to reiterate the importance of reading the library documentation and encourage you to do the same. You can find the documentation here: `https://matplotlib.org`. On the official Matplotlib website, you would find the documentation for each function, news of latest releases and ongoing development, and a list of third-party packages, as well as tutorials and galleries of example plots.

However, building advanced and sophisticated plots by reading through documentation from scratch means a much steeper learning curve and a lot more time spent, especially when the documentation is regularly updated for better comprehension. This book aims to provide the reader with a guided road-map to accelerate the learning process, save time and effort, and put theory into practice. The online manuals can serve as the atlases you can turn to whenever you want to explore further.

The Matplotlib source code is available on GitHub at `https://github.com/matplotlib/matplotlib`. We encourage our readers to fork it and add their ideas!

Output formats and backends

Matplotlib enables users to obtain output plots as static figures. The plots can also be piped and made responsive through interactive backends.

Static output formats

Static images are the most commonly used output format for reporting and presentation purposes, and for our own quick inspection of data. Static images can be classified into two distinct categories.

Raster images

Raster is the classic image format that provides support to a wide variety of image files, including PNG, JPG and BMP. Each raster image can be seen as a dense array of color values. For raster images, resolution matters.

The amount of image details kept is measured in **dots per inch** (**DPI**). The higher the DPI value (that is, the more pixel dots kept in it), the clearer the resultant image would be, even when stretched to a larger size. Of course, the file size and computational resources needed for the rendering would increase accordingly.

Vector images

For vector images, instead of a matrix of discrete color dots, information is saved as paths, which are lines joining dots. They scale without losing any details:

- SVG
- PDF
- PS

Setting up Matplotlib

Now that we have a comprehensive overview of the capabilities and functionalities of Matplotlib, we are ready to get our hands dirty and work through some examples. We will begin after ensuring that we have set up the Matplotlib environment. Follow along the steps discussed to set up the environment.

Installing Python

Since version 2.0, Matplotlib supports both Python 2.7 and 3.4+. We are using Python 3 in this book, which is the latest stable Python version. You can download Python from `http:/ /www.python.org/download/`.

Python installation for Windows

Python comes as an installer or zipped source code for Windows. We recommend the executable installer. Choose the right computer architecture for the best performance. You can call Python in the Command Prompt by pressing the Windows + *R* keys and typing `cmd.exe`, as shown in the following screenshot:

Python installation for macOS

macOS natively comes with Python 2.7. To install Python 3.4+, download the installation wizard and follow the instructions. Following is a screenshot of the wizard at the first step:

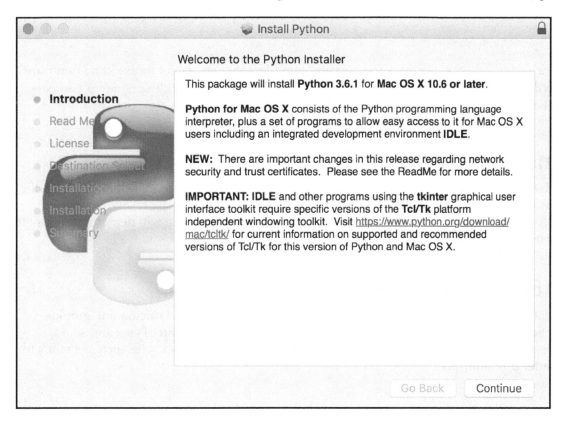

Some Python packages require Xcode command-line tools to compile properly. Xcode can be obtained from the Mac App Store. To install the command-line tools, enter the following command in the Terminal: `xcode-select --install`. Then follow the installation prompts.

Python installation for Linux

Most Linux distributions have Python 3.4 preinstalled. You may confirm this by typing `python3` in the Terminal. If you see the following, it means Python 3.4 is present:

```
Python 3.6.3 (default, Oct 6 2017, 08:44:35) [GCC 5.4.0 20160609] on linux
Type "help", "copyright", "credits" or "license" for more information. >>>
```

If the Python shell does not appear at the command, you can install Python 3 with `apt`, the Linux software management tool:

```
sudo apt update
sudo apt install Python3 build-essential
```

The `build-essential` package contains compilers that are useful for building non-pure Python packages. Meanwhile, you may need to substitute `apt` with `apt-get` if you have Ubuntu 14.04 or older.

Installing Matplotlib

Matplotlib requires a large number of dependencies. We recommend installing Matplotlib by a Python package manager, which will help you to automatically resolve and install dependencies upon each installation or upgrade of a package. We will demonstrate how to install Matplotlib with `pip`.

About the dependencies

Matplotlib depends on a host of Python packages for background calculation, graphic rendering, interaction, and more. They are NumPy, libpng, and FreeType, and so on. Depending on the usage, users can install additional backend packages, such as PyQt5, for a better user interface.

Installing the pip Python package manager

We recommend installing Matplotlib using the Python package manager `pip`; it resolves basic dependencies automatically. `pip` is installed with `Python 2 >= 2.7.9` or `Python 3 >= 3.4` binaries.

If `pip` is not installed, you may do so by downloading `get-pip.py` from `http://bootstrap.pypa.io/get-pip.py`, and running it in the console:

```
python3 get-pip.py
```

To upgrade `pip` to the latest version, do this:

```
pip3 install --upgrade pip
```

The documentation for `pip` can be found at `http://pip.pypa.io`.

Installing Matplotlib with pip

Enter `python3 -m pip install matplotlib` on the Terminal/Command Prompt to install. Add a `--user` option for `pip install` for users without root/admin rights where necessary.

Setting up Jupyter Notebook

To create our plots, we need a user-friendly development environment.

Jupyter Notebook provides an interactive coding ground to edit and run your code, display the results, and document them neatly. Data and methods can be loaded to the memory for reuse within a session. As each notebook is hosted as a web server, you can connect to notebook instances running at a remote server on a browser.

If you are excited to try it out before installing, you may go to `https://try.jupyter.org` and open a Python 3 notebook.

To install Jupyter, type this in your console:

```
python3 -m pip install jupyter
```

Starting a Jupyter Notebook session

Just type `jupyter notebook` in the console. This will start a Jupyter Notebook session as a web server.

By default, a notebook session should pop up on your default browser. To manually open the page, type `localhost:8888` as the URL. Then you will enter the following home page of the Jupyter Notebook:

You can choose to host the notebook on different ports, for instance, when you are running multiple notebooks. You can specify the port to use with the `--port=<customportnum>` option.

Since the release of 4.3, token authentication has been added to Jupyter, so you may be asked for a token password before entering the notebook home page, as shown in the following screenshot:

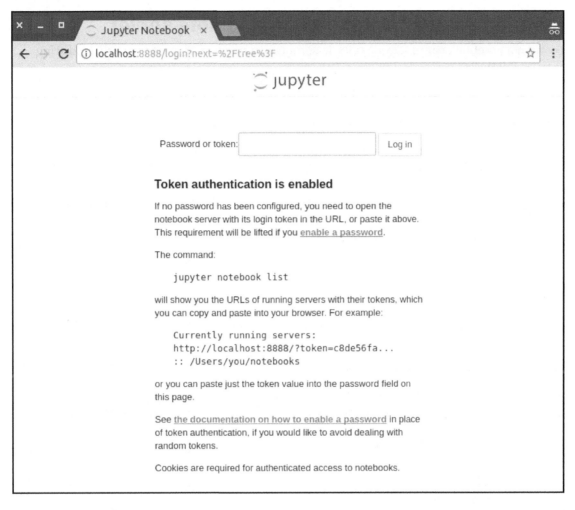

To retrieve the token, such as when visiting the running notebook from a different browser or machine, you may call `jupyter notebook list` from the console:

```
claire  jupyter notebook list
Currently running servers:
http://localhost:8888/?token=192bf3d3cf73190e795572c69374942cb7a54922a2175862 :: /home/claire
```

Running Jupyter Notebook on a remote server

To open a notebook running on a remote server, you may set up port forwarding during SSH, as follows:

```
ssh -L 8888:localhost:8888 mary@remoteserver
```

Then you may open the notebook again with `localhost:8888` as the URL.

When multiple users are running Jupyter Notebooks on the same server on the same port (say the default, `8888`) and each uses the same port forwarding, there is a possibility that your notebook content will be forwarded to another user who cannot read his/her own content without changing the port. While this might be fixed with later releases, it is recommended to change the port from the default.

To upgrade from a previous version, run the following command:

```
pip3 install --upgrade matplotlib
```

`pip` will automatically collect and install the Matplotlib dependencies for you.

Editing and running code

A Jupyter Notebook has boxes called **cells**. It begins with the text input area for code editing, known as the gray box cell, by default. To insert and edit the code do the following:

1. Click inside the gray box.
2. Type your Python code inside it.
3. Click on the play button or press *Shift + Enter* to run the current cell and move the cursor to the next cell:

```
In [4]:  import logging,sys
         print("Let's run some code.")

         print("Sure :)")

         n = 1+1
         print(n)

         print(Oops)

         Let's run some code.
         Sure :)
         2

         ---------------------------------------------------------------
         ----
         NameError                               Traceback (most recent call l
         ast)
         <ipython-input-4-54a3410c52d8> in <module>()
               7 print(n)
               8
         ----> 9 print(Oops)

         NameError: name 'Oops' is not defined
```

Once a cell is run, the relevant data and methods are loaded to the memory and can be used across cells in the same notebook kernel. No reloading is needed unless for an intended change. This saves effort and time in debugging and reloading large datasets.

Manipulating notebook kernel and cells

You can use the toolbar at the top to manipulate cells and the kernel. The available functions are annotated as follows:

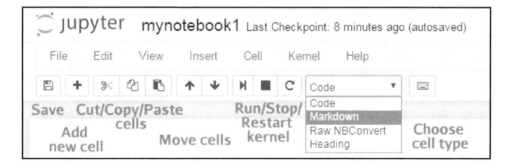

Verify your output amount before running a cell! A huge output stream doesn't usually kill your console, but it can easily crash your browser and notebook in a matter of seconds. This issue has been addressed since Jupyter 4.2 by stopping large output. However, it does not guarantee to capture all non-stop output. Therefore, readers are advised to exercise caution and avoid attempts to obtain large output results in a notebook cell. Consider slicing it for a glimpse or obtaining output in another file:

```
In [1]:  while 1:
             print("Stop me! >.<")

         Stop me! >.<
         Stop me! >.<
         Stop me! >.<
         Stop me! >.<
         Stop me! >.<
         Stop me! >.<
         Stop me! >.<
         Stop me! >.<
         Stop me! >.<
         Stop me! >.<
         Stop me! >.<
         Stop me! >.<
         Stop me! >.<
         Stop me! >.<
         Stop me! >.<
         Stop me! >.<
         Stop me! >.<
         Stop me! >.<
         Stop me! >.<
```

Embed your Matplotlib plots

Matplotlib is highly integrated into Jupyter Notebook. Use the Jupyter built-in *magic* command %matplotlib inline (set as default in the current release) to display resultant plots as static image output at each cell:

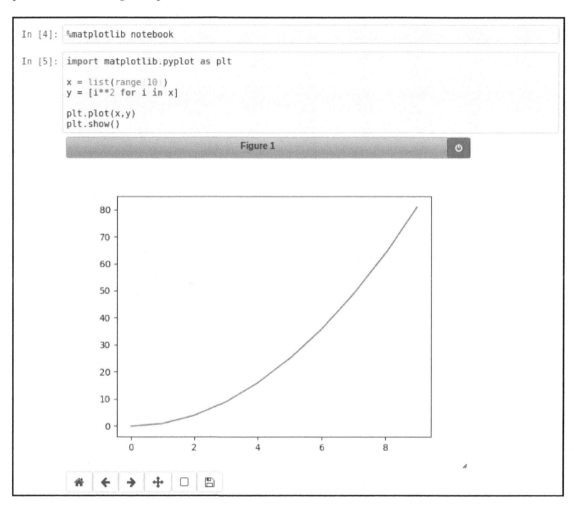

Alternatively, you can run a magic cell command—`%matplotlib notebook` to use the interactive Matplotlib GUI for zooming or rotating in the same output area:

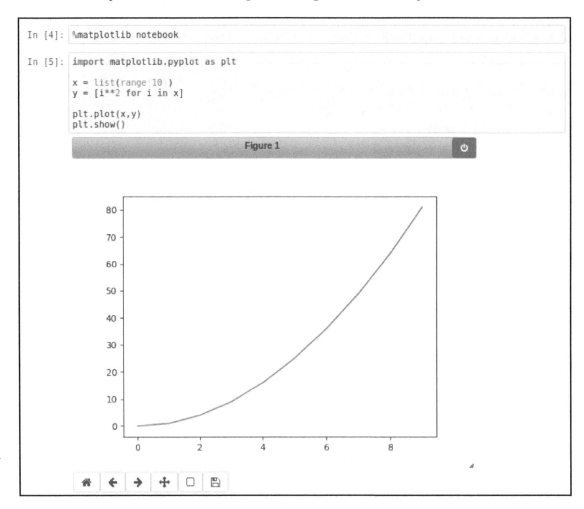

Documenting in Markdown

Jupyter Notebook supports Markdown syntax for organized documentation:

1. Select **Markdown** from the drop-down list in the toolbar.
2. Write your notes in the gray input box.
3. Click on **Run** or *Shift + Enter*:

```
Title: My first notebook
==
# Header 1
## Header 2

This is the content of my notebook.

I am __BOLD__.
- I want to make a point
* so do I


1. Let's have some order here
2. Some *more* order
    - I need some hierarchy
    - *italic. Isn't it chic?*

> I love Python :D

```
print("Hello world!")
print("I am ready to learn Matplotlib!")
```

```

After running the cell, the text will be styled in the display:

Title: My first notebook

Header 1

Header 2

This is the content of my notebook.

I am **BOLD**.

- I want to make a point
- so do I

1. Let's have some order here
2. Some *more* order

    - I need some hierarchy
    - *italic. Isn't it chic?*

    I love Python :D

```
print("Hello world!")
print("I am ready to learn Matplotlib!")
```

You can find a detailed Markdown cheat sheet by Adam Pritchard at `https://github.com/adam-p/markdown-here/wiki/Markdown-Cheatsheet`.

Save your hard work!

Jupyter Notebook auto-saves itself every 2 minutes. As good practice, you should save it yourself more often by clicking on the floppy icon on the toolbar, or more conveniently by *Ctrl* + *S*.

Each project you open on Jupyter is saved as the JSON-based `.ipynb` notebook format:

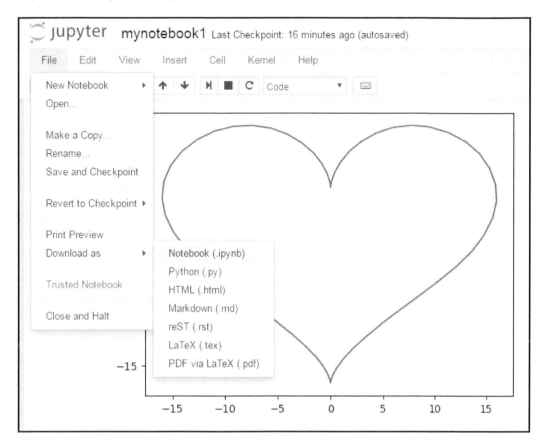

The `.ipynb` notebook is portable across different Jupyter servers. Notebooks can be exported as basic runnable Python script `.py`, Markdown `.md` for documentation, and web page format `.html` for instant display of the flow of your project without having the readers install Jupyter Notebook in advance. It also supports LaTex format and PDF conversion via LaTex upon installation of the dependency Pandoc. If interested, you may check out the installation instructions at `http://pandoc.org/installing.html`.

Summary

Woo-hoo! We've taken our first steps in our Matplotlib journey together. You can rest assured you have a comprehensive understanding of Matplotlib's capabilities and also have the requisite environment set up. Now that we have successfully ventured into data visualization and gotten our feet wet, let's go ahead and build our first plots!

Getting Started with Matplotlib

2

Now that we are familiar with the capabilities and functionalities of Matplotlib and all geared up with the Python environment, let's go straight ahead and create our first plots.

In this chapter, we will learn how to:

- Draw basic line and scatter plots
- Overlay multiple data series on the same plots
- Adjust grids, axes, and labels
- Add a title and legend
- Save created plots as separate files
- Configure Matplotlib global settings

Loading data

Before we start plotting, we need to import the data we intend to plot and get familiar with basic plotting commands in Matplotlib. Let's start going through these basic commands!

While working on data visualization projects, we need to ensure that we have basic familiarity and understanding of the tools used for data processing. Before we begin, let's briefly revise the most common data structures you will encounter when handling data with Python.

List

This is the most basic Python data structure; it stores a collection of values. While you can store any data type as an element in a Python list, for our purpose of data visualization, we mostly handle lists of numerical values as data input, or at, most, lists with elements of the same data type, such as strings to store text labels.

A list is specified by square brackets, `[]`. To initiate an empty list, assign `[]` to a variable by `l = []`. To create a list, we can write the following:

```
fibonacci = [1,1,2,3,5,8,13]
```

Sometimes, we may want to get a list of arithmetic sequences. We may do so by using `list(range(start,stop,step))`.

See the following example:

```
In [1]: fifths = list(range(10,30,5))
        fifths
Out[1]: [10, 15, 20, 25]

In [2]: list(range(10,30,5))==[10, 15, 20, 25]
Out[2]: True
```

Unlike Python 2.7, in Python 3.x, you cannot use the `range()` object interchangeably with a list.

NumPy array

NumPy allows the creation of n-dimensional arrays, which is where the name of the data type, `numpy.ndarray`, comes from. It handles many sophisticated scientific and matrix operations. It provides many linear algebra and random number functionalities.

NumPy lies at the core of many calculations that computationally enable Matplotlib and many other Python packages. It is therefore a dependency for many common packages and often comes along with Python distributions. For instance, it provides the fundamental data structure for SciPy, a package that handles statistical calculations useful in science and many other areas.

To import NumPy, input this:

```
import numpy as np
```

To create a NumPy array from lists, use the following:

```
x = np.array([2,3,1,0])
```

You can also create non-integral arithmetic series with NumPy by using `np.linspace(start,stop,number)`.

See the following example:

```
In [1]: np.linspace(3,5,20)
Out[1]: array([ 3.        ,  3.10526316,  3.21052632,  3.31578947,
3.42105263,
         3.52631579,  3.63157895,  3.73684211,  3.84210526,  3.94736842,
         4.05263158,  4.15789474,  4.26315789,  4.36842105,  4.47368421,
         4.57894737,  4.68421053,  4.78947368,  4.89473684,  5.        ])
```

Matrix operations can be applied across NumPy arrays. Here is an example of multiplying two arrays:

```
In [2]: a = np.array([1, 2, 1])
In [3]: b = np.array([2, 3, 8])
In [4]: a*b
Out[4]: array([2, 6, 8])
```

pandas DataFrame

You may often see `df` appearing on Python-based data science resources and literature. It is a conventional way to denote the pandas DataFrame structure. pandas lets us perform the otherwise tedious operations on tables (data frames) with simple commands, such as `dropna()`, `merge()`, `pivot()`, and `set_index()`.

pandas is designed to streamline handling processes of common data types, such as time series. While NumPy is more specialized in mathematical calculations, pandas has built-in string manipulation functions and also allows custom functions to be applied to each cell via `apply()`.

Before use, we import the module with the conventional shorthand as:

```
pd.DataFrame(my_list_or_array)
```

To read data from existing files, just use the following:

```
pd.read_csv()
```

For tab-delimited files, just add '\t' as the separator:

```
pd.read_csv(sep='\t')
```

pandas supports data import from a wide range of common file structures for data handling and processing, from `pd.read_xlsx()` for Excel and `pd.read_sql_query()` for SQL databases to the more recently popular JSON, HDF5, and Google BigQuery.

pandas provides a collection of handy operations for data manipulation and is considered a must-have in a Python data scientist's or developer's toolbox.

 We encourage our readers to seek resources and books on our Mapt platform to get a better and intimate understanding of the pandas library usage.

To fully understand and utilize the functionalities, you may want to read more from the official documentation:

```
http://pandas.pydata.org/pandas-docs/stable/
```

Our first plots with Matplotlib

We have just revised the basic ways of data handling with Python. Without further ado, let's create our first "Hello World!" plot example.

Importing the pyplot

To create a pandas DataFrame from objects such as lists and ndarrays, you may call:

```
import pandas as pd
```

To start creating Matplotlib plots, we first import the plotting API `pyplot` by entering this command:

```
import matplotlib.pyplot as plt
```

This will start your plotting routine.

In Jupyter Notebook, you need to import modules once you begin a notebook session after starting the kernel.

Line plot

After importing `matplotlib.pyplot` as `plt`, we draw line plots with the `plt.plot()` command.

Here is a code snippet for a simple example of plotting the temperature of the week:

```
# Import the Matplotlib module
import matplotlib.pyplot as plt

# Use a list to store the daily temperature
t = [22.2,22.3,22.5,21.8,22.5,23.4,22.8]

# Plot the daily temperature t as a line plot
plt.plot(t)

# Show the plot
plt.show()
```

After you run the code, the following plot will be displayed as the output in the notebook cell:

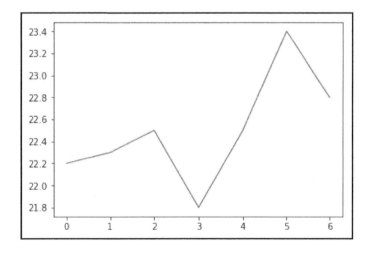

When a single parameter is parsed, the data values are assumed to be on the *y* axis, with the indices on the *x* axis.

Remember to conclude each plot with `plt.show()`. If you forget this, a plot object will be shown as the output instead of the plot. If you do not overwrite the plot with other plotting commands, you can call `plt.show()` in the next running cell to display the plot. The following is a screenshot made to illustrate the case:

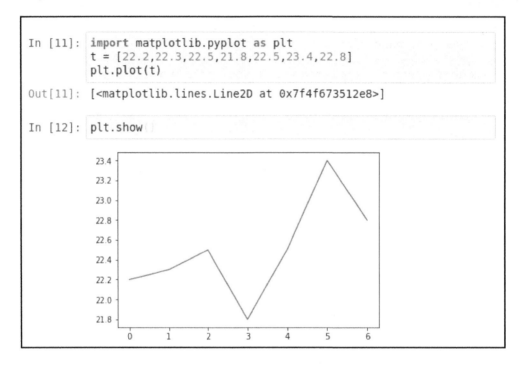

Also, if you run the plotting commands multiple times before calling `plt.show()`, multiple plots or plots with unexpected elements (for example, changed color) will appear in the output area the next time you add the line back and run. We can demonstrate this by duplicating the same plotting commands in two cells running consecutively before showing the plot. In the following screenshot, you will see a change in color from the default blue as previously, to brown. This is due to the blue, line plotted with the first command being covered with a second brown line from the second command:

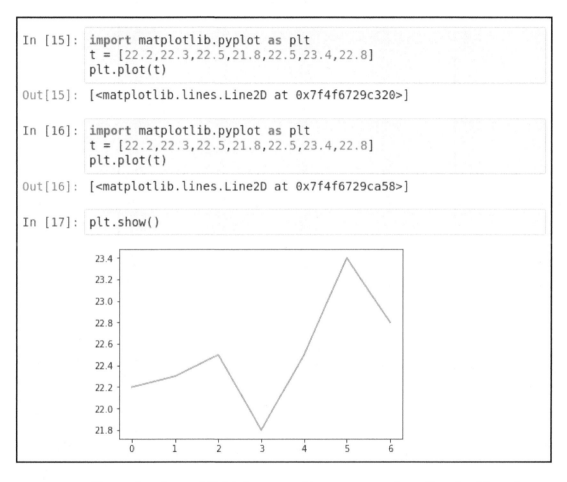

```
In [15]:   import matplotlib.pyplot as plt
           t = [22.2,22.3,22.5,21.8,22.5,23.4,22.8]
           plt.plot(t)

Out[15]:   [<matplotlib.lines.Line2D at 0x7f4f6729c320>]

In [16]:   import matplotlib.pyplot as plt
           t = [22.2,22.3,22.5,21.8,22.5,23.4,22.8]
           plt.plot(t)

Out[16]:   [<matplotlib.lines.Line2D at 0x7f4f6729ca58>]

In [17]:   plt.show()
```

Do not be alarmed if this happens. You can rerun the cell and achieve the desired result.

Suppressing function output: Sometimes the plot may show up without calling `plt.show()`, but the line of the `matplotlib` object also shows up without giving much useful information. We can put a semicolon (`;`) at the end of a code line to suppress its input. For instance, in the following quick example, we will not see the Matplotlib object `[<matplotlib.lines.Line2D at 0x7f6dc6afe2e8>]` appear in the output when we put `;` after the plotting command:

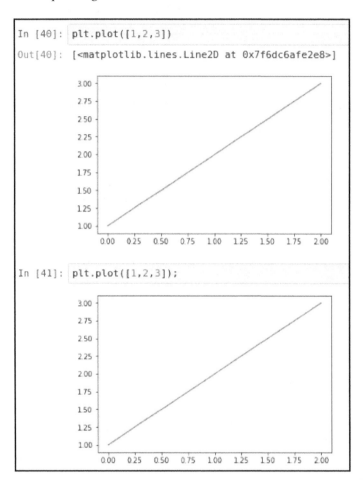

To specify a customized *x*-axis, simply supply it as the first argument to `plt.plot()`. Let's say we plot the temperatures from the date 11th. We can plot temperatures t against a list of dates d by calling `plt.plot(d,t)`. Here is the result, where you can observe the specified dates on the *x* axis:

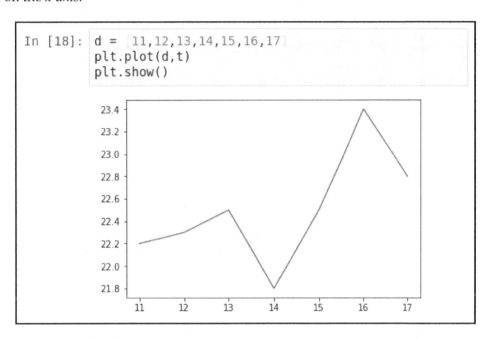

```
In [18]:   d = 11,12,13,14,15,16,17
           plt.plot(d,t)
           plt.show()
```

Scatter plot

Another basic plot type is scatter plot, a plot of dots. You can draw it by calling `plt.scatter(x,y)`. The following example shows a scatter plot of random dots:

```
import numpy as np
import matplotlib.pyplot as plt

# Set the random seed for NumPy function to keep the results reproducible
np.random.seed(42)

# Generate a 2 by 100 NumPy Array of random decimals between 0 and 1
r = np.random.rand(2,100)

# Plot the x and y coordinates of the random dots on a scatter plot
plt.scatter(r[0],r[1])
```

```
# Show the plot
plt.show()
```

The following plot is the result of the preceding code:

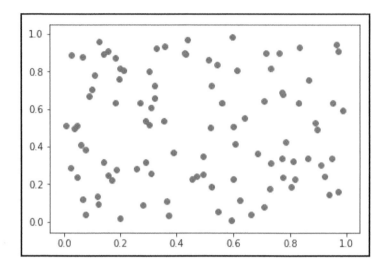

Overlaying multiple data series in a plot

We can stack several plotting commands before concluding a plot with `plt.show()` to create a plot with multiple data series. Each data series can be plotted with the same or different plot types. The following are examples of line plots and scatter plots with multiple data series, as well as a combination of both plot types show trends.

Multiline plots

For example, to create a multiline plot, we can draw a line plot for each data series before concluding the figure. Let's try plotting the temperatures of three different cities with the following code:

```
import matplotlib.pyplot as plt

# Prepare the data series
d = [11,12,13,14,15,16,17]
t0 = [15.3,15.4,12.6,12.7,13.2,12.3,11.4]
t1 = [26.1,26.2,24.3,25.1,26.7,27.8,26.9]
t2 = [22.3,20.6,19.8,21.6,21.3,19.4,21.4]
```

```
# Plot the lines for each data series
plt.plot(d,t0)
plt.plot(d,t1)
plt.plot(d,t2)

plt.show()
```

Here is the plot generated by the preceding code:

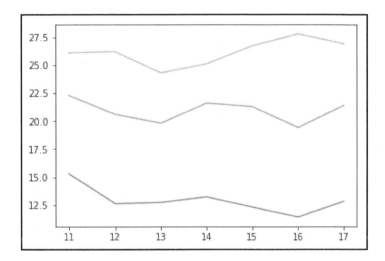

This example is adapted from the maximum temperatures of three cities in a week in December 2017. From the graph, can you recognize which two lines are more likely to be representative of cities from the same continent?

Scatter plot to show clusters

While we have seen a scatter plot of random dots before, scatter plots are most useful with representing discrete data points that show a trend or clusters. Each data series will be plotted in different color per plotting command by default, which helps us distinguish the distinct dots from each series. To demonstrate the idea, we will generate two artificial clusters of data points using a simple random number generator function in NumPy, shown as follows:

```
import matplotlib.pyplot as plt

# seed the random number generator to keep results reproducible
np.random.seed(123)
```

```
# Generate 10 random numbers around 2 as x-coordinates of the first data
series
x0 = np.random.rand(10)+1.5

# Generate the y-coordinates another data series similarly
np.random.seed(321)
y0 = np.random.rand(10)+2
np.random.seed(456)
x1 = np.random.rand(10)+2.5
np.random.seed(789)
y1 = np.random.rand(10)+2
plt.scatter(x0,y0)
plt.scatter(x1,y1)

plt.show()
```

We can see from the following plot that there are two artificially created clusters of dots colored blue (approximately in the left half) and orange (approximately in the right half) respectively:

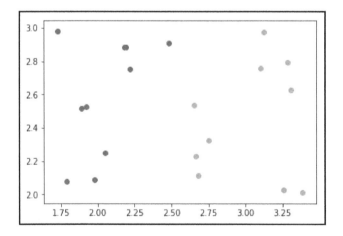

There is another way to generate clusters and plot them on scatter plots. We can generate clusters of data points for testing and demonstration more directly using the make_blobs() function in a package called sklearn, which is developed for more advanced data analysis and data mining, as shown in the following snippet. We can specify the colors according to the assigned feature (cluster identity):

```
import matplotlib.pyplot as plt
from sklearn.datasets import make_blobs

# make blobs with 3 centers with random seed of 23
```

```
blob_coords,features = make_blobs(centers=3, random_state=23)

# plot the blobs, with c value set to map colors to features
plt.scatter(blob_coords[:, 0], blob_coords[:, 1], marker='x', c=features)
plt.show()
```

As the `make_blob` function generates dots based on isotropic Gaussian distribution, we can see from the resultant plot that they are better clustered as three distinct blobs of dots centralized at three points:

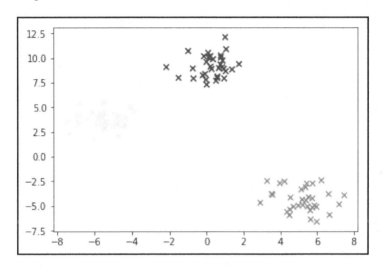

scikit-learn is a powerful Python package that provides many different simple functions for data mining and data analysis. It has a versatile suite of algorithms for classification, regression, clustering, dimension reduction, and modeling. It also allows data preprocessing and pipelining multiple processing stages.

For getting familiar with the scikit-learn library, we can use the datasets preloaded in package, such as the famous iris petals, or generate datasets according to the specified distribution as shown before. Here we'll only use the data to illustrate a simple visualization using scatter plot, and we won't go into the details just yet. More examples are available and can be found by clicking on this link:

`http://scikit-learn.org/stable/auto_examples/datasets/plot_random_dataset.html`

The previous example is a demonstration of an easier way to map dot color with labeled features, if any. The details of `make_blobs()` and other scikit-learn functions are out of our scope of introducing basic plots in this chapter.

We encourage our readers to seek resources and books on our Mapt platform to get a better understanding of the scikit-learn library usage.

Alternatively, readers can also read the scikit-learn documentation here: `http://scikit-learn.org`.

Adding a trendline over a scatter plot

Multiple plot types can be overlaid on top of each other. For example, we can add a trendline over a scatter plot. The following is an example of adding a trendline to 10 y coordinates with slight deviations from a linear relationship with the x coordinates:

```
import numpy as np
import matplotlib.pyplot as plt

# Generate th
np.random.seed(100)
x = list(range(10))
y = x+np.random.rand(10)-0.5

# Calculate the slope and y-intercept of the trendline
fit = np.polyfit(x,y,1)

# Add the trendline
yfit = [n*fit[0] for n in x]+fit[1]
plt.scatter(x,y)
plt.plot(yfit,'black')

plt.show()
```

We can observe from the following plot that the trendline overlays the upward sloping dots:

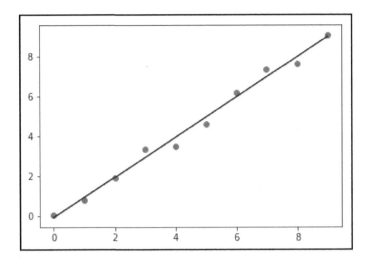

Adjusting axes, grids, labels, titles, and legends

We have just learned how to turn numerical values into dots and lines with Matplotlib. By default, Matplotlib optimizes the display by calculating various values in the background, such as the reasonable axis range and font sizes. However, good visualization often requires more design input to suit our custom data visualization needs and purpose. Moreover, text labels are needed to make figures informative in many cases. In the following sections, we will demonstrate the methods to adjust these elements.

Adjusting axis limits

While Matplotlib automatically chooses the range of x and y axis limits to spread data onto the whole plotting area, sometimes we want some adjustment, such as to show 100% as maximum instead of somewhere lower. To set the limits of x and y axes, we use the commands `plt.xlim()` and `plt.ylim()`. In our daily temperature example, the auto-scaling makes the temperature changes of less than 2 degrees Celsius seem very dramatic. Here is how we can adjust it, say, to show 0 degrees as the lower limit on the y axis for temperatures of the first 5 days only:

```
import matplotlib.pyplot as plt

d = [11,12,13,14,15,16,17]
```

```
t0 = [15.3,12.6,12.7,13.2,12.3,11.4,12.8]
t1 = [26.1,26.2,24.3,25.1,26.7,27.8,26.9]
t2 = [22.3,20.6,19.8,21.6,21.3,19.4,21.4]

plt.plot(d,t0)
plt.plot(d,t1)
plt.plot(d,t2)

# Set the limit for each axis
plt.xlim(11,15)
plt.ylim(0,30)

plt.show()
```

The preceding code produces a plot with the *y* axis ranging from **0** to **30**, as follows:

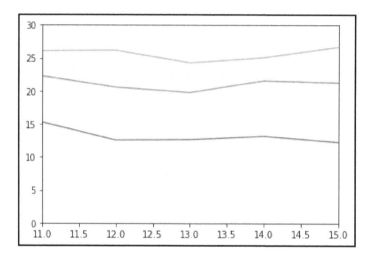

Adding axis labels

To give meaning to the values on the *x* and *y* axes, we need information about the nature and type of data, and its corresponding units. We can provide this piece of information by placing axis labels with plt.xlabel() or plt.ylabel().

Let us continue with our example plot of multi-city temperatures. We shall add plt.xlabel('Temperature (°C)') and plt.ylabel('Date') to label the axes to produce the following plot:

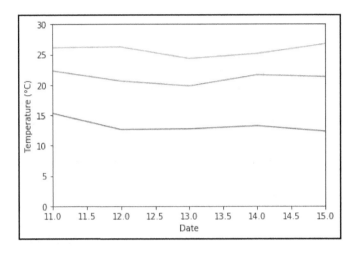

Similar to many other Matplotlib functions involving text, it is possible to set the text properties, such as font size and color within the `plt.xlabel()` and `plt.ylabel()` functions, by passing the properties as parameters. Here, we specified a bolder font weight for the labels for some hierarchy:

```
plt.xlabel('Date',size=12,fontweight='semibold')
plt.ylabel('Temperature (°C)',size=12,fontweight='semibold')
```

As you can see, Matplotlib supports inline adjustment of fonts for many text elements. Here, we have specified a bolder font weight for the labels for some hierarchy:

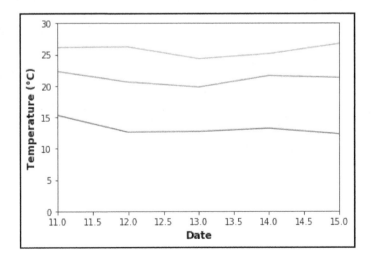

Adding a grid

While a blank plot background is clean, sometimes we may like to get some reference gridlines for better reference, such as in the multiline case.

We can turn on the background gridlines by calling `plt.grid(True)` before `plt.show()`. For example, we can add this command to the preceding multi-city temperature plot to obtain the following plot:

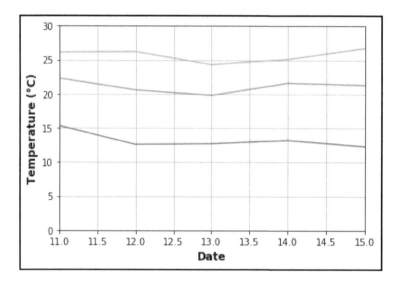

Similarly, when we do not want the grid any longer, such as when using styles with gridlines as the default, we can use `plt.grid(False)` to remove the grid.

Detailed styling options will be discussed in the next chapter. The grid in the preceding example distinctly stands out too much and interferes with the interpretation of the line plots. Grid line properties, such as line width, color, and dash patterns, are adjustable within the `plt.grid()` command; here is a brief example of making the grid more subtle:

```
plt.grid(True,linewidth=0.5,color='#aaaaaa',linestyle='-')
```

As seen in the following plot, the grid lines become lighter and less interfering with the data lines in comparison to the default grid color in the plot in the last example:

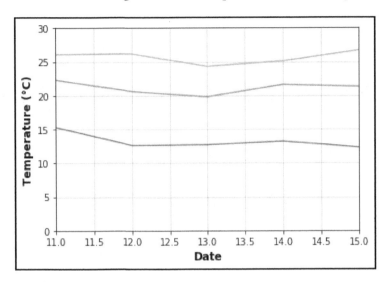

Titles and legends

Depending on where and how our plots will be presented, they may or may not be accompanied by figure caption that describes the background and results that the data plot is illustrating. We may need to add a title to succinctly summarize and communicate the result.

Meanwhile, although axis labels suffice to identify data series for some figure types, such as bar plots and box plots, there may be cases where we need an extra legend key for this purpose. The following are ways to add and adjust these text elements to make our plot more informative.

Adding a title

To describe the information of the plotted data, we can give a title to our figure. This can be done simply with the command `plt.title(yourtitle)`:

```
plt.title("Daily temperature of 3 cities in the second week of December")
```

Again, we can specify text style properties. Here we set the title font to be larger than other labels:

```
plt.title("Daily temperature of 3 cities in the second week of December",
size=14, fontweight='bold')
```

The following is the plot with title added:

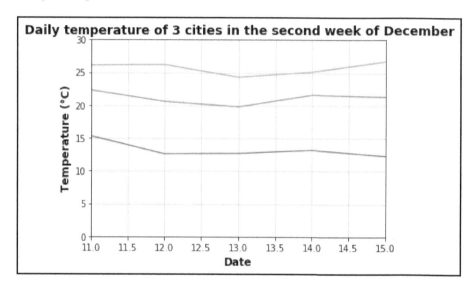

Adding a legend

To match data series on plots with their labels, such as by their line styles and marker styles, we add the following:

```
plt.legend()
```

The label of each data series can be specified within each `plt.plot()` command with the `label` parameter.

By default, Matplotlib chooses the best location to minimize overlap with data points and add transparency to the legend face color in case of overlapping. However, this does not always guarantee the location to be ideal in each case. To adjust the location, we can't pass `loc` settings , such as by using `plt.legend(loc='upper left')`.

Possible `loc` settings are as follows:

- `'best'`: 0 (only implemented for axes' legends)
- `'upper right'`: 1
- `'upper left'`: 2
- `'lower left'`: 3
- `'lower right'`: 4
- `'right'`: 5 (the same as 'center right'; for back-compatibility)
- `'center left'`: 6
- `'center right'`: 7
- `'lower center'`: 8
- `'upper center'`: 9
- `'center'`: 10

You can also set `loc` as normalized coordinates with respect to the parent, which is usually the axes' area; that is, edges of axes are at 0 and 1. For instance, `plt.legend(loc=(0.5,0.5))` sets the legend right in the middle.

Let's try to set the legend to our multiline plot in the lower-right corner with absolute coordinates, `plt.legend(loc=(0.64,0.1))`, as shown in the following created plot:

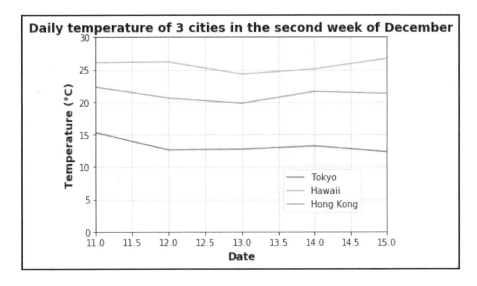

A complete example

To get further acquainted with Matplotlib functions, let us plot a multiline plot with axes, labels, title, and legend configured in one single snippet.

In this example, we take real-world data from the World Bank on agriculture. As the world population continues to grow, food security continues to be an important global issue. Let us have a look at the production data of a few major crops in the recent decade by plotting a multiline plot with the following code:

```
Data source: https://data.oecd.org/agroutput/crop-production.htm
OECD (2017), Crop production (indicator). doi: 10.1787/49a4e677-en
(Accessed on 25 December 2017)
# Import relevant modules
import pandas as pd
import matplotlib.pyplot as plt

# Import dataset
crop_prod = pd.read_csv('OECD-THND_TONNES.txt',delimiter='\t')
years = crop_prod[crop_prod['Crop']=='SOYBEAN']['Year']
rice = crop_prod[crop_prod['Crop']=='RICE']['Value']
wheat = crop_prod[crop_prod['Crop']=='WHEAT']['Value']
maize = crop_prod[crop_prod['Crop']=='MAIZE']['Value']
soybean = crop_prod[crop_prod['Crop']=='SOYBEAN']['Value']

# Plot the data series
plt.plot(years, rice, label='Rice')
plt.plot(years, wheat, label='Wheat')
plt.plot(years, maize, label='Maize')
plt.plot(years, soybean, label='Soybean')

# Label the x- and y-axes
plt.xlabel('Year',size=12,fontweight='semibold')
plt.ylabel('Thousand tonnes',size=12,fontweight='semibold')

# Add the title and legend
plt.title('Total OECD crop production in 1995-2016', size=14,
fontweight='semibold')
plt.legend()

# Show the figure
plt.show()
```

From the resultant plot, we can observe the production of maize > wheat > soybean > rice, a generally growing trend of crop production and a steady growth of soybean production:

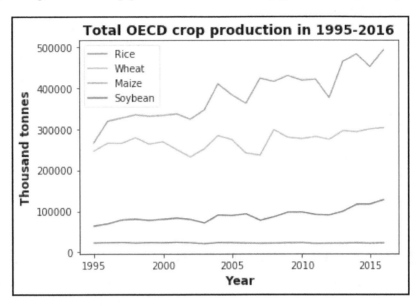

Saving plots to a file

To save a figure, we put `plt.savefig(outputpath)` at the end of plotting commands. It can be used in place of `plt.show()`, to directly save the figure without displaying it.

If you want to save the figure as a file as well as display it on the notebook output, you can call both `plt.savefig()` and `plt.show()`.

Reversing the order can result in the plot elements being cleaned up, leaving a blank canvas for the saved figure file.

Setting the output format

`plt.savefig()` automatically detects the file extension of the specified output path, and generates the corresponding file format if it is supported. If no file extension is specified in the input, a PNG format file would be obtained as output with the default backend. This supports a number of image formats, including PNG, JPG, PDF, and PostScript:

```
import numpy as np
import matplotlib.pyplot as plt
y = np.linspace(1,2000)
x = 1.0/np.sin(y)
plt.plot(x,y,'green')
plt.xlim(-20,20)
plt.ylim(1000,2400)
plt.show()
plt.savefig('123')
```

Setting the figure resolution

Depending on the format, location, and purpose of display, each figure may require a different scale of resolution. Generally, large printed materials, such as posters, would require higher resolution. We can set the resolution by specifying the **dot per inch** (**DPI**) value, like this for example:

```
plt.savefig(dpi=300)
```

For a *8x12* squared inches figure and output with 300 DPI, there will be *(8x300)x(12x300) = 2400x3600* pixels in the image.

Jupyter support

Matplotlib is well integrated into Jupyter Notebook natively; such integration allows the plots to be displayed directly as static images as the output of each notebook cell. At times, we might be interested in the interactive GUI of Matplotlib, such as for zooming or panning a plot to view from different angles. We can continue working in the Jupyter Notebook with some simple steps.

Interactive navigation toolbar

To access the interactive navigation toolbar in a Jupyter Notebook, first call the Jupyter cell magic:

```
%matplotlib notebook
```

We will demonstrate with a plot with a more dynamic shape:

```
import numpy as np
import matplotlib.pyplot as plt

y = np.linspace(1,2000)
x = 1.0/np.sin(y)

plt.plot(x,y,'green')
plt.xlim(-20,20)
plt.ylim(1000,2400)

plt.show()
```

As shown in the illustration, here we have a Christmas-tree-shaped plot embedded within a GUI box:

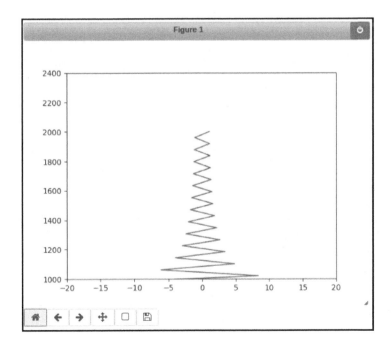

You can find a tool bar in the bottom-left corner. The button functions from left to right are as follows:

- **Home logo**: Reset original view
- **Left arrow**: Back to previous view
- **Right arrow**: Forward to next view
- **Four-direction arrow**: Pan by holding down the left mouse key; zoom with the right arrow key on the screen
- **Rectangle**: Zoom by dragging rectangle on the plot
- **Floppy disk icon**: Download the plot

Here is an example of panning by dragging on the plot:

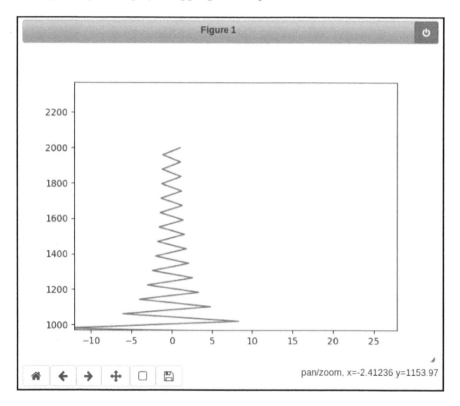

The following illustration shows the result of zooming by dragging a rectangle over the plot:

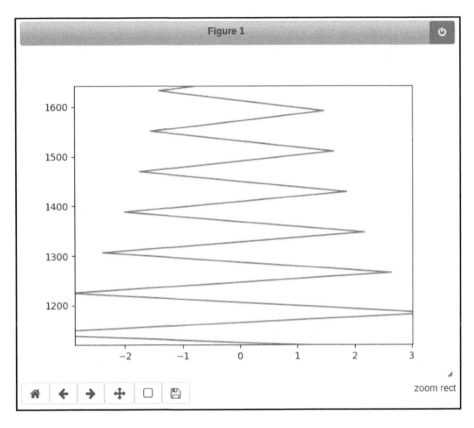

To revert to inline output mode, use the cell magic `%matplotlib inline`, or click on the power button in the top-right corner.

Configuring Matplotlib

We have learned to tweak a few major elements in a Matplotlib plot. When we recurrently generate figures of similar style, it would be nice to have a way to store and apply the persistent global settings. Matplotlib offers a few options for configuration.

Configuring within Python code

To keep settings throughout the current session, we can execute `matplotlib.rcParams` to override configuration file settings.

For instance, we can set the font size of all text in plots to 18 with the following:

```
matplotlib.rcParams['font.size'] = 18
```

Alternatively we can call the `matplotlib.rc()` function. As `matplotlib.rc()` just changes one property, to change multiple settings, we can use the function `matplotlib.rcParams.update()`, and pass parameters in the form of a dictionary of key-value pairs:

```
matplotlib.rcParams.update({'font.size': 18, 'font.family': 'serif'})
```

Reverting to default settings

To revert to default settings, you can call `matplotlib.rcdefaults()` or `matplotlib.style.use('default')`.

Global setting via configuration rc file

If you have a set of configurations that you want to apply globally without setting every time, you can set the `matplotlibrc` default values. To make persistent and selective changes on a certain set of parameters, we store the options in an `rc` configuration file.

Finding the rc configuration file

On Linux/Unix systems, you can set a global configuration for all users on the machine by editing `/etc/matplotlibrc` for `$HOME/.matplotlib/matplotlib/rc` or `~/.config/matplotlib/matplotlibrc`.

On Windows, the default `matplotlibrc` file may be placed in `C:\Python35\Lib\site-packages`. To find the path of the currently active `matplotlibrc` file, we can use the `matplotlib_fname()` function of Matplotlib in Python shell as follows:

```
In [1]: import matplotlib as mpl
        mpl.matplotlib_fname()
Out[1]: '/home/mary/.local/lib/python3.6/site-packages/matplotlib/mpl-
data/matplotlibrc'
```

The rc configuration file is found under
`$INSTALL_DIR/matplotlib/mpl-data/matplotlibrc`,
where `$INSTALL_DIR` is where you installed Matplotlib, which usually
looks like `python3.6/site-packages/`. The rc file in the installation
directory will be overwritten at each update. To keep the changes
persistent across version updates, please keep them in the local
configuration directory, such
as `'/home/mary/.config/matplotlib/matplotlibrc'`.

Editing the rc configuration file

The basic format of the file is in the form of `option: value`. For example, to keep the
legend always on the right, we put:

```
legend.loc: right
```

Matplotlib provides massive configurability of plots, and there are several places to control
the customization:

- **Global machine configuration file**: Matplotlib is configured for each user using
  the global machine configuration file
- **User configuration file**: A unique file for each user, where they can overwrite the
  global configuration file choosing their own settings (note that the user can
  execute a Matplotlib-related code anytime)
- **Configuration file in the current directory**: The current script or program can be
  customized specifically by using this directory

This is particularly useful in situations when different programs have different needs, and
using an external configuration file is better than hardcoding those settings in the code.

Summary

Congratulations! We are now familiar with the basic plotting techniques using Matplotlib
syntax! Remember, the success of a data visualization project relies heavily upon making
appealing visuals.

In the next chapters, we will learn how to beautify our plots and select the right kind of plot
that communicates our data effectively!

3
Decorating Graphs with Plot Styles and Types

In the previous chapter, we learned some basic concepts to draw line and scatter plots with Matplotlib, and made adjustments to a few elements. Now that we are familiar with the Matplotlib syntax, we are ready to go further and explore the potential of Matplotlib.

In this chapter, we will discuss:

- Color specification
- Line style customization
- Point style customization
- More native plot types
- Inserting text and other annotations
- Considerations in plot styling

Controlling the colors

Color is an essential element in any visual. It can have a huge impact on how graphics are perceived. For example, sharp color contrast can be used to highlight a focus; a combination of several distinct colors is useful in setting up a hierarchy.

In Matplotlib 2, colors have been set by default to better differentiate between categories; and to perceive continuous numerical values more intuitively, yet we often need better control over the colors to represent our data. In this section, we will introduce the common color options in Matplotlib.

Default color cycle

A color cycle is a list of colors used to control the color of a series of elements automatically, such as each data series in multiline plots. In Matplotlib 2.0, the default color cycle has expanded from 7 to 10 colors using the *category10* palette in **Data-Driven Documents (D3)** https://github.com/d3 and Vega, a declarative language for visualization grammar. These colors are designed to show good contrast between distinct categories. Each color is named 'C0' to 'C9', and can be called in manually by specifying a color in the preset color cycle. Here is a toy example of a multiline plot with each color in the default cycle:

```
import matplotlib.pyplot as plt
for i in range(10):
    plt.plot([i]*5,c='C'+str(i),label='C'+str(i))
plt.xlim(0,5)
plt.legend()
plt.show()
```

The following is the figure output. The legend displays the name of each color in the default cycle:

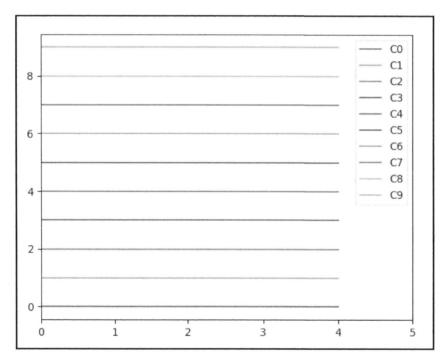

To access the hexadecimal codes of the colors, you may use the following code:

```
import matplotlib as mpl
mpl.rcParams['axes.prop_cycle']
```

Single-lettered abbreviations for basic colors

There are several common colors with built-in, single-lettered standard abbreviations for quick use. They are listed as follows:

- 'b': Blue
- 'g': Green
- 'r': Red
- 'c': Cyan
- 'm': Magenta
- 'y': Yellow
- 'k': Black
- 'w': White

Standard HTML color names

When we want to quickly build a palette from a wider range of colors, names in plain English may be more intuitive to start with than numerical code. There are more than a hundred different color names that are supported by HTML on all modern browsers. They are well supported in Matplotlib, for example, salmon, orange, yellow-green, chocolate, and cornflower blue.

You can find the full list with matched colors and names at: https://matplotlib.org/examples/color/named_colors.html. The corresponding hexadecimal code is available at: https://www.w3schools.com/colors/colors_names.asp.

RGB or RGBA color code

A color can also be specified as a tuple of three to four float numbers between zero and one, such as (0.1,0.1,0.2) or (0.2,0.2,0.3,0.8). The first three numbers define how much red, green, and blue light should be mixed into the desired color output. The optional fourth number is the alpha value to control the transparency level.

Hexadecimal color code

Similar to RGBA values, hexademical (hex) color codes control the amount of red, green, and blue light. They also control transparency with a two-digit hex number, each starting with a hash sign '#', for instance, '#81d8d0ec'. Therefore, pure red, green, blue, black, and white's hex codes are '#ff0000', '#00ff00', '#0000ff', '#000000', and '#ffffff', respectively.

Depth of grayscale

You can specify any value within *0-1* in a string of a float number, such as '0.5'. A smaller number gives a darker shade of gray.

Colormaps

Colormaps map numerical values to a range of colors.

Since Matplotlib 2.0, the default colormap has been changed from 'jet', which spans the visible light spectrum from red to blue, to 'viridis', which is a perceptually uniform continuum from yellow to blue. This makes it more intuitive to perceive continuous values:

```python
import numpy as np
import matplotlib.pyplot as plt

N = M = 200
X, Y = np.ogrid[0:20:N*1j, 0:20:M*10]
data = np.sin(np.pi * X*2 / 20) * np.cos(np.pi * Y*2 / 20)

fig, (ax2, ax1) = plt.subplots(1, 2, figsize=(7, 3)) # cmap=viridis by
default
im = ax1.imshow(data, extent=[0, 200, 0, 200])
ax1.set_title("v2.0: 'viridis'")
fig.colorbar(im, ax=ax1, shrink=0.85)

im2 = ax2.imshow(data, extent=[0, 200, 0, 200], cmap='jet')
fig.colorbar(im2, ax=ax2, shrink=0.85)
ax2.set_title("classic: 'jet'")

fig.tight_layout()
plt.show()
```

Check out the following image generated with the preceding code to understand what perceptual color uniformity means:

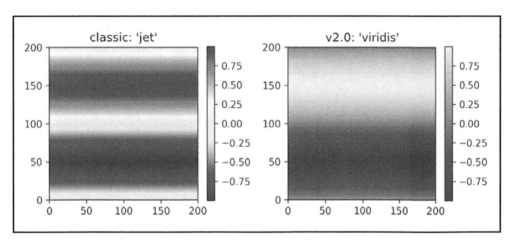

Matplotlib also provides a number of preset colormaps that are optimized for displaying diverging values or qualitative categories. Feel free to check them out at: `https://matplotlib.org/2.1.0/tutorials/colors/colormaps.html`.

Creating custom colormaps

We can set up our own colormap. This is useful when customizing heatmaps and surface plots.

A simple way to create a custom linear colormap is to prepare a list of colors and allow Matplotlib to handle the transition. Let's look at the following example:

```
import numpy as np
import matplotlib.pyplot as plt
import matplotlib.colors

# Create a 30 random dots
np.random.seed(52)
x,y,c = zip(*np.random.rand(30,3))

# Create a custom linear colormap
cmap = matplotlib.colors.LinearSegmentedColormap.from_list("",
["red","yellow","green"])
```

```
plt.scatter(x,y,c=c, cmap=cmap)
plt.colorbar()
plt.show()
```

Here, we have a scatter plot with a colormap set up on our own, morphing from red through yellow to green:

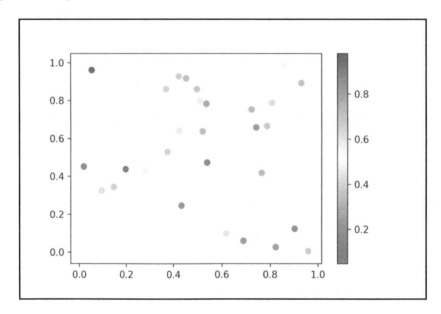

Line and marker styles

We have demonstrated how to draw line plots and scatter plots in the previous chapter. We know that scatter plots are made up of dots denoting each data point, whereas line plots are generated by joining dots of data points. In Matplotlib, the marker to mark the location of data points can be customized to have different styles, including shape, size, color, and transparency. Similarly, the line segments joining the data points as well as different 2D lines that share the same class in the object-oriented Matplotlib structure can have their styles adjusted, as briefly demonstrated in the grid section of the previous chapter. Adjusting marker and line styles is useful in making the data series more distinguishable, and sometimes for aesthetic considerations. In this section, we will go through the details and implementation methods of marker and line styles in Matplotlib.

Marker styles

For markers denoting data points, we can adjust their shapes, sizes, and colors. By default, Matplotlib draws markers as single round dots. Here, we introduce the methods of adjustment.

Choosing the shape of markers

There are dozens of available markers to denote data points. They are grouped into unfilled markers and the bolder filled_markers. Here are a few examples:

- 'o': Circle
- 'x': Cross
- '+': Plus sign
- 'P': Filled plus sign
- 'D': Filled diamond
- 's': Square
- '^': Triangle

We can access the keys and names of all available marker shapes under mpl.lines.Line2D.markers. The following is a code snippet for an overview of all our marker shapes:

```
import matplotlib.pyplot as plt
from matplotlib.lines import Line2D

for i,marker in enumerate(Line2D.markers):
    plt.scatter(i%10,i,marker=marker,s=100) # plot each of the markers in
size of 100
plt.show()
```

Here is the graphical output of the markers:

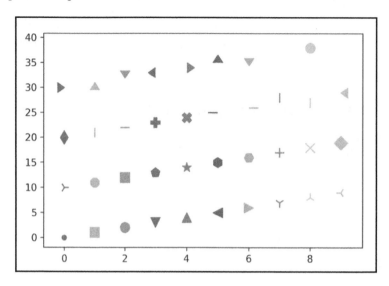

Using custom characters as markers

Matplotlib supports the use of custom characters as markers, which now include mathtext and emoji. To use characters as custom markers, we concatenate two dollar signs '$', each in front of and behind the character, and we pass them as the `marker` parameter.
The notations starting with a backslash '\', such as '\clubsuit', are in mathtext, which will be introduced later in this chapter (in the text and annotations section).

Here is an example of a scatter plot of markers in mathematical symbols and an emoji:

```
import matplotlib.pyplot as plt
from matplotlib.lines import Line2D

custom_markers = ['$'+x+'$' for x in ['\$','\%','\clubsuit','\sigma','😎']]
for i,marker in enumerate(custom_markers):
    plt.scatter(i%10,i,marker=marker,s=500) # plot each of the markers in
size of 100
plt.show()
```

As seen from the following figure, we have successfully used symbols, a Greek alphabet, as well as an emoji as custom markers in a scatter plot:

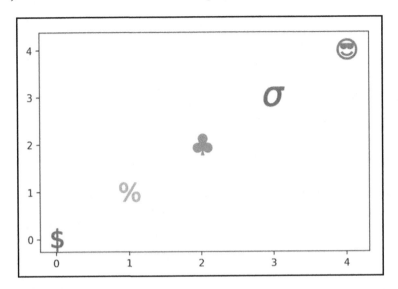

Adjusting marker sizes and colors

In a scatter plot, we can specify the marker size with the parameter s and the marker color with c in the plt.scatter() function.

To draw markers on line plots, we first specify the shape of the markers in the plt.plot() function, such as marker='x'. Marker colors follow the line color.

Please note that scatter plots accept list types as size and color values, convenient in visualizing clusters, while line plots only accept a single value per data series.

Let's look at the following example:

```
import numpy as np
import matplotlib.pyplot as plt
import matplotlib.colors

# Prepare a list of integers
n = list(range(5))

# Prepare a list of sizes that increases with values in n
s = [i**2*100+100 for i in n]
```

```
# Prepare a list of colors
c = ['red','orange','yellow','green','blue']

# Draw a scatter plot of n points with sizes in s and colors in c
plt.scatter(n,n,s=s,c=c)

# Draw a line plot with n points with black cross markers of size 12
plt.plot(n,marker='x',color='black',ms=12)

# Set axis limits to show the markers completely
plt.xlim(-0.5,4.5)
plt.ylim(-1,5)

plt.show()
```

This code generates a figure of a scatter plot with marker sizes increasing with the data values, and a line plot with cross-shaped markers of a fixed size:

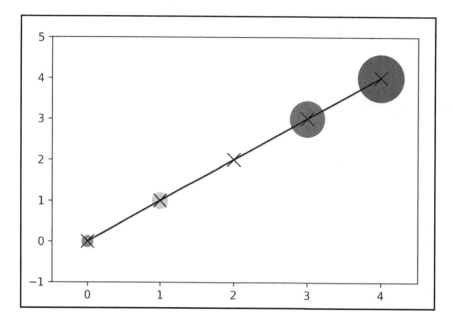

Fine-tuning marker styles with keyword arguments

We can have further refined control over marker styles with some more keyword arguments. For example, for `plt.plot()`, we can change the `markeredgecolor`, `markeredgewidth`, and `markerfacecolor`.

Here is a code example:

```
import numpy as np
import matplotlib.pyplot as plt
import matplotlib.colors

# Prepare data points
x = list(range(5))
y = [1]*5

# Set the face color, edge color, and edge width of markers
plt.plot(x,y,marker='o',ms=36,markerfacecolor='floralwhite',markeredgecolor
='slateblue',markeredgewidth=10)

plt.show()
```

This is the result of adding the extra keyword arguments:

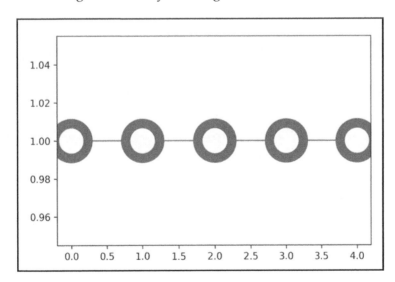

Line styles

Lines are among the most frequently occurring elements in Matplotlib visualization, from those representing data series to those marking axes, grids, and outlines of any shape. Hence, it is important to understand how we can adjust line style. Lines in Matplotlib are controlled by the `Line2D` class. The object-oriented structure of Matplotlib makes it easy to adjust line styles through keyword arguments with similar grammar in each API. Here, we shall introduce the several most commonly tuned aspects of Matplotlib lines.

Color

Setting the color of the lines in a line plot is as simple as adding a `color` or its shorthand `c` parameter to the `plt.plot()` command. The color option is available in many other Matplotlib APIs as well.

Line thickness

The thickness is set by the `linewidth` or `lw` parameter in most Matplotlib elements involving lines, including line plots.

Dash patterns

Dash patterns of lines are designated by the `linestyle` or `ls` parameter. It can sometimes be used as a positional argument for convenience. For example, in line plots, we can specify the following:

- `'solid'` or `'-'`: Solid line; default
- `'dashed'` or `'--'`: Equally spaced dashes
- `'dashdot'` or `'-.'`: Alternate dashes and dots
- `'.'`: Loose dotted line
- `':'`: Packed dotted line
- `'None'`, `' '`, `''`: No visible line
- `(offset, on-off-dash-seq)`: Customized dashes

The following is an example of lines in different dash patterns:

```
import matplotlib.pyplot as plt

# Prepare 4 data series of sine curves
y = [np.sin(i) for i in np.arange(0.0, 10.0, 0.1)]

dash_capstyles = ['-','--','-.','.',':']

# Plot each data series in different cap dash styles
for i,x in enumerate(dash_capstyles):
    plt.plot([n*(i+1) for n in y],x,label=x)

plt.legend(fontsize=16,loc='lower left')
plt.show()
```

We can see the effect of each dash style in the following figure:

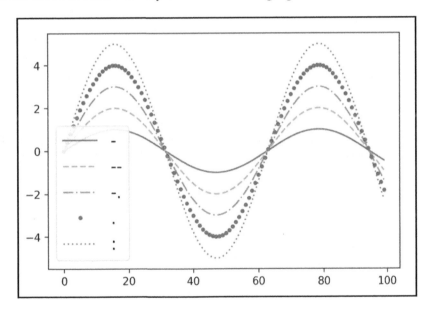

Designing a custom dash style

Matplotlib does not limit us to its preset line styles. In fact, we can design our own dash patterns by specifying the length and space for each repeating dash unit, such as (0, (5,3,1,3,1,3)).

Cap styles

Another parameter for tuning is `dash_capstyle`. It controls the style of the dash ends:

- `'butt'`: Blunt end
- `'projecting'`: Extends in length
- `'round'`: Rounded end

To demonstrate the different cap styles, we have a code snippet of a multiline plots with thick lines to enlarge the dashes:

```
import matplotlib.pyplot as plt

# Prepare 4 data series of sine curves
y = list(range(10))

dash_capstyles = ['butt','projecting','round']

# Plot each data series in different cap dash styles
for i,x in enumerate(dash_capstyles):
 plt.plot([n*(i+1) for n in y],lw=10,ls='--',dash_capstyle=x,label=x)

plt.legend(fontsize=16)
plt.show()
```

From the following figure, we can clearly see how blunt and round dashes give different impressions of sharpness and subtlety:

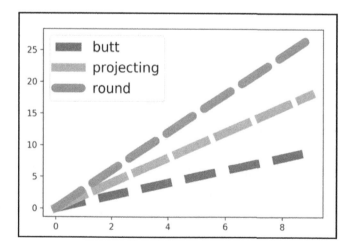

Spines

Spines in Matplotlib refer to the lines surrounding the axes of the plotting area. We can set each spine to have different line styles or to be invisible.

To begin, we first access the axes with `plt.gca()`, where **gca** stands for **get current axes**, and store it in a variable, say `ax`.

We then adjust the properties of each spine in `ax.spines` with either `'top'`, `'right'`, `'bottom'`, or `'left'`. The common settings include line widths, color, and visibility, which is demonstrated in the following code snippet.

The following is an example to remove the top and right spines, often seen as a convention in certain scientific plots, and to enhance visual simplicity in general. It is also common to thicken the remaining spines. The change in color is shown as a demonstration. We can adjust it to suit our overall design where the plot is displayed:

```python
import matplotlib.pyplot as plt

y = list(range(4))
plt.plot(y)

# Store the current axes as ax
ax = plt.gca()

# Set the spine properties
ax.spines['left'].set_linewidth(3)
ax.spines['bottom'].set_linewidth(3)
ax.spines['left'].set_color('darkblue')
ax.spines['bottom'].set_color('darkblue')
ax.spines['right'].set_visible(False)
ax.spines['top'].set_visible(False)

plt.show()
```

This will create a graph of blue spines on the left and bottom:

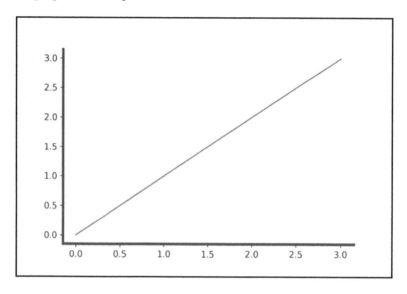

More native Matplotlib plot types

Besides the most basic scatter and line plots, Matplotlib provides a versatile collection of plot types to serve different data visualization purposes. In this section, we will introduce the rationale of plot type selection and the usage of each type.

Choosing the right plot

A successful visualization must communicate the message well. In order to achieve this goal, we need to have a good understanding of the nature of our data as well as the advantages and limitations of each plot type in illustrating different relationships in data.

In choosing the right plot type to display, we have the following considerations:

- Number of variables
- Distribution of data
- Relationships between data series

Histogram

Histograms are useful in surveying the distribution of data. For example, we can plot data on a histogram when we want to see some age groups distributed in a population, light exposure in a photograph, or the amount of precipitation in each month in a city.

In Matplotlib, we call the `plt.hist()` function with a linear array. Matplotlib will automatically group the set of data points into `bins` and plot out the frequencies for each bin in bars. We can also specify the bin size by `plt.hist(array,bins=binsize)`.

Here is an example of plotting a randomly generated binomial distribution:

```
import numpy as np
import matplotlib.pyplot as plt

np.random.seed(8)
x = np.random.binomial(100, 0.5, size=10000)
plt.hist(x,bins=20) # or plt.hist(x,20)
plt.show()
```

The histogram produced is as follows:

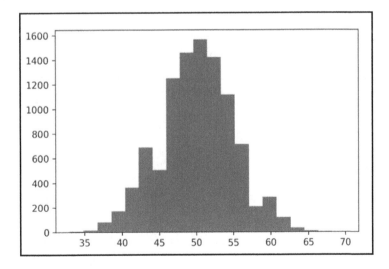

Bar plot

Bar plots are useful for comparing absolute levels of discrete data series. They are created by the function `plt.bar(labels,heights)` in Matplotlib.

Let's look at the example of the market capitalization of today's much hyped cryptocurrencies. The five top cryptocurrencies in terms of market capitalization are shown here:

```python
import matplotlib.pyplot as plt

# Data retrieved from https://coinmarketcap.com on Jan 8, 2018
# Prepare the data series
cc = ['BTC','XRP','ETH','BCH','ADA']
cap = [282034,131378,107393,49999,26137]

# Plot the bar chart
plt.bar(cc,cap)
plt.title('Market capitalization of five top cryptocurrencies in Jan 2018')
plt.xlabel('Crytocurrency')
plt.ylabel('Market capitalization (million USD)')
plt.show()
```

We can see from the following figure that instead of following the input order, Matplotlib outputs a figure of bars with labels sorted alphabetically:

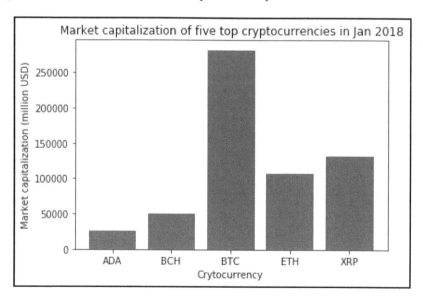

To create bar plots with bars in the designated order, we can make use of Pandas and its Matplotlib integration. The procedure is as follows:

1. Create a Pandas DataFrame df
2. Plot the bar chart with df.plot(kind='bar')
3. Set the labels of xticks
4. Adjust the other plot properties
5. Show the plot with plt.show()

Please note that, by default, df.plot() includes a legend. We need to specify legend=False to turn it off.

Here is an example to reorder the bar plot in the previous output figure:

```
import pandas as pd
import matplotlib.pyplot as plt

df = pd.DataFrame({'cc':cc,'cap':cap}, legend=False)

ax = df.plot(kind='bar')
ax.set_xticklabels(df['cc'])

plt.title('Market capitalization of five top cryptocurrencies in Jan 2018')
plt.xlabel('Crytocurrency')
plt.ylabel('Market capitalization (million USD)')
plt.show()
```

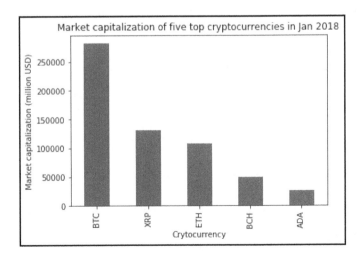

Setting bar plot properties

We can set the `width`, `color`, and `bottom` coordinates of the bars as keyword arguments in `plt.bar()`.

The bar `width` is set in ratios, whereas the color is set as introduced in the earlier section of this chapter.
For data that may include experimental or measurement errors, we can input lists of `yerr` (and `xerr`) values to show the accuracy.

Drawing bar plots with error bars using multivariate data

We can easily create bar plots with multiple data series with Pandas `df.plot()`. This API also allows us to easily add error bars by supplying the `xerr` and `yerr` parameters. Let's have a look at an example that demonstrates the usage of this function along with bar property adjustment.

The following code snippet draws a multibar plot to show the performance of an imaginary drug to treat inflammation, by comparing the level of an inflammatory protein before and after treatment of a drug and placebo as control:

```
import pandas as pd
import matplotlib.pyplot as plt

# Prepare the data series
labels_drug = ['Drug (Before)', 'Drug (After)']
labels_placebo = ['Placebo (Before)', 'Drug (After)']
drug = [2.88,1.42]
placebo = [2.72,2.68]
yerr_drug = [0.12,0.08]
yerr_placebo = [0.24,0.13]

df = pd.DataFrame([drug,placebo])
df.columns = ['Before', 'After']
df.index = ['Drug','Placebo']

# Plot the bar chart with error bars
df.plot(kind='bar',width=0.4,color=['midnightblue','cornflowerblue'],\
        yerr=[yerr_drug,yerr_placebo])

plt.title('Effect of Drug A Treatment')
plt.xlabel('Condition')
plt.ylabel('[hsCRP] (mg/L)')
```

```
plt.xticks(rotation=0) # to keep the xtick labels horizontal
plt.legend(loc=(0.4,0.8))

plt.show()
```

Here, you get a paired bar chart for two conditions. It seems the drug may have some effect compared to the placebo control. Can you think of more examples of data to draw multibar plots?

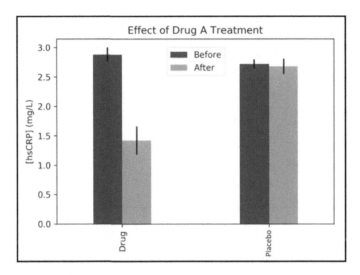

Besides using Pandas, we can also call multiple `plt.bar()` commands to draw multiple series of bar charts. Note that we will have to shift the coordinates so that the bars do not overlap each other.

Mean-and-error plots

For experimental sciences, a data point is often averaged from several repeats of experiments, necessitating the need to show the error range to illustrate the precision level. In this case, mean-and-error plots may be more suitable than bar charts. In Matplotlib, mean-and-error plots are generated by the `plt.errorbar()` API.

When the positive errors and negative errors are the same, we can input 1D arrays to error values to draw symmetric error bars. Otherwise, we input 2D arrays of [`positive errors, negative errors`] for asymmetric error bars. While it is more common to have plots with y errors only, error values for both x and y axes are supported.

By default, Matplotlib draws a line linking each error bar, with format `fmt` set to `'.-'`. For discrete datasets, we can add the keyword argument `fmt='.'` to remove the line. Let's go through a simple example:

```
import matplotlib.pyplot as plt
import numpy as np

# Prepare data for a sine curve
x = np.arange(0, 5, 0.3)
y = np.sin(-x)

# Prepare random error to plot the error bar
np.random.seed(100)
e1 = 0.1 * np.abs(np.random.randn(len(y)))

# Plotting the error bar
plt.errorbar(x, y, yerr=e1, fmt='.-')
plt.show()
```

We now get a sine curve with error bars, as follows. Try to substitute it with some real testing data you get:

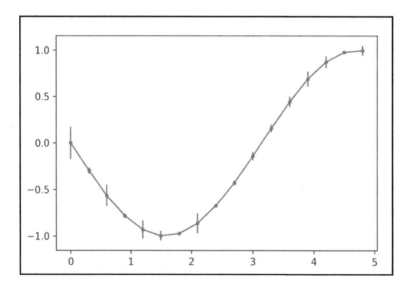

Pie chart

Pie chart is a circular representation of component ratios. The angle, and hence the arc length of each sector ratio (also called **wedges**), presents the proportion that each component accounts for, relative to the whole.

Matplotlib provides the `plt.pie()` function to draw pie charts. We can label each sector with `labels` as well as the percentage with `autopct` automatically. For different ways to customize the string format of the percentages, you may refer to: `https://pyformat.info/`. To maintain the circular shape of our pie chart, we specify the same width and length for a square figure with `plt.figure(figsize=(n,n))`.

Here, we have an example of web server usage in the first week of January 2017:

```
# Data obtained from https://trends.builtwith.com/web-server on Jan 06,
2017
import matplotlib.pyplot as plt
plt.figure(figsize=(4,4))

x = [0.31,0.3,0.14,0.1,0.15]
labels = ['nginx','Apache','IIS','Varnish','Others']
plt.pie(x,labels=labels,autopct='%1.1f%%')
plt.title('Web Server Usage Statistics')
plt.show()
```

The resultant pie chart is as follows:

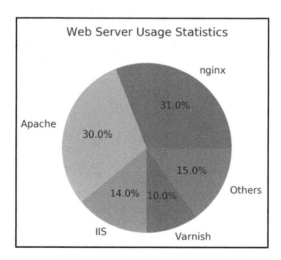

We can also separate each sector by passing a list of ratios to the keyword argument `explode`. For example, adding the argument `explode=[0.1]*5` to the preceding `plt.pie()` plot will generate the following result:

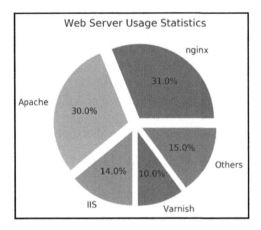

Please note that if the input array sums up to less than 1, the output pie chart will be incomplete, as shown in the following example:

```
import matplotlib.pyplot as plt
plt.figure(figsize=(4,4))
x = [0.1,0.3]
plt.pie(x)
plt.show()
```

As seen here, instead of a full circle, we have an incomplete fan-shaped plot:

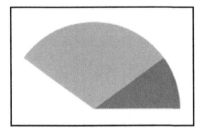

In that case, we have to explicitly specify the ratio of each term. For instance, in the preceding example, change `x = [0.1,0.3]` to `x = [0.25,0.75]`.

Polar chart

A polar chart is used to display multivariate data and is also known as a radar chart or a spider chart. It is often seen in illustrations of strength in different aspects of different objects for comparison, such as the evaluation of the price and various specifications of a piece of hardware, or the abilities of a game character.

Moreover, polar plots are also useful in drawing mathematical functions, which we are going to demonstrate here. In Matplotlib, we draw polar charts with the command `plt.polar()`. Apart from the x, y coordinate system we are familiar with, polar coordinates are used for polar charts, angles, and radii. The central point is called the **pole**. Note that Matplotlib takes a degree unit for the angle input.
Here is the code to draw a polar rose:

```
import numpy as np
import matplotlib.pyplot as plt

theta = np.arange(0., 2., 1./180.)*np.pi
plt.polar(3*theta, theta/6)
plt.polar(theta, np.cos(6*theta))
plt.polar(theta, [1.2]*len(theta))

plt.savefig('mpldev_03_polarrose.png')
plt.show()
```

This is the result. How many petals do you see in the rose?

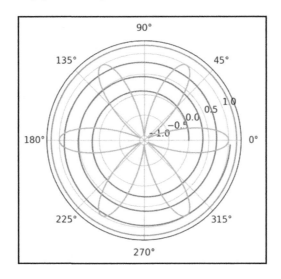

We can also make use of the polar coordinate system to create charts such as a heatmap of wind speed of the earth in geography, or the surface temperature of a round object for engineers. We will leave these advanced uses for you as an exercise when you have completed this book.

Controlling radial and angular grids

There are two functions to control the radial and angular grids: `rgrid()` and `thetagrid()` respectively. We can pass the `radii`, `labels`, and `angle` arguments to the `rgrid()` function, and `angles`, `labels`, and `frac` to the `thetagrid()` function, respectively.

Text and annotations

To enhance the understanding of plot details, we may sometimes add in text annotations for explanation. We will now introduce the methods of adding and adjusting text in Matplotlib plots.

Adding text annotations

We can add text to our plot by calling `plt.text(x,y,text)`; we specify the x and y coordinates and the text string.
Here is a quick example:

```
plt.text(0.25,0.5,'Hello World!',fontsize=30)
plt.show()
```

You can see in this figure the **Hello World!** message appearing in the center of the plot:

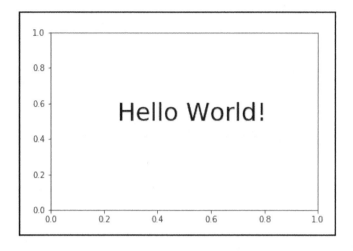

Font

Here are some of the common font properties adjustable in Matplotlib:

- **Font size**: Float or relative size, for example, smaller and x-large
- **Font weight**: For example, bold or semibold
- **Font style**: For example, italic
- **Font family**: For example, Arial
- **Rotation**: Angle in degrees; it is vertical or horizontal

 Matplotlib now supports unicode and emoji.

Mathematical notations

As a plotting tool, mathematical notations are common. We can use the in-built mathtext or LaTeX to render mathematical symbols in Matplotlib.

Mathtext

To create a mathtext notation, we precede a string with r, such as `r'$\alpha'`. The following is a short code for demo:

```
plt.title(r'$\alpha > \beta$')
plt.show()
```

Alpha plus beta in the following plot are printed by MathTex:

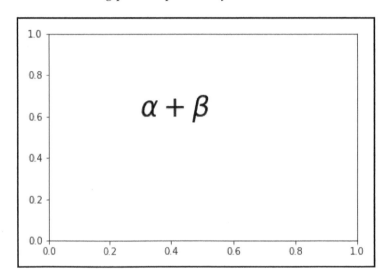

LaTeX support

Matplotlib supports LaTeX, although it renders slower than mathtext; accordingly, it allows more flexible text rendering. Here are more details of the LaTeX usage: `https://matplotlib.org/users/usetex.html`.

External text renderer

If we have LaTeX installed, we can allow the external LaTeX engine to render the text elements by `matplotlib.rc('text', usetex='false')`.

Arrows

To point out specific features in a plot, we can draw arrows with the function
`plt.arrow()`. This code illustrates the different available styles of arrow annotations:

```
import matplotlib.pyplot as plt

plt.axis([0, 9, 0, 18])
arrstyles = ['-', '->', '-[', '<-', '<->', 'fancy', 'simple', 'wedge']
for i, style in enumerate(arrstyles):
 plt.annotate(style, xytext=(1, 2+2*i), xy=(4, 1+2*i), \
 arrowprops=dict(arrowstyle=style))
connstyles=["arc", "arc,angleA=10,armA=30,rad=15", \
 "arc3,rad=.2", "arc3,rad=-.2", "angle", "angle3"]

for i, style in enumerate(connstyles):
 plt.annotate("", xytext=(6, 2+2*i), xy=(8, 1+2*i), \
 arrowprops=dict(arrowstyle='->', connectionstyle=style))

plt.show()
```

It generates the following figure to list the available arrow shapes for annotation:

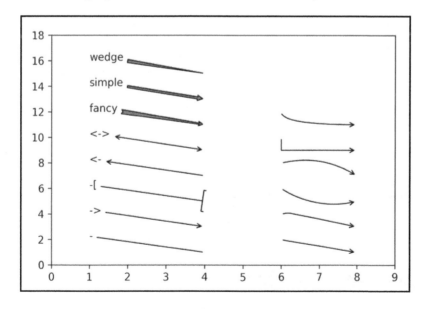

Using style sheets

We have learned to style our plots step by step so far. For more persistent and portable settings, we can apply a predefined global style via the `matplotlib.style` module:

```
## Available styles
 Matplotlib provides a number of pre-built style sheets. You can check them
out by with `matplotlib.style.available`.


import matplotlib as mpl
mpl.style.available

Out[1]: ['seaborn-talk',
'seaborn-poster',
'_classic_test',
'seaborn-ticks',
'seaborn-paper',
'ggplot',
'seaborn',
'seaborn-dark',
'seaborn-bright',
'seaborn-pastel',
'fivethirtyeight',
'Solarize_Light2',
'classic',
'grayscale',
'bmh',
'seaborn-dark-palette',
'seaborn-whitegrid',
'seaborn-white',
'dark_background',
'seaborn-muted',
'fast',
'seaborn-notebook',
'seaborn-darkgrid',
'seaborn-colorblind',
'seaborn-deep']
```

Applying a style sheet

We can call `plt.style.use(stylename)` to apply a style. This function takes in built-in style sheets, local paths, and URLs.

Creating own style sheet

You can also create your own style sheet. For the specifications of a Matplotlib style sheet file, please refer to the documentation page at: `http://matplotlib.org/users/ customizing.html`.

Resetting to default styles

The effects set by style sheets are sustained through new plots. To reset to the default parameters, call `plt.rcdefaults()`.

Aesthetics and readability considerations in styling

As visualization is about delivering messages, the more we think from the reader's perspective, the more effective it will be. An attractive graphic catches more attention. The easier to read a plot is, the more likely are readers to understand the message. Here are several basic principles in designing data plots.

Suitable font styles

The hierarchy can use no more than three levels of font family, weight, and sizes. Use less fancy font families, Sans Serif font if possible. Make sure the font size is large enough to be legible

Serif versus Sans Serif

Serif means decorative edges on alphabets. And sans means without in French. As the names imply, Sans Serif fonts are plainer and more simplistic than Serif fonts in general. Let's take the most popular examples of default fonts in Microsoft Office. Times New Roman used in Office 2007 and before is a Serif font, whereas the newer Calibri is a Sans Serif font.

Effective use of colors

- Use sharper color contrasts for emphasis and distinction
- Use extra colors with discretion, for example, one color only for one data series
- Be friendly for readers with a color weakness; for example, avoid red-green combinations

Keeping it simple

"Less is more."

– Andrea del Sarto (The Faultless Painter) by Robert Browning

This quote spells out the basic principle of the preceding suggestions. The philosophy of minimalist design inspires much of the most brilliant work, from architecture to graphic design. While the use of different colors and styles creates distinction and hierarchy as well as adding attractiveness to our graphics, we must reduce the fanciness wherever possible. This helps our readers focus on the major message, and also helps keep a professional impression for our figures.

Summary

Congratulations! You have now mastered the most commonly used plots and the basic methods to customize plots. We are now ready to move on to more advanced Matplotlib usage.

In the next chapter, we will cover more plot types with the help of third-party packages, methods to optimize displays for multiple plots and axes in certain scales, as well as showing pixels in images. Stay tuned!

4
Advanced Matplotlib

In previous chapters, we have learnt the versatile usage of basic Matplotlib APIs to create and customize various plot types. In order to create more suitable visuals for our data, there are more advanced techniques to make more refined figures. In fact, we can leverage not only the native Matplotlib functionalities but also a number of third-party packages built on top of Matplotlib. They provide easy ways to create more advanced plots that are also aesthetically styled by default. We can then make use of Matplotlib techniques to refine our data plots.

In this chapter, we would further explore the advanced usage of Matplotlib. We would learn how to group multiple relevant plots into subplots in one figure, using non-linear scale axis scales, plotting images, and creating advanced plots with the help of some popular third-party packages. Here are the detailed list of topics we would cover:

- Drawing subplots
- Using non-linear axis scales
- Plotting images
- Using Pandas-Matplotlib plotting integration
    - Hexbin plots on bivariate datasets
- Using Seaborn to construct:
    - Kernel density estimation plots for bivariate data
    - Heatmaps with and without hierarchical clustering
    - `mpl_finance` to plot finance data
- 3D plotting with `Axes3D`
- Using Basemap and GeoPandas to visualize geographical data

Drawing Subplots

In designing layouts of visual aids, it is often necessary to organize multiple relevant plots into panels in the same figure, such as when illustrating different aspects of the same dataset. Matplotlib provides a few ways to create figures with multiple subplots.

Initiating a figure with plt.figure()

The `plt.figure()` API is the API that is used to initiate a figure that serves as the base canvas. It takes in arguments that determines the number of figures and parameters such as size and background color of the plot image. It displays a new area as the canvas for plotting `axes` when called. We wouldn't obtain any graphical output unless we add other plotting elements. If we were to call `plt.show()` at this point, we would see a Matplotlib `figure` object being returned, as shown in the following screen capture:

```
In [1]:  import matplotlib.pyplot as plt
         plt.figure()
         plt.show |

         <matplotlib.figure.Figure at 0x7efea014dd30>
```

When we are plotting simple figures that involve only a single plot, without the need for multiple panels, we can omit calling `plt.figure()`. If `plt.figure()` is not called or if no argument is supplied to `plt.figure()`, then a single figure is initiated by default, equivalent to `plt.figure(1)`. If the dimension ratio of a figure is crucial, we should adjust it by passing a tuple of (`width, height`) as the `figsize` argument here.

Initiating subplots as axes with plt.subplot()

To initiate the axes plot instances that actually frame each plot, we can use `plt.subplot()`. It takes three parameters: number of rows, number of columns, and plot number. When the total number of plots is less than 10, we can omit the delimiting commas in the input arguments. Here is a code snippet example:

```
import matplotlib.pyplot as plt
# Initiates a figure area for plotting
fig = plt.figure()

# Initiates six subplot axes
ax1 = plt.subplot(231)
```

```
ax2 = plt.subplot(232)
ax3 = plt.subplot(233)
ax4 = plt.subplot(234)
ax5 = plt.subplot(235)
ax6 = plt.subplot(236)

# Print the type of ax1
print(type(ax1))

# Label each subplot with corresponding identities
ax1.text(0.3,0.5,'231',fontsize=18)
ax2.text(0.3,0.5,'232',fontsize=18)
ax3.text(0.3,0.5,'233',fontsize=18)
ax4.text(0.3,0.5,'234',fontsize=18)
ax5.text(0.3,0.5,'234',fontsize=18)
ax6.text(0.3,0.5,'236',fontsize=18)

plt.show()
```

The preceding code generates the following figure. Note how the subplots are ordered from left to right, top to bottom. When adding actual plot elements, it is essential to place them accordingly:

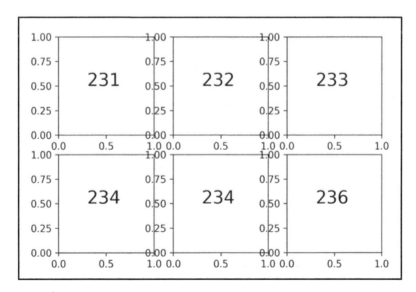

Also note that printing the type of one of the axes returns `<class 'matplotlib.axes._subplots.AxesSubplot'>` as a result.

Adding subplots with plt.figure.add_subplot()

There is an `add_subplot()` function similar to `plt.subplot()` under `plt.figure()` that allows us to create additional subplots under the same figure. Similar to `plt.subplot()`, it takes the row number, column number, and plot number as input arguments and allows arguments without commas for fewer than 10 plots.

We can also initiate the first subplot using this function. This code is a quick example:

```
import matplotlib.pyplot as plt

fig = plt.figure()
ax = fig.add_subplot(111)

plt.show()
```

This creates an empty plot area enclosed by four spines containing the *x* axis and *y* axis, as shown below. Note that we must call the `add_subplot()` function under a `figure` but not by `plt`:

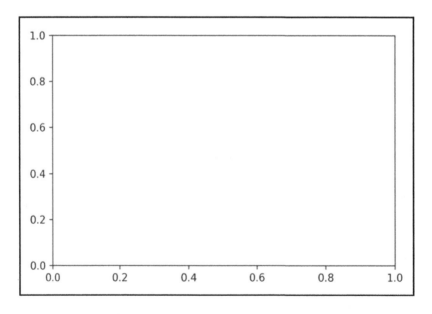

Let us further compare the differences between `fig.add_subplot()`.
and `plt.subplot()`. Here, we would be creating three empty subplots with different sizes and face colors.

We will first use try using `fig.add_subplot()`:

```
import matplotlib.pyplot as plt

fig = plt.figure()
ax1 = fig.add_subplot(111,facecolor='red')
ax2 = fig.add_subplot(121,facecolor='green')
ax3 = fig.add_subplot(233,facecolor='blue')

plt.show()
```

We get three overlapping subplots on the same figure, as shown below:

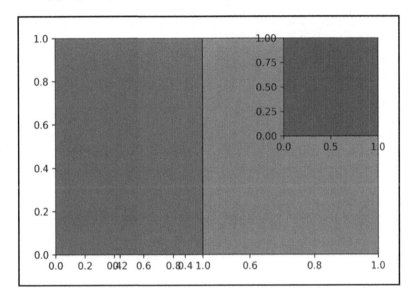

Next, we replace `fig.add_subplot()` with `plt.subplot()`:

```
import matplotlib.pyplot as plt

fig = plt.figure() # Note this line is optional here
ax1 = plt.subplot(111,facecolor='red')
ax2 = plt.subplot(121,facecolor='green')
ax3 = plt.subplot(233,facecolor='blue')

plt.show()
```

Notice in the following image that the red `ax1` subplot cannot be displayed:

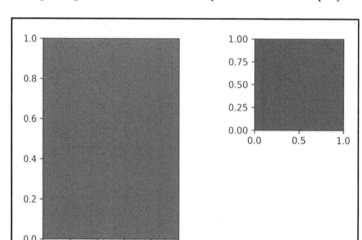

If we have already plotted the first subplot using `plt.subplot()` and would like to create additional subplots, we can call the `plt.gcf()` function to retrieve the `figure` object and store it as a variable. Then, we can call `fig.add_subplot()` as shown in the example before.

Hence, the following code is an alternative way to generate the three overlapping subplots:

```
import matplotlib.pyplot as plt

ax1 = plt.subplot(111,facecolor='red')
fig = plt.gcf() # get current figure
ax2 = fig.add_subplot(121,facecolor='green')
ax3 = fig.add_subplot(233,facecolor='blue')

plt.show()
```

Initiating an array of subplots with plt.subplots()

When we need to create a larger number of subplots of the same size, it can be quite inefficient to generate them one by one with the `plt.subplot()` or `fig.add_subplot()` function. In this case, we can call `plt.subplots()` to generate an array of subplots at once.

`plt.subplots()` takes in the number of rows and columns as input parameters, and returns a `Figure` together with a grid of subplots stored in a NumPy array. When there is no input parameter, `plt.subplots()` is equivalent to `plt.figure()` plus `plt.subplot()` by default.

Here is a code snippet for demonstration:

```python
import matplotlib.pyplot as plt

fig, axarr = plt.subplots(1,1)
print(type(fig))
print(type(axarr))

plt.show()
```

From the resultant screenshot , we can observe that `plt.subplots()` also returns the `Figure` and `AxesSubplot` objects:

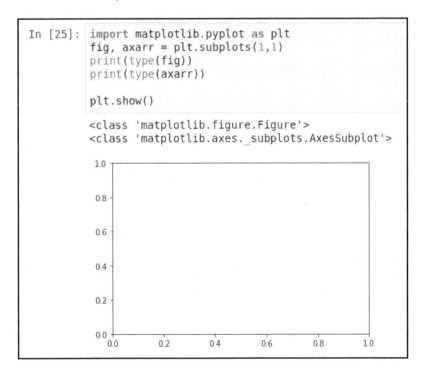

The next example illustrates a more useful case of `plt.subplots()`.

This time, we will create a figure of 3x4 subplots and label each in a nested `for` loop:

```
import matplotlib.pyplot as plt

fig, axarr = plt.subplots(3,4)
for i in range(3):
    for j in range(4):
        axarr[i][j].text(0.3,0.5,str(i)+','+str(j),fontsize=18)

plt.show()
```

Again, we can observe from this figure that the subplots are ordered in rows and then columns, as seen in the preceding examples:

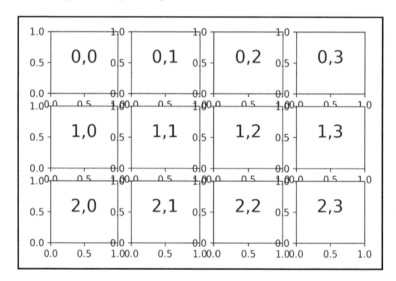

It is also possible to supply only one input parameter to `plt.subplots()`, which will be interpreted as the specified number of plots vertically stacked in rows. As the `plt.subplots()` function has essentially incorporated the `plt.figure()` function, we can also specify the figure dimensions by providing input to the `figsize` argument:

```
import numpy as np
import matplotlib.pyplot as plt

x = np.arange(0.0, 1.0, 0.01)
y1 = np.sin(8*np.pi*x)
y2 = np.cos(8*np.pi*x)
```

```
# Draw 1x2 subplots
fig, axarr = plt.subplots(2,figsize=(8,6))

axarr[0].plot(x,y1)
axarr[1].plot(x,y2,'red')

plt.show()
```

Note that the type of `axarr` is `<class 'numpy.ndarray'>`.

The preceding code results in the following figure with two rows of subplots:

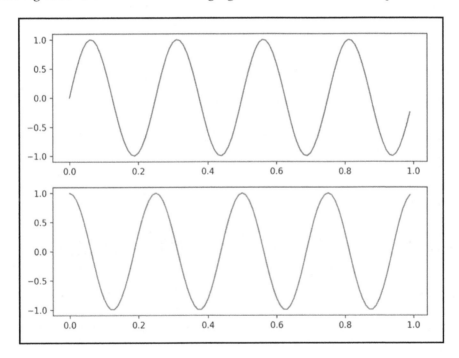

Shared axes

When using `plt.subplots()`, we can specify that the subplots should share the *x* axis and/or *y* axis to avoid cluttering.

Returning to the 3x4 subplots example earlier, suppose we turn on the shared axes option in `plt.subplots()` by supplying `sharex=True` and `sharey=True` as arguments, as in:

```
fig, axarr = plt.subplots(3,4,sharex=True,sharey=True)
```

We now obtain the following figure. Compared to the preceding example, it looks neater with the subplot axis labels removed except for the leftmost and bottom ones:

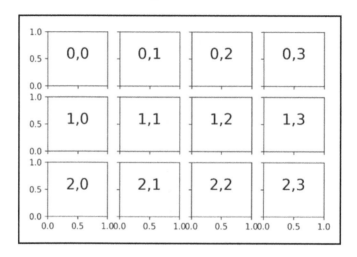

Setting the margin with plt.tight_layout()

Next, we can adjust the alignment. We may want to adjust the margin between each subplot, or leave no margin instead of having rows and columns of discrete boxes. In this case, we can use the `plt.tight_layout()` function. By default, it fits all subplots into the figure area when no parameters are supplied. It takes the keyword arguments `pad`, `w_pad`, and `h_pad` to control the padding around subplots. Let's look at the following code example:

```
import matplotlib.pyplot as plt

fig, axarr = plt.subplots(3,4,sharex=True,sharey=True)
for i in range(3):
    for j in range(4):
        axarr[i][j].text(0.3,0.5,str(i)+','+str(j),fontsize=18)

plt.tight_layout(pad=0, w_pad=-1.6, h_pad=-1)
```

We see from the following figure that the now there is no space between subplots, but there's some overlap of axis ticks.

We will learn how to adjust tick properties or to remove ticks in a later section:

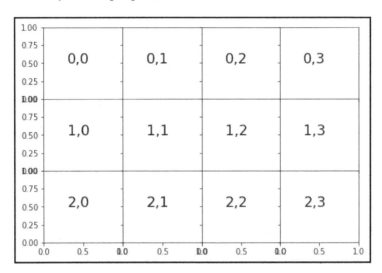

Aligning subplots of different dimensions with plt.subplot2grid()

While `plt.subplots()` provides a handy way to create grids of same-sized subplots, at times we may need to combine subplots of different sizes in a group. This is when `plt.subplot2grid()` comes into use.

`plt.subplot2grid()` takes in three to four parameters. The first tuple specifies the overall dimensions of the grid. The second tuple determines where in the grid the top left corner of a subplot starts. Finally we describe the subplot dimensions using the `rowspan` and `colspan` arguments.

Here is a code example to showcase the usage of this function:

```
import matplotlib.pyplot as plt

axarr = []
axarr.append(plt.subplot2grid((3,3),(0,0)))
axarr.append(plt.subplot2grid((3,3),(1,0)))
axarr.append(plt.subplot2grid((3,3),(0,2), rowspan=3))
```

```
axarr.append(plt.subplot2grid((3,3),(2,0), colspan=2))
axarr.append(plt.subplot2grid((3,3),(0,1), rowspan=2))

axarr[0].text(0.4,0.5,'0,0',fontsize=16)
axarr[1].text(0.4,0.5,'1,0',fontsize=16)
axarr[2].text(0.4,0.5,'0,2\n3 rows',fontsize=16)
axarr[3].text(0.4,0.5,'2,0\n2 cols',fontsize=16)
axarr[4].text(0.4,0.5,'0,1\n2 rows',fontsize=16)

plt.show()
```

The following is the resultant plot. Notice how the subplots of different sizes are aligned:

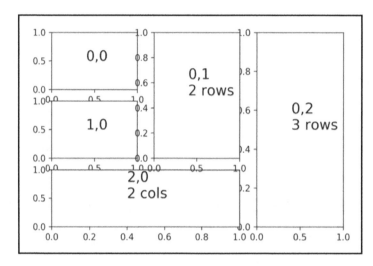

Drawing inset plots with fig.add_axes()

It is not a must for subplots to align side by side. In some occasions, such as when zooming in or out, we can also embed subplots on top of the parent plot layer. This can be done by `fig.add_axes()`. To add a subplot, here is the basic usage:

```
fig = plt.figure() # or fig = plt.gcf()
fig.add_axes([left, bottom, width, height])
```

The `left,` `bottom,` `width,` and `height` parameters are specified relative to the parent figure in terms of `float.` Note that `fig.add_axes()` returns an axes object, so you may store it as a variable such as `ax = fig.add_axes([left, bottom, width, height])` for further adjustments.

The following is a complete example where we try to plot the overview in a smaller embedded subplot:

```
import numpy as np
import matplotlib.pyplot as plt

fig = plt.figure()
np.random.seed(100)
# Prepare data
x = np.random.binomial(1000,0.6,1000)
y = np.random.binomial(1000,0.6,1000)
c = np.random.rand(1000)

# Draw the parent plot
ax = plt.scatter(x,y,s=1,c=c)
plt.xlim(580,650)
plt.ylim(580,650)

# Draw the inset subplot
ax_new = fig.add_axes([0.6, 0.6, 0.2, 0.2])
plt.scatter(x,y,s=1,c=c)
plt.show()
```

Let's check out the result in the figure:

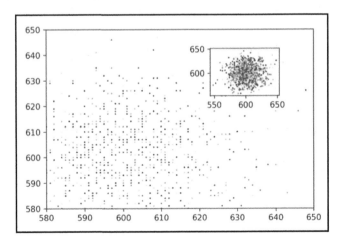

Adjusting subplot dimensions post hoc with plt.subplots_adjust

We can adjust the dimensions of a subplot with `plt.subplots_adjust()`, which takes in any combinations of parameters—`left`, `right`, `top`, and `bottom`—each defined relative to the parent axes.

Adjusting axes and ticks

In data visualization, it is often not enough to only display the trend in a relative sense. An axis scale is essential to facilitate value estimation for proper interpretation. Ticks are markers on an axis that denote the scale for this purpose. Depending on the nature of data and figure layout, we often need to adjust the scale and tick spacing to provide enough information without clutter. In this section, we are going to introduce the customization methods.

Customizing tick spacing with locators

There are two sets of ticks to mark coordinates on each axis: major and minor ticks. By default, Matplotlib tries to automatically optimize the tick spacing and format based on the data input. Wherever manual adjustment is needed, it can be done through setting these four locators: `xmajorLocator`, `xminorLocator`, `ymajorLocator`, `yminorLocator` via the function `set_major_locator`, or `set_minor_locator` on the respective axis. The following is a usage example, where `ax` is an axes object:

```
ax.xaxis.set_major_locator(xmajorLocator)
ax.xaxis.set_minor_locator(xminorLocator)
ax.yaxis.set_major_locator(ymajorLocator)
ax.yaxis.set_minor_locator(yminorLocator)
```

Here, we list the common locators and their usage.

Removing ticks with NullLocator

When `NullLocator` is used, ticks are removed from view.

Locating ticks in multiples with MultipleLocator

As the name implies, `MultipleLocator` generates ticks in multiples of a user-specified base. For example, if we would like our ticks to mark integers instead of floats, we can initialize the base by `MultipleLocator(1)`.

Locators to display date and time

For time series plotting, Matplotlib provides a list of tick locators to serve as datetime markers:

- `MinuteLocator`
- `HourLocator`
- `DayLocator`
- `WeekdayLocator`
- `MonthLocator`
- `YearLocator`
- `RRuleLocator`, which allows arbitrary date tick specification
- `AutoDateLocator`
- `MultipleDateLocator`

To plot time series, we can also use Pandas to specify the datetime format for data in the *x* axis.

Time series data can be resampled by aggregation methods such as `mean()`, `sum()`, or a custom function.

Customizing tick formats with formatters

Tick formatters control the formats of tick labels. It is used similarly to tick locators, as follows:

```
ax.xaxis.set_major_formatter(xmajorFormatter)
ax.xaxis.set_minor_formatter(xminorFormatter)
ax.yaxis.set_major_formatter(ymajorFormatter)
ax.yaxis.set_minor_formatter(yminorFormatter)
```

Using a non-linear axis scale

Depending on the distribution of our data, a linear scale may not be the best way to fit in all useful data points in a figure. In this case, we may need to modify the scale of the axes into a log or symmetric log scale. In Matplotlib, this can be done by `plt.xscale()` and `plt.yscale()` before defining the axes, or by `ax.set_xscale()` and `ax.set_yscale()` after an axis is defined.

We do not need to change the scale of the entire axis. To display a part of the axis in linear scale, we adjust the linear threshold with the argument `linthreshx` or `linthreshy`. To obtain a smooth continuous line, we can also mask the non-positive numbers with the argument `nonposx` or `nonposy`.

The following code snippet is an example of the different axis scales. For a simpler illustration, we only change the scale in the `y` axis. Similar operations can be applied to the `x` axis:

```
import numpy as np
import matplotlib.pyplot as plt

# Prepare 100 evenly spaced numbers from -200 to 200
x = np.linspace(-1000, 1000, 100)
y = x * 2
# Setup subplot with 3 rows and 2 columns, with shared x-axis.
# More details about subplots will be discussed in Chapter 3.
f, axarr = plt.subplots(2,3, figsize=(8,6), sharex=True)
for i in range(2):
    for j in range(3):
        axarr[i,j].plot(x, y)
        # Horizontal line (y=10)
        axarr[i,j].scatter([0], [10])

# Linear scale
axarr[0,0].set_title('Linear scale')

# Log scale, mask non-positive numbers
axarr[0,1].set_title('Log scale, nonposy=mask')
axarr[0,1].set_yscale('log', nonposy='mask')

# Log scale, clip non-positive numbers
axarr[0,2].set_title('Log scale, nonposy=clip')
axarr[0,2].set_yscale('log', nonposy='clip')

# Symlog
axarr[1,0].set_title('Symlog scale')
```

```
axarr[1,0].set_yscale('symlog')

# Symlog scale, expand the linear range to -100,100 (default=None)
axarr[1,1].set_title('Symlog scale, linthreshy=100')
axarr[1,1].set_yscale('symlog', linthreshy=100)

# Symlog scale, expand the linear scale to 3 (default=1)
# The linear region is expanded, while the log region is compressed.
axarr[1,2].set_title('Symlog scale, linscaley=3')
axarr[1,2].set_yscale('symlog', linscaley=3)
plt.show()
```

Let's compare the results of each axis scale in the following figure:

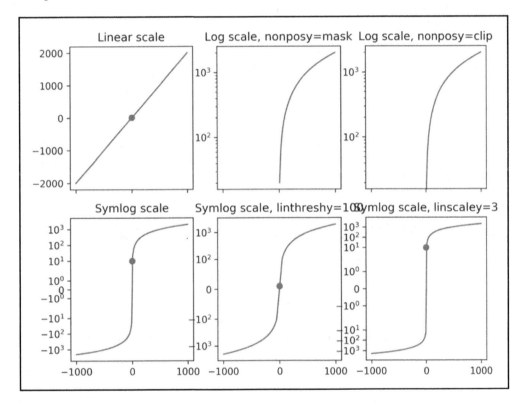

More on Pandas-Matplotlib integration

Pandas provides the DataFrame data structure commonly used in handling multivariate data. When we usually use the Pandas package for data I/O, storage, and preprocessing, it also provides a number of native integrations with Matplotlib for quick visualization.

To create these plots, we can call `df.plot(kind=plot_type)`, `df.plot.scatter()`, and so on. Here is a list of available plot types:

- `line`: Line plot (default)
- `bar`: Vertical bar plot
- `barh`: Horizontal bar plot
- `hist`: Histogram
- `box`: Boxplot
- `kde`: **Kernel Density Estimation (KDE)** plot
- `density`: The same as `kde`
- `area`: Area plot
- `pie`: Pie plot

We have created some of the simpler graphs in the previous chapters. Here, we will take the density plot as an example for discussion.

Showing distribution with the KDE plot

Similar to a histogram, the KDE plot is a method to visualize the shape of data distribution. It uses kernel smoothing to create smooth curves and is often combined with a histogram. It is useful in exploratory data analysis.

In the following example, we will compare the income in various age groups across different countries, with data obtained from surveys binned with different age groupings.

Here is the code for data curation:

```
import pandas as pd
import matplotlib.pyplot as plt

# Prepare the data
# Weekly earnings of U.S. wage workers in 2016, by age
# Downloaded from Statista.com
# Source URL:
https://www.statista.com/statistics/184672/median-weekly-earnings-of-full-t
```

```
ime-wage-and-salary-workers/
us_agegroups = [22,29.5,39.5,49.5]
# Convert to a rough estimation of monthly earnings by multiplying 4
us_incomes = [x*4 for x in [513,751,934,955]]

# Monthly salary in the Netherlands in 2016 per age group excluding
overtime (Euro)
# Downloaded from Statista.com
# Source URL:
https://www.statista.com/statistics/538025/average-monthly-wage-in-the-neth
erlands-by-age/
# take the center of each age group
nl_agegroups = [22.5, 27.5, 32.5, 37.5, 42.5, 47.5, 52.5]
nl_incomes = [x*1.113 for x in [1027, 1948, 2472, 2795, 2996, 3069, 3070]]

# Median monthly wage analyzed by sex, age group, educational attainment,
occupational group and industry section
# May-June 2016 (HKD)
# Downloaded form the website of Censor and Statistics Department of the
HKSAR government
# Source URL:
https://www.censtatd.gov.hk/fd.jsp?file=D5250017E2016QQ02E.xls&product_id=D
5250017&lang=1
hk_agegroups = [19.5, 29.5, 39.5, 49.5]
hk_incomes = [x/7.770 for x in [11900,16800,19000,16600]]
```

Let's now draw the KDE plots for comparison. We have prepared a reusable function to plot the three pieces of data with less repetition in the code:

```
import seaborn as sns
def kdeplot_income_vs_age(agegroups,incomes):
    plt.figure()
    sns.kdeplot(agegroups,incomes)
    plt.xlim(0,65)
    plt.ylim(0,6000)
    plt.xlabel('Age')
    plt.ylabel('Monthly salary (USD)')
    return

kdeplot_income_vs_age(us_agegroups,us_incomes)
kdeplot_income_vs_age(nl_agegroups,nl_incomes)
kdeplot_income_vs_age(hk_agegroups,hk_incomes)
```

Now we can look at the results, which are from top to bottom for the US, the Netherlands, and Hong Kong, respectively:

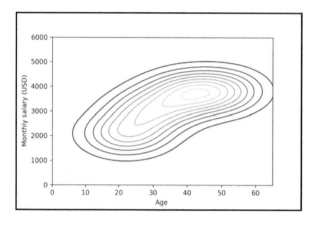

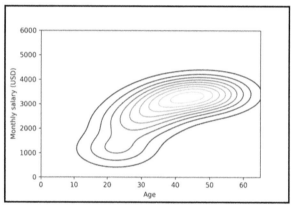

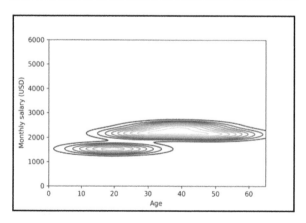

Of course, the figure is not a very accurate reflection of the original data, as extrapolation was involved before any tweaking (for instance, we do not have child labor data here, but the contours extend even to children below age **10**). Yet, we can observe a general difference in the pattern of income structures between ages **20** and **50** across the three economies, and to what extent the downloaded public data is comparable. We may then be able to suggest surveys with more useful groupings and perhaps to get more raw data points to suit our analyses.

Showing the density of bivariate data with hexbin plots

Scatter plot is a common method to show the distribution of data in a more raw form. But when data density goes over a threshold, it may not be the best visualization method as points can overlap and we lose information about the actual distribution.

A hexbin map is a way to improve the interpretation of data density, by showing the data density in an area by color intensity.

Here is an example to compare the visualization of the same dataset that aggregates in the center:

```
import pandas as pd
import numpy as np
# Prepare 2500 random data points densely clustered at center
np.random.seed(123)

df = pd.DataFrame(np.random.randn(2500, 2), columns=['x', 'y'])
df['y'] = df['y'] = df['y'] + np.arange(2500)
df['z'] = np.random.uniform(0, 3, 2500)

# Plot the scatter plot
ax1 = df.plot.scatter(x='x', y='y')
# Plot the hexbin plot
ax2 = df.plot.hexbin(x='x', y='y', C='z',
reduce_C_function=np.max,gridsize=25)

plt.show()
```

This is the scatter plot in `ax1`. We can see that many data points are overlapping:

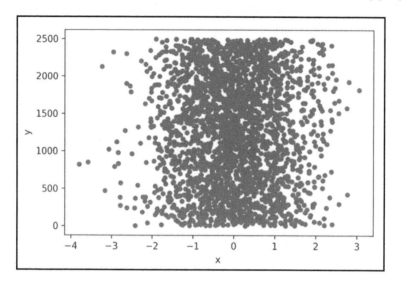

As for the hexbin map in `ax2`, although not all discrete raw data points are shown, we can clearly see the variation of data distribution in the center:

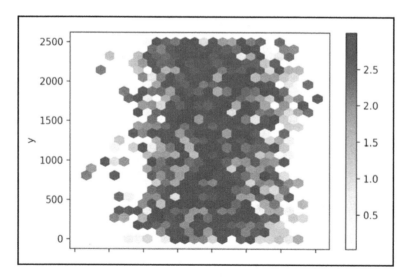

Expanding plot types with Seaborn

To install the Seaborn package, we open the terminal or command prompt and call `pip3 install --user seaborn`. For each use, we import the library by `import seaborn as sns`, where `sns` is a commonly used shorthand to save typing.

Visualizing multivariate data with a heatmap

A heatmap is a useful visualization method to illustrate multivariate data when there are many variables to compare, such as in a big data analysis. It is a plot that displays values in a color scale in a grid. It is among the most common plots utilized by bioinformaticians to display hundreds or thousands of gene expression values in one plot.

With Seaborn, drawing a heatmap is just one line away from importing the library. It is done by calling `sns.heatmap(df)`, where `df` is the Pandas DataFrame to be plotted. We can supply the `cmap` parameter to specify the color scale (`"colormap"`) to be used. You can revisit the previous chapter for more details on colormap usage.

To get a feel for heatmap, in the following example, we demonstrate the usage with the specification of the 7th and 8th generations of Intel Core CPUs, which involves dozens of models and four chosen metrics. Before looking at the plotting code, let's look at the structure of the Pandas DataFrame that stores the data:

```
# Data obtained from https://ark.intel.com/#@Processors
import pandas as pd

cpuspec = pd.read_csv('intel-cpu-7+8.csv').set_index('Name')
print(cpuspec.info())
cpuspec.head()
```

From the following screen capture of the output, we see that we simply put the labels as the index and different properties in each column:

```
<class 'pandas.core.frame.DataFrame'>
Index: 65 entries, i7-8809G to m3-7Y30
Data columns (total 5 columns):
Core            65 non-null int64
Max Frequency   49 non-null float64
Base Frequency  65 non-null float64
Cache           65 non-null int64
Gen             65 non-null int64
dtypes: float64(2), int64(3)
memory usage: 3.0+ KB
None
```

Name	Core	Max Frequency	Base Frequency	Cache	Gen
i7-8809G	4	4.2	3.1	8	8
i7-8709G	4	4.1	3.1	8	8
i7-8706G	4	4.1	3.1	8	8
i7-8705G	4	4.1	3.1	8	8
i7-8700K	6	4.7	3.7	12	8

Notice that there are 16 models that do not support boosting without the **Max Frequency** property value. It makes sense to consider the **Base Frequency** as the maximum for our purpose here. We will fill in the **NA** values with the `'Max Frequency'` by the corresponding `'Base Frequency'`:

```
cpuspec['Max Frequency'] = cpuspec['Max Frequency'].fillna(cpuspec['Base
Frequency'])
```

Now, let's draw the heatmap with the following code:

```
import matplotlib.pyplot as plt
import seaborn as sns

plt.figure(figsize=(13,13))
sns.heatmap(cpuspec.drop(['Gen'],axis=1),cmap='Blues')
plt.xticks(fontsize=16)
plt.show()
```

Simple, isn't it? Only one line of code actually draws the heatmap. This is also an example of how we can use basic Matplotlib code to adjust other fine details of the plot, such as figure dimensions and the `xticks` font size in this case. Let's look at the result:

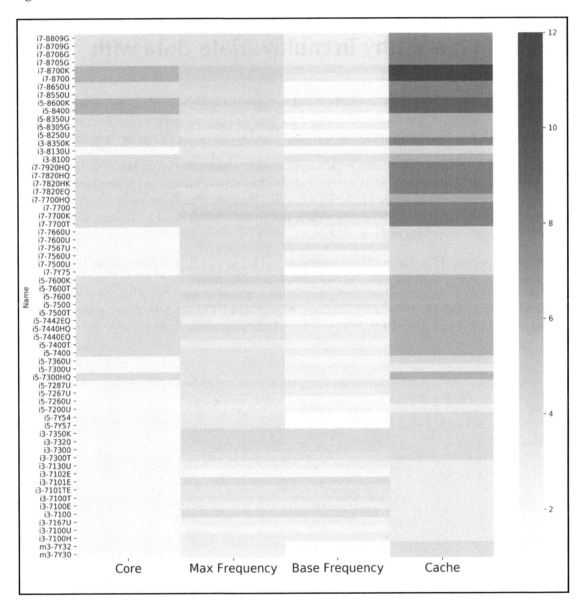

From the figure, even if we have absolutely no idea about these CPU models, we can easily infer something from the darker colors at the top among the i7 models. They are designed for higher performance with more core and cache space.

Showing hierarchy in multivariate data with clustermap

Sometimes, a heatmap illustration can be hard to interpret when there are too many alternating color bands. This is because our data may not be ordered in terms of similarity. In this case, we need to group more similar data together in order to see the structure.

For this purpose, Seaborn offers the `clustermap` API, which is a combination of heatmap and dendrogram. A dendrogram is a tree-shaped graph that clusters more similar variables under the same branches/leaves. Drawing a dendrogram involves generally unsupervised hierarchical clustering, which is run in the background by default when we call the `clustermap()` function.

Besides unsupervised clustering, if we have a priori knowledge of certain labels, we can also show it in colors with the `row_colors` keyword argument.

Here, we extend from the preceding heatmap example of CPU models, draw a clustered heatmap, and label the generation as row colors. Let's look at the code:

```
import seaborn as sns

row_colors = cpuspec['Gen'].map({7:'#a2ecec',8:'#ecaabb'}) # map color
values to generation
sns.clustermap(cpuspec.drop(['Gen'],axis=1),standard_scale=True,cmap='Blues
',row_colors=row_colors);
```

Again, calling the API is just as simple as the earlier heatmap, and we have generated the following figure:

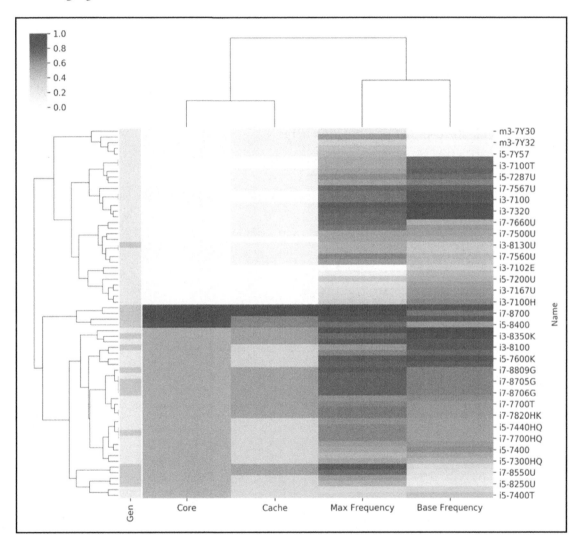

Other than being helpful in showing multiple properties of a larger number of samples, with some tweaking, clustermap can also be used in pairwise clustering to show the similarity among samples with all the available properties considered together.

To draw a pairwise clustering heatmap, we have to first calculate the correlation between samples from the various property values, convert the correlation matrix into a distance matrix, and then perform hierarchical clustering to generate linkage values for dendrogram plotting. We use the `scipy` package for this purpose. To understand more about linkage calculation methods, please refer to the SciPy documentation.

We will provide the user-defined function here:

```
from scipy.cluster import hierarchy
from scipy.spatial import distance
import seaborn as sns

def
pairwise_clustermap(df,method='average',metric='cityblock',figsize=(13,13),
cmap='viridis',**kwargs):
    correlations_array = np.asarray(df.corr())

    row_linkage = hierarchy.linkage(
    distance.pdist(correlations_array), method=method)

    col_linkage = hierarchy.linkage(
    distance.pdist(correlations_array.T), method=method)

    g = sns.clustermap(correlations, row_linkage=row_linkage,
col_linkage=col_linkage, \
    method=method, metric=metric, figsize=figsize, cmap=cmap,**kwargs)
    return g
```

Here is the result of the pairwise clustering plot:

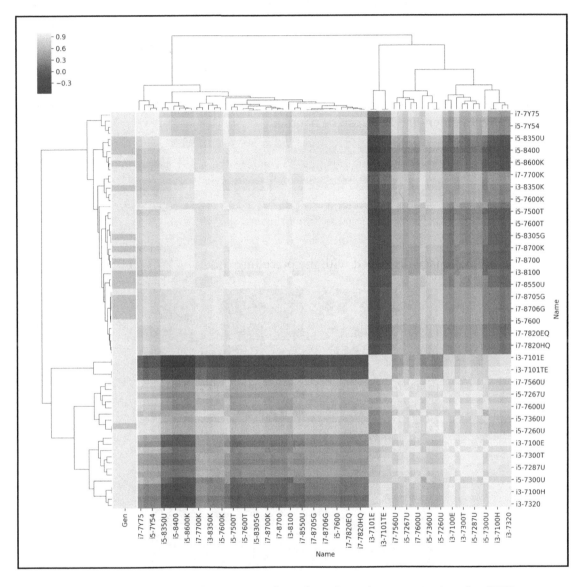

From both heatmaps, we can observe that, based on these four properties, the CPUs seem to be better clustered by the product line suffix such as **U**, **K**, and **Y** than by brand modifiers such as **i5** and **i7**. When we approach data, this is among the analytical skills where observation of the similarity within a large group is required.

Image plotting

In analyzing images, the first step is to convert colors into numerical values. Matplotlib provides APIs to read and show an image matrix of RGB values.

The following is a quick code example of reading an image into a NumPy array with `plt.imread('image_path')`, and we show it with `plt.imshow(image_ndarray)`. Make sure that the Pillow package is installed so that more image types other than PNG can be handled:

```
import matplotlib.pyplot as plt
# Source image downloaded under CC0 license: Free for personal and
commercial use. No attribution required.
# Source image address:
https://pixabay.com/en/rose-pink-blossom-bloom-flowers-693155/
img = plt.imread('ch04.img/mpldev_ch04_rose.jpg')
plt.imshow(img)
```

Here is the original image displayed with the preceding code:

After showing the original image, we will try to work with transforming the image by changing the color values in the image matrix. We will create a high-contrast image by setting the RGB values to either 0 or 255 (max) at the threshold of 160. Here is how to do so:

```
# create a copy because the image object from `plt.imread()` is read-only
imgcopy = img.copy()
imgcopy[img<160] = 0
imgcopy[img>=160] = 255
plt.imshow(imgcopy)
plt.show()
```

This is the result of the transformed image. By artificially increasing the contrast, we have created a pop art image!

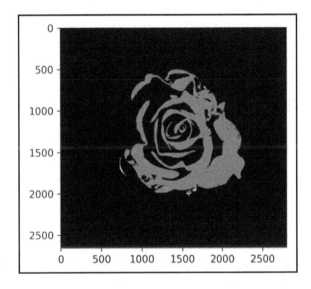

To demonstrate a more practical use for the image processing feature of Matplotlib, we will demonstrate MNIST. MNIST is a famous dataset of handwritten digits. It is often used in tutorials of machine learning algorithms. Here, we will not go into details of machine learning but rather will try to recreate the scenario where we visually inspect the dataset during the exploratory data analysis stage.

We can download the entire MNIST dataset from the official site at http://yann.lecun.com/exdb/mnist/. To ease our discussion and introduce useful package for Python machine learning, we load the data from Keras, which is a high-level API that facilitates neural network implementation. The MNIST dataset from the Keras package contains 70,000 images, arranged in tuples of coordinates and corresponding labels to facilitate model training and testing when building neural networks.

Let's first import the package:

```
from keras.datasets import mnist
```

The data is loaded only when load_data() is called. Because Keras is intended for training, the data is returned in tuples of training and testing datasets, each containing the actual image color values and labels, named X and y by convention here:

```
(X_train,y_train),(X_test,y_test) = mnist.load_data()
```

When initially called, load_data() may take some time to download the MNIST dataset from the online database.

We can inspect the dimensions of the data as follows:

```
for d in X_train, y_train, X_test, y_test:
    print(d.shape)
```

Here is the output:

```
(60000, 28, 28)
(60000,)
(10000, 28, 28)
(10000,)
```

Finally let's take one of the images in the X_train set and plot it in black and white with plt.imshow():

```
plt.imshow(X_train[123], cmap='gray_r')
```

From the following figure, we can easily read seven with our bare eyes. In the case of solving real image recognition problems, we may sample some mis-called images and consider strategies to optimize our training algorithms:

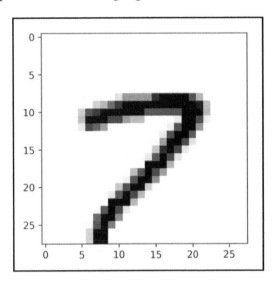

Financial plotting

There are situations where more raw values per time point are needed to understand a trend for prediction. The candlestick plot is a commonly used visualization in technical analysis in finance to show a price trend, most often seen in the stock market. To draw a candlestick plot, we can use the `candlestick_ohlc` API in the `mpl_finance` package.

`mpl_finance` can be downloaded from GitHub. After cloning the repository in the Python site-packages directory, call `python3 setup.py install` in the terminal to install it.

`candlestick_ohlc()` takes the input of a Pandas DataFrame with five columns: `date` in floating-point numbers, `open`, `high`, `low`, and `close`.

In our tutorial, we use the cryptocurrency market values as an example. Let's again look at the data table we obtained:

```
import pandas as pd
# downloaded from kaggle "Cryptocurrency Market Data" dataset curated by
user jvent
# Source URL: https://www.kaggle.com/jessevent/all-crypto-currencies
crypt = pd.read_csv('crypto-markets.csv')
print(crypt.shape)
crypt.head()
```

Here is the how the table looks:

(679183, 13)

Out[18]:

	slug	symbol	name	date	ranknow	open	high	low	close	volume	market	close_ratio	spread
0	bitcoin	BTC	Bitcoin	2013-04-28	1	135.30	135.98	132.10	134.21	0	1500520000	0.5438	3.88
1	bitcoin	BTC	Bitcoin	2013-04-29	1	134.44	147.49	134.00	144.54	0	1491160000	0.7813	13.49
2	bitcoin	BTC	Bitcoin	2013-04-30	1	144.00	146.93	134.05	139.00	0	1597780000	0.3843	12.88
3	bitcoin	BTC	Bitcoin	2013-05-01	1	139.00	139.89	107.72	116.99	0	1542820000	0.2882	32.17
4	bitcoin	BTC	Bitcoin	2013-05-02	1	116.38	125.60	92.28	105.21	0	1292190000	0.3881	33.32

Let's select the first cryptocurrency, Bitcoin, as our example. The following code selects the OHLC values in the month of December 2017 and sets the index as `date` in the datetime format:

```
from matplotlib.dates import date2num
btc =
crypt[crypt['symbol']=='BTC'][['date','open','high','low','close']].set_ind
ex('date',drop=False)
btc['date'] = pd.to_datetime(btc['date'], format='%Y-%m-
%d').apply(date2num)
btc.index = pd.to_datetime(btc.index, format='%Y-%m-%d')
btc = btc['2017-12-01':'2017-12-31']
btc = btc[['date','open','high','low','close']]
```

Next, we will draw the candlestick plot. Recall the techniques to set axis ticks to fine-tune time markers:

```
import matplotlib.pyplot as plt
from matplotlib.dates import WeekdayLocator, DayLocator, DateFormatter,
MONDAY
from mpl_finance import candlestick_ohlc
# from matplotlib.finance import candlestick_ohlc deprecated in 2.0 and
removed in 2.2
```

```
fig, ax = plt.subplots()

candlestick_ohlc(ax,btc.values,width=0.8)
ax.xaxis_date() # treat the x data as dates
ax.xaxis.set_major_locator(WeekdayLocator(MONDAY)) # major ticks on the
Mondays
ax.xaxis.set_minor_locator(DayLocator()) # minor ticks on the days
ax.xaxis.set_major_formatter(DateFormatter('%Y-%m-%d'))

# Align the xtick labels
plt.setp(ax.get_xticklabels(), horizontalalignment='right')

# Set x-axis label
ax.set_xlabel('Date',fontsize=16)

# Set y-axis label
ax.set_ylabel('Price (US $)',fontsize=16)
plt.show()
```

`mpl_finance` can be installed by running the following command:

pip3 install --user
https://github.com/matplotlib/mpl_finance/archive/master.zip

We can observe that the rapid rise of Bitcoin values in early December turns its direction in mid-December 2017:

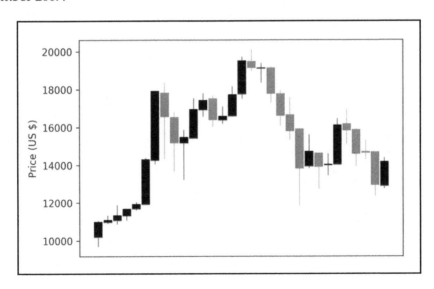

3D plots with Axes3D

We have so far discussed plotting in two dimensions. In fact, there are numerous occasions where we may need 3D data visualizations. Examples include illustrating more complex mathematical functions, terrain features, fluid dynamics in physics, as well as just showing one more facet of our data.

In Matplotlib, it can done by `Axes3D` in the `mplot3d` library within `mpl_toolkits`.

We just need to specify `projection='3d'` when defining an axes object after importing the library. Next, we just have to define the axes with x, y, and z coordinates. Supported plot types include scatter plot, line plot, bar plot, contour plots, wireframe plots, and surface plots with or without triangulation.

The following is an example of drawing a 3D surface plot:

```
import numpy as np
import matplotlib.pyplot as plt
from mpl_toolkits.mplot3d import Axes3D


fig = plt.figure()
ax = fig.add_subplot(111, projection='3d')

x = np.linspace(-2, 2, 60)
y = np.linspace(-2, 2, 60)
x, y = np.meshgrid(x, y)
r = np.sqrt(x**2 + y**2)
z = np.cos(r)
surf = ax.plot_surface(x, y, z, rstride=2, cstride=2, cmap='viridis',
linewidth=0)
```

 Matplotlib Axes3D is useful for plotting simple 3D plots with the usual Matplotlib syntax and appearance. For advanced scientific 3D plotting with Python demanding high rendering, it is recommended to use the Mayavi package. Here is the official website of the project for more details: `http://code.enthought.com/pages/mayavi-project.html`.

From the following screenshot, we see that the color gradient also helps in portraying the shape of the 3D plot:

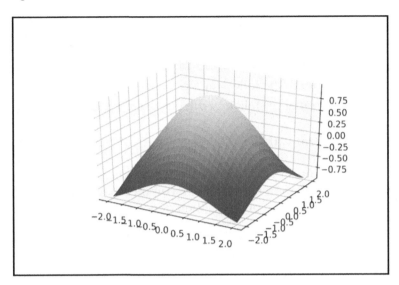

Geographical plotting

To demonstrate the power of Matplotlib with third-party packages, we will illustrate its usage in spatial analysis. Since the invention of satellites, a myriad of useful **Geographics Information System (GIS)** data has been generated to facilitate various analyses, from natural phenomena to human activities.

To utilize this data, there are common Python packages integrated with Matplotlib to show spatial data on a map, such as Basemap, GeoPandas, Cartopy, and Descartes. In this final section of the chapter, we will briefly introduce the usage of the first two packages.

Basemap

Basemap is among the most popular Matplotlib-based plotting toolkits to plot over world maps. It is a handy way to show any geographical location.

To install Basemap, do this:

1. Unpack in $Python3_dir/site-packages/mpl_toolkits
2. Enter the Basemap installation directory: cd $basemap_dir
3. Enter the geos directory in the Basemap directory: cd $basemap/geos-3.3.3
4. Install the GEOS library via ./configure, make, and make install
5. Install PyProj (refer to the following tip)
6. Return to the Basemap installation directory and run python3 setup.py install
7. Set the environment variable PROJ_DIR=$pyproj_dir/lib/pyproj/data

Basemap requires PyProj as a dependency, where there are recurrent reports of installation failures. We recommend installing from GitHub with prior installation of the Cython dependency.

1. Clone the PyProj GitHub repository from https://github.com/jswhit/pyproj into the Python site packages directory
2. Install the Cython dependency with pip install --user cython
3. Enter the PyProj directory and install using python3 setup.py install

For Windows users, it could be easier to install via Anaconda with the command prompt conda install -c conda-forge geopandas.

As a brief introduction, we will show how to draw our beautiful Earth with shaded terrain with the following code snippet:

```
from mpl_toolkits.basemap import Basemap
import matplotlib.pyplot as plt

# Initialize a Basemap object
# Use orthogonal spherical projection
# Adjust the focus by setting the latitude and longitude
map = Basemap(projection='ortho', lat_0=20, lon_0=80)

# To shade terrain by relief. This step may take some time.
map.shadedrelief()
```

```
# Draw the country boundaries in white
map.drawcountries(color='white')
plt.show()
```

Here is how the plot looks:

Besides showing the earth as a sphere with orthogonal projection as shown in the preceding figure, we can also set `projection='cyl'` to use the Miller Cylindrical projection for a flat rectangular illustration.

Basemap provides plenty map drawing functions, such as drawing coastlines and plotting data over maps with hexbin or streamplot. Their details can be found in the official tutorials at `http://basemaptutorial.readthedocs.io`. As in-depth geographical analysis is beyond the scope of this book, we will leave a more specific exploration of its usage as an exercise for interested readers.

GeoPandas

GeoPandas is a geographical plotting package integrated with Matplotlib. It has comprehensive functionalities to read common GIS file formats.

To use GeoPandas, we will import the library as follows:

```
import geopandas as gpd
import matplotlib.pyplot as plt
```

In the following example, we will explore the climate change data prepared by the World Bank Group.

We have selected the projection of precipitation in 2080-2099 based on scenario B1: a convergent world with global population peaking in mid-century and then declining. The storyline describes economies becoming more service- and information-oriented, with the introduction of clean and resource-efficient technologies but without additional climate initiatives.

As input, we have downloaded the shapefile (.shp), which is one of the standard formats used in geographical data analysis:

```
# Downloaded from the Climate Change Knowledge portal by the World Bank
Group
# Source URL: http://climate4development.worldbank.org/open/#precipitation
world_pr = gpd.read_file('futureB.ppt.totals.median.shp')
world_pr.head()
```

We can look at the first few rows of the GeoPandas DataFrame. Note that the shape data is stored in the geometry column:

	ANNUAL	FID	ANN90	ANN10	UNCERTAIN	UCP	geometry
0	27.169403	0_0	43.493927	-9.617419	53.11	1.95	POLYGON ((-181 -81, -181 -79, -179 -79, -179 -...
1	29.888596	1_0	46.822582	-10.193469	57.02	1.91	POLYGON ((-179 -81, -179 -79, -177 -79, -177 -...
2	32.919357	2_0	51.010445	-10.960211	61.97	1.88	POLYGON ((-177 -81, -177 -79, -175 -79, -175 -...
3	36.056152	3_0	52.492485	-11.570847	64.06	1.78	POLYGON ((-175 -81, -175 -79, -173 -79, -173 -...
4	38.931015	4_0	52.384979	-12.343842	64.73	1.66	POLYGON ((-173 -81, -173 -79, -171 -79, -171 -...

Next, we will add borders to the world map to better identify the locations:

```
# Downloaded from thematicmapping.org
# Source URL http://thematicmapping.org/downloads/world_borders.php
world_borders = gpd.read_file('TM_WORLD_BORDERS_SIMPL-0.3.shp')
world_borders.head()
```

Here we inspect the GeoPandas DataFrame. The shape information is also stored in the `geometry` as expected:

	FIPS	ISO2	ISO3	UN	NAME	AREA	POP2005	REGION	SUBREGION	LON	LAT	geometry
0	AC	AG	ATG	28	Antigua and Barbuda	44	83039	19	29	-61.783	17.078	(POLYGON ((-61.68666800000003 17.0244410000001...
1	AG	DZ	DZA	12	Algeria	238174	32854159	2	15	2.632	28.163	POLYGON ((2.963610000000017 36.802216, 4.78583...
2	AJ	AZ	AZE	31	Azerbaijan	8260	8352021	142	145	47.395	40.430	(POLYGON ((45.08332252502441 39.76804542541504...
3	AL	AL	ALB	8	Albania	2740	3153731	150	39	20.068	41.143	POLYGON ((19.43621399999998 41.02106500000001,...
4	AM	AM	ARM	51	Armenia	2820	3017661	142	145	44.563	40.534	POLYGON ((45.15387153625488 41.1986026763916, ...

The geometry data will be plotted as filled polygons. To draw the edges only, we will generate the geometry of borders by `GeoSeries.boundary`:

```
# Initialize an figure and an axes as the canvas
fig,ax = plt.subplots()

# Plot the annual precipitation data in ax
world_pr.plot(ax=ax,column='ANNUAL')

# Draw the simple worldmap borders
world_borders.boundary.plot(ax=ax,color='#cccccc',linewidth=0.6)

plt.show()
```

Now, we have obtained this result:

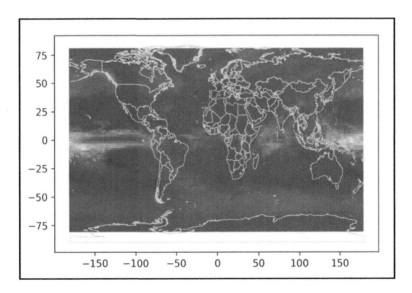

The website also provides data for another scenario, A2, which describes a very heterogeneous world, with local identities preserved. How will the picture look? Will it look similar or strikingly different? Let's download the file to find out!

Again, GeoPandas provides many APIs for more advanced usage. Readers can refer to `http://geopandas.org/` for the full documentation or further details.

Summary

Congratulations! We have come a long way in our advanced usage of Matplotlib. In this chapter, we learned how to draw and share axes between subplots, use a non-linear axis scale, adjust tick formatters and locators, plot images, create advanced plots with Seaborn, create a candlestick plot for financial data, draw simple 3D plots with Axes3D, and visualize geographic data with Basemap and GeoPandas.

You're all set to dig deeper into integrating these skills with your desired applications. In the next few chapters, we will be working with the different backends supported by Matplotlib. Stay tuned!

Embedding Matplotlib in GTK+3

5

We have worked on quite a few examples so far, and now have a good foundation from which to use Matplotlib to generate data plots and figures. While using Matplotlib alone is very handy in generating interactive figures, experimenting with datasets, and understanding substructures of data, there may be instances where we want an application to acquire, parse, and display our data.

In this chapter, we will study examples on how to embed Matplotlib in applications through GTK+3.

Installing and setting up GTK+3

Setting up GTK+3 is fairly simple and straightforward. There are quite a few ways to install GTK+3 depending on your OS version and environment.

We encourage our readers refer to the link: `https://python-gtk-3-tutorial.readthedocs.io/en/latest/install.html` for the latest updates and information on installation.

At the time of writing this book, the official website advises users to install GTK+3 through JHBuild. However, users have experienced a compatibility issue with JHBuild with the macOS El Capitan.

We recommend macOS users to use the package manager `brew` to install GTK+3.

GTK+3 can be installed simply if you have `brew` installed in your macOS:

```
#Installing the gtk3 package
brew install gtk3
#Installing PyGObject
brew install pygobject3
```

For Linux systems such as Ubuntu, GTK+3 is installed by default. For sophisticated and advanced users who prefer a more customized approach to installing GTK+3, we encourage referring their website to obtain the most recently updated information.

 We have observed that GTK+3 visualization is not as compatible with IPython Notebook. We encourage you to run the code on the Terminal for best results.

A brief introduction to GTK+3

Before exploring the various examples and applications, let's first acquire a brief, high-level understanding of the GTK+3.

GTK+3 contains a set of graphical control elements (widgets) and is a highly usable, feature-rich toolkit used to develop graphical user interfaces. It has cross-platform compatibility and is relatively easy to use. GTK+3 is an object-oriented widget toolkit written in the C programming language. Therefore, when running GTK+3 in Python, we need a wrapper to call the functions in the GTK+3 library. In this case, PyGObject is a Python module that serves as the wrapper and saves us time by not having to learn two languages to plot our figures. PyGObject exclusively supports GTK+3 or later versions. If you prefer to use GTK+2 in your application, we recommend using PyGTK instead.

Together with the Glade GUI builder, they provide a very powerful application development environment.

Introduction to the GTK+3 signal system

GTK+3 is an event-driven toolkit, which means it is always dormant in a loop function and waiting (*listening*) for events to occur; then it passes control to the appropriate function. Examples of events are a click on a button, menu item activation, ticking a checkbox, and so forth. When widgets receive an event, they frequently emit one or more signals. That signal will then evoke functions that you have connected to, in this case known as **callbacks**. This passing of control is done using the concept of signals.

Although the terminology is almost identical, GTK+3 signals are not the same as Unix system signals and are not implemented using them.

When an *event* such as the press of a mouse button occurs, the appropriate signal is emitted by the click that received the widget. This is one of the most important parts of how GTK+3 works. There are signals that all widgets inherit, such as *destroy* and *delete-event*, and there are signals that are widget-specific, such as toggling on a toggle button. To make the signal framework functional, we need to set up a signal handler to catch those signals and call the appropriate function.

From a more abstract point of view, a generic example is as follows:

```
handler_id = widget.connect("Event", callback, data )
```

`widget`, shown in this generic example, is an instance of a widget we created earlier. It can display widgets, buttons, toggles, or text data entry. Each widget has its own particular *event* that must occur for it to respond. If the widget is a button, and when there is an action such as a click, a signal is issued. The `callback` argument is the name of the callback function. The callback function will be executed when the *event* has occurred. Finally, the `data` argument includes any data that should be passed when the signal is generated; this is optional and can be left out if the *callback* function requires no argument.

Here is our first sample of GTK+3:

```
#In here, we import the GTK module in order to access GTK+3's classes and
functions
#We want to make sure we are importing GTK+3 and not any other version of
the library
#Therefore we require_version('Gtk','3.0')
import gi
gi.require_version('Gtk', '3.0')
from gi.repository import Gtk

#This line uses the GTK+3 functions and creates an empty window
window = Gtk.Window(title="Hello World!")
#We created a handler that connects window's delete event to ensure the
application
#is terminated if we click on the close button
window.connect("destroy",Gtk.main_quit)
#Here we display the window
```

```
window.show_all()
#This tells the code to run the main loop until Gtk.main_quit is called
Gtk.main()
```

To run this code, readers can either copy and paste or it save the code into a file named `first_gtk_example.py` and run it in the Terminal as follows:

python3 first_gtk_example.py

The readers should be able to create an empty 200x200 pixel window (by default when not specified otherwise), shown as follows:

Figure 1

To fully appreciate the usefulness of GTK3+, it is advisable that the code be written as a PyGObject.

The following code demonstrates a modified, slightly more complicated example of having two click buttons in one window, each performing different tasks!

Readers should install `cairocffi` through `pip3` before running the examples in this chapter:

`pip3 install cairocffi`

The `cairocffi` library is a CFFI-based drop-in replacement for Pycairo, and is necessary in this case. Now let's delve into the code:

```
#Again, here we import the GTK module
import gi
gi.require_version('Gtk', '3.0')
from gi.repository import Gtk

#From here, we define our own class, namely TwoClicks.
#This is a sub-class of Gtk.Window
class TwoClicks(Gtk.Window):
    #Instantiation operation will creates an empty object
    #Therefore, python3 uses __init__() to *construct* an object
    #__init__() will be automatically invoked when the object is being
created!
    #You can call this the constructor in Python3
    #Noted that *self* here indicates the reference of the object created
from this class
    #Anything starting with self.X refers to the local function or
variables of the object itself!
    def __init__(self):
        #In here, we are essentially constructing a Gtk.Window object
        #And parsing the information title="Hello world" to the constructor
of Gtk.Window
        #Therefore, the window will have a title of "Hello World"
        Gtk.Window.__init__(self, title="Hello World")
        #Since we have two click buttons, we created a horizontally
oriented box container
        #with 20 pixels placed in between children - the two click buttons
        self.box = Gtk.Box(spacing=100)
        #This assigns the box to become the child of the top-level window
        self.add(self.box)
        #Here we create the first button - click1, with the title "Print
once!" on top of it
        self.click1 = Gtk.Button(label="Print once!")
        #We assign a handler and connect the *Event* (clicked) with the
*callback/function* (on_click1)
        #Noted that, we are now calling the function of the object itself
        #Therefore we are using *self.onclick1
        self.click1.connect("clicked", self.on_click1)
        #Gtk.Box.pack_start() has a directionality here, it positions
widgets from left to right!
        self.box.pack_start(self.click1, True, True, 0)
        #The same applies to click 2, except that we connect it with a
different function
        #which prints Hello World 5 times!
        self.click2 = Gtk.Button(label="Print 5 times!")
```

```
        self.click2.connect("clicked", self.on_click2)
        self.box.pack_start(self.click2, True, True, 0)
    #Here defines a function on_click1 in the Class TwoClicks
    #This function will be triggered when the button "Print once!" is
clicked
    def on_click1(self, widget):
        print("Hello World")
    #Here defines a function on_click2 in the Class TwoClicks
    #This function will be triggered when the button "Print 5 times!" is
clicked
    def on_click2(self, widget):
        for i in range(0,5):
            print("Hello World")

#Here we instantiate an object, namely window
window = TwoClicks()
#Here we want the window to be close when the user click on the close
button
window.connect("delete-event", Gtk.main_quit)
#Here we display the window!
window.show_all()
#This tells the code to run the main loop until Gtk.main_quit is called
Gtk.main()
```

Here is what you will get from the preceding snippet:

Figure 2

Clicking on different buttons will result in obtaining different outcomes on the Terminal.

This example serves as an introduction to the **object-oriented programming (OOP)** style. OOP is fairly sophisticated for novice users, yet it is one of the best ways to arrange one's code, create modules, and make it more readable and usable for other programmers. Although novice users may not have noticed, we have already used a lot of OOP concepts in the first four chapters.

By understanding `init()` and `self`, we are now ready to delve into more advanced programming skills. So, let's try some more advanced examples! What if we want to embed some of the plots we have made into GTK+3 windows? We do the following:

```
#Same old, importing Gtk module, we are also importing some other stuff
this time
#such as numpy and the backends of matplotlib
import gi, numpy as np, matplotlib.cm as cm
gi.require_version('Gtk', '3.0')
from gi.repository import Gtk

#From here, we are importing some essential backend tools from matplotlib
#namely the NavigationToolbar2GTK3 and the FigureCanvasGTK3Agg
from matplotlib.backends.backend_gtk3 import NavigationToolbar2GTK3 as
NavigationToolbar
from matplotlib.backends.backend_gtk3agg import FigureCanvasGTK3Agg as
FigureCanvas
from matplotlib.figure import Figure

#Some numpy functions to create the polar plot
from numpy import arange, pi, random, linspace

#Here we define our own class MatplotlibEmbed
#By simply instantiating this class through the __init__() function,
#A polar plot will be drawn by using Matplotlib, and embedded to GTK3+
window
class MatplotlibEmbed(Gtk.Window):

    #Instantiation
    def __init__(self):
        #Creating the Gtk Window
        Gtk.Window.__init__(self, title="Embedding Matplotlib")
        #Setting the size of the GTK window as 400,400
        self.set_default_size(400,400)

        #Readers should find it familiar, as we are creating a matplotlib
figure here with a dpi(resolution) 100
        self.fig = Figure(figsize=(5,5), dpi=100)
        #The axes element, here we indicate we are creating 1x1 grid and
putting the subplot in the only cell
        #Also we are creating a polar plot, therefore we set projection as
'polar
        self.ax = self.fig.add_subplot(111, projection='polar')

        #Here, we borrow one example shown in the matplotlib gtk3 cookbook
        #and show a beautiful bar plot on a circular coordinate system
        self.theta = linspace(0.0, 2 * pi, 30, endpoint=False)
```

```
        self.radii = 10 * random.rand(30)
        self.width = pi / 4 * random.rand(30)
        self.bars = self.ax.bar(self.theta, self.radii, width=self.width,
bottom=0.0)

        #Here defines the color of the bar, as well as setting it to be
transparent
        for r, bar in zip(self.radii, self.bars):
            bar.set_facecolor(cm.jet(r / 10.))
            bar.set_alpha(0.5)
        #Here we generate the figure
        self.ax.plot()

        #Here comes the magic, a Vbox is created
        #VBox is a containder subclassed from Gtk.Box, and it organizes its
child widgets into a single column
        self.vbox = Gtk.VBox()
        #After creating the Vbox, we have to add it to the window object
itself!
        self.add(self.vbox)

        #Creating Canvas which store the matplotlib figure
        self.canvas = FigureCanvas(self.fig)  # a Gtk.DrawingArea
        # Add canvas to vbox
        self.vbox.pack_start(self.canvas, True, True, 0)

        # Creating toolbar, which enables the save function!
        self.toolbar = NavigationToolbar(self.canvas, self)
        self.vbox.pack_start(self.toolbar, False, False, 0)

#The code here should be self-explanatory by now! Or refer to earlier
examples for in-depth explanation
window = MatplotlibEmbed()
window.connect("delete-event", Gtk.main_quit)
window.show_all()
Gtk.main()
```

In this example, we created a vertical box and put both the canvas (with the figure) and the toolbar in it:

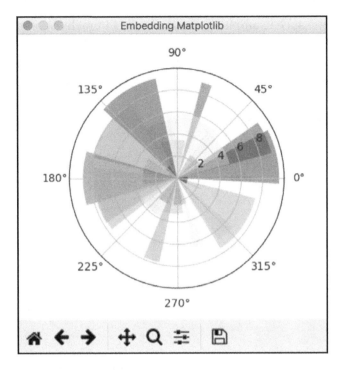

Figure 3

It seems like it is fairly easy to incorporate Matplotlib figures right into GTK+3, doesn't it? If you have your own figure that you wish to plug it into the GTK+3 engine, simply expand on the *polar* plot example and then you can start playing with your own figure with this template!

One additional thing we did here is create a toolbar and put it at the bottom of the figure. Remember that we are using a VBox in organizing the widgets? V in this case stands for vertical, which organizes data from top to bottom. Therefore, when putting the toolbar after the canvas, we have such an ordering. The toolbar is a great place to modify and save your figures elegantly.

So let's try a few more examples and see how we can create some interactive plots by combining GTK+3 and Matplotlib. One very important concept is event connections with Matplotlib through canvas; this can be achieved by calling the `mpl_connect()` function.

There are many good examples that can be found on the *Matplotlib Cookbook* online.

Let's walk through one such example that provides an interactive zoom-in function. Here is a preview of the output of the code:

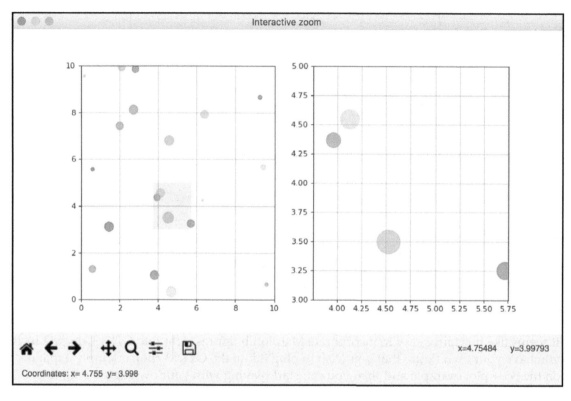

Figure 4

The window comprises two subplots; the plot on the left side is the big picture, while the plot on the right side is the zoomed-in version. The area chosen for enlargement is designated by the gray box on the left, and the gray box is movable along the click of your mouse. This may sound complicated but it can easily be accomplished by just a few lines of code. We would suggest readers first read the following code featuring the class `DrawPoints` and try to trace the logic starting from `window = Gtk.Window()`.

Here's an in-depth explanation of the code:

```
#Same old, importing Gtk module, we are also importing some other stuff
this time
#such as numpy and the backends of matplotlib
import gi, numpy as np, matplotlib.cm as cm
gi.require_version('Gtk', '3.0')
```

```
from gi.repository import Gtk

#From here, we are importing some essential backend tools from matplotlib
#namely the NavigationToolbar2GTK3 and the FigureCanvasGTK3Agg
from numpy import random
from matplotlib.backends.backend_gtk3 import NavigationToolbar2GTK3 as
NavigationToolbar
from matplotlib.backends.backend_gtk3agg import FigureCanvasGTK3Agg as
FigureCanvas
from matplotlib.figure import Figure
from matplotlib.patches import Rectangle

#Here we created a class named DrawPoints
class DrawPoints:
    #Upon initiation, we create 4 randomized numpy array, those are for the
coordinates, colors and size of dots
    #on the scatter plot. After that we create a figure object, put in two
subplots and create a canvas to store
    #the figure.
    def __init__(self):
        #Namely we are creating 20 dots, therefore n = 20
        self.n = 20
        #X and Y coordinates
        self.xrand = random.rand(1,self.n)*10
        self.yrand = random.rand(1,self.n)*10
        #Sizes
        self.randsize = random.rand(1,self.n)*200
        #Colors
        self.randcolor = random.rand(self.n,3)
        #Here creates the figure, with a size 10x10 and resolution of 80dpi
        self.fig = Figure(figsize=(10,10), dpi=80)
        #Stating that we are creating two plots side by side and adding
        #self.ax as the first plot by add_subplot(121)
        self.ax = self.fig.add_subplot(121)
        #Adding the second subplot by stating add_subplot(122)
        self.axzoom = self.fig.add_subplot(122)
        #Create a canvas to store the figure object
        self.canvas = FigureCanvas(self.fig)
    #Here draw the scatterplot on the left
    def draw(self):
        #Here is the key - cla(), when we invoke the draw() function, we
have to clear the
        #figure and redraw it again
        self.ax.cla()
        #Setting the elements of the left subplot, in this case - grid
        self.ax.grid(True)
        #Set the maximum value of X and Y-axis in the left subplot
        self.ax.set_xlim(0,10)
```

```
        self.ax.set_ylim(0,10)
        #Draw the scatter plot with the randomized numpy array that we
created earlier in __init__(self)
        self.ax.scatter(self.xrand, self.yrand, marker='o',
s=self.randsize, c=self.randcolor, alpha=0.5)
    #This zoom function is invoked by updatezoom() function outside of the
class Drawpoints
    #This function is responsible for things:
    #1. Update X and Y coordinates based on the click
    #2. invoke the draw() function to redraw the plot on the left, this is
essential to update the position
    # of the grey rectangle
    #3. invoke the following drawzoom() function, which will "Zoom-in" the
designated area by the grey rectangle
    # and will redraw the subplot on the right based on the updated X & Y
coordinates
    #4. draw a transparent grey rectangle based on the mouse click on the
left subplot
    #5. Update the canvas
    def zoom(self, x, y):
        #Here updates the X & Y coordinates
        self.x = x
        self.y = y
        #invoke the draw() function to update the subplot on the left
        self.draw()
        #invoke the drawzoom() function to update the subplot on the right
        self.drawzoom()
        #Draw the transparent grey rectangle at the subplot on the left
        self.ax.add_patch(Rectangle((x - 1, y - 1), 2, 2, facecolor="grey",
alpha=0.2))
        #Update the canvas
        self.fig.canvas.draw()
    #This drawzoom function is being called in the zoom function
    #The idea is that, when the user picked a region (rectangle) to zoom,
we need to redraw the zoomed panel,
    #which is the subplot on the right
    def drawzoom(self):
        #Again, we use the cla() function to clear the figure, and getting
ready for a redraw!
        self.axzoom.cla()
        #Setting the grid
        self.axzoom.grid(True)
        #Do not be confused! Remember that we invoke this function from
zoom, therefore self.x and self.y
        #are already updated in that function. In here, we are simply
changing the X & Y-axis minimum and
        #maximum value, and redraw the graph without changing any element!
        self.axzoom.set_xlim(self.x-1, self.x+1)
```

```
        self.axzoom.set_ylim(self.y-1, self.y+1)
        #By changing the X & Y-axis minimum and maximum value, the dots
that are out of range will automatically
        #disappear!
        self.axzoom.scatter(self.xrand, self.yrand, marker='o',
s=self.randsize*5, c=self.randcolor, alpha=0.5)

def updatecursorposition(event):
    '''When cursor inside plot, get position and print to statusbar'''
    if event.inaxes:
        x = event.xdata
        y = event.ydata
        statbar.push(1, ("Coordinates:" + " x= " + str(round(x,3)) + "  y=
" + str(round(y,3))))

def updatezoom(event):
    '''When mouse is right-clicked on the canvas get the coordiantes and
send them to points.zoom'''
    if event.button!=1: return
    if (event.xdata is None): return
    x,y = event.xdata, event.ydata
    points.zoom(x,y)

#Readers should be familiar with this now, here is the standard opening of
the Gtk.Window()
window = Gtk.Window()
window.connect("delete-event", Gtk.main_quit)
window.set_default_size(800, 500)
window.set_title('Interactive zoom')

#Creating a vertical box, will have the canvas, toolbar and statbar being
packed into it from top to bottom
box = Gtk.Box(orientation=Gtk.Orientation.VERTICAL)
#Adding the vertical box to the window
window.add(box)

#Instantiate the object points from the Class DrawPoints()
#Remember that at this point, __init__() of DrawPoints() are invoked upon
construction!
points = DrawPoints()
#Invoke the draw() function in the object points
points.draw()

#Packing the canvas now to the vertical box
box.pack_start(points.canvas, True, True, 0)

#Creating and packing the toolbar to the vertical box
toolbar = NavigationToolbar(points.canvas, window)
```

```
box.pack_start(toolbar, False, True, 0)

#Creating and packing the statbar to the vertical box
statbar = Gtk.Statusbar()
box.pack_start(statbar, False, True, 0)

#Here is the magic that makes it happens, we are using mpl_connect to link
the event and the canvas!
#'motion_notify_event' is responsible for the mouse motion sensing and
position updating
points.fig.canvas.mpl_connect('motion_notify_event', updatecursorposition)
#'button_press_event' is slightly misleading, in fact it is referring to
the mouse button being pressed,
#instead of a GTK+3 button being pressed in this case
points.fig.canvas.mpl_connect('button_press_event', updatezoom)

window.show_all()
Gtk.main()
```

As you can see from the preceding example, event handling and picking are the elements that makes the interaction part much easier than we imagine. Therefore, it is important to have a quick review of the available event connections that are part of the `FigureCanvasBase`:

Event name	Class and description
button_press_event	**MouseEvent:** Mouse button is pressed
button_release_event	**MouseEvent:** Mouse button is released
scroll_event	**MouseEvent:** Mouse scroll wheel is rolled
motion_notify_event	**MouseEvent:** Mouse motion
draw_event	**DrawEvent:** Canvas draw
key_press_event	**KeyEvent:** Key is pressed
key_release_event	**KeyEvent:** Key is released
pick_event	**PickEvent:** An object in the canvas is selected
resize_event	**ResizeEvent:** Figure canvas is resized
figure_enter_event	**LocationEvent:** Mouse enters a new figure
figure_leave_event	**LocationEvent:** Mouse leaves a figure
axes_enter_event	**LocationEvent:** Mouse enters a new axis

axes_leave_event	**LocationEvent:** Mouse leaves an axis

Installing Glade

Installing Glade is very straightforward; you can either obtain the source file from its web page, or simply use Git to obtain the latest version of source code. Here is the command for obtaining Glade through Git:

```
git clone git://git.gnome.org/glade
```

Designing the GUI using Glade

Designing the GUI using Glade is straightforward. Just start the Glade program and you will see this interface (from macOS, or something similar if using another OS):

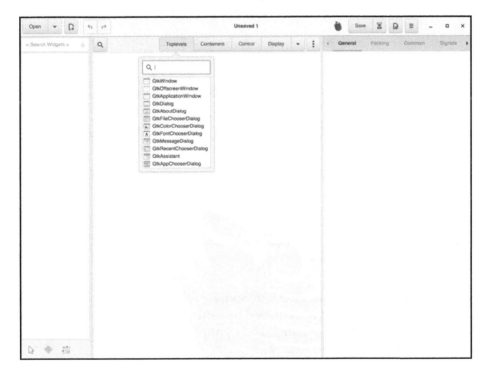

Figure 5

Let's now explore the Glade interface. There are four main buttons that we will be using primarily in Glade; **Toplevels**, **Containers**, **Control**, and **Display**. The preceding screenshot shows that `GtkWindow` is listed in `Toplevels`, which serves as the basic unit for construction. Let's click on `GtkWindow` and see the resulting action:

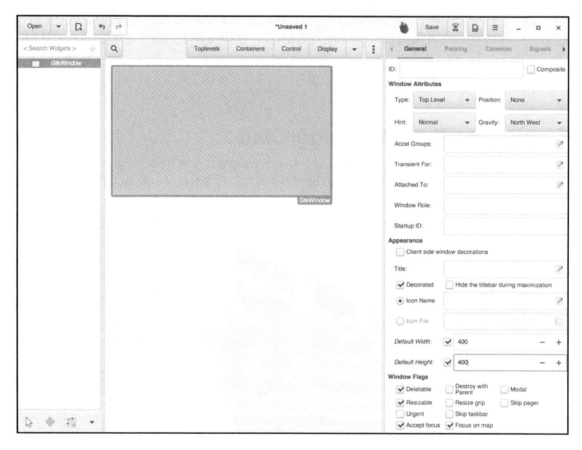

Figure 6

Now a GtkWindow is being constructed and nothing is inside. Let's set the size of this GtkWindow to: 400x400. This can be achieved by setting the default width and height as 400 in the lower section of the right panel. The right panel is currently illustrating the **General** properties of this GtkWindow.

Remember that we used vertical boxes a lot in the previous examples? Let's add a vertical box to the GtkWindow! This can be achieved by clicking on **Containers** and choosing **GtkBox**, as shown here:

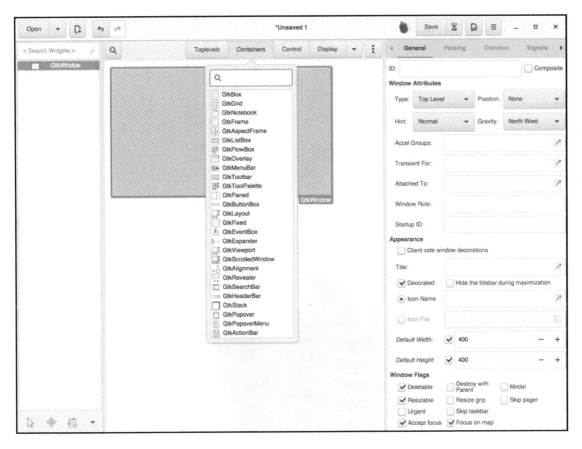

Figure 7

After choosing **GtkBox**, click on the **GtkWindow** in the middle panel and a GtkBox will be created as a sub-module or a sub-window of the GtkWindow. This can be confirmed by checking the left panel as shown here:

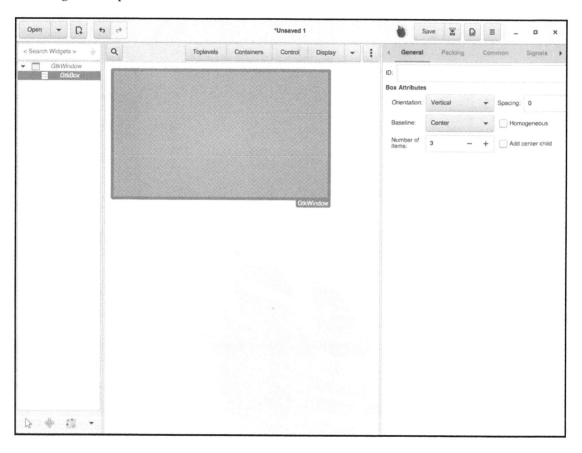

Figure 8

GtkBox is below **GtkWindow** and indented on the left panel. Since we are picking vertical box, the *orientation* in **General** is *vertical*. One can even specify the spacing and number of items that will be included in the GtkBox. Let's add a menu bar onto the top vertical box. This can be done as shown in *Figure 9*. In **Containers**, pick **GtkMenubar** and click on the top vertical box. It will fit in a menu bar with the following options: **File**, **Edit**, **View**, and **Help**.

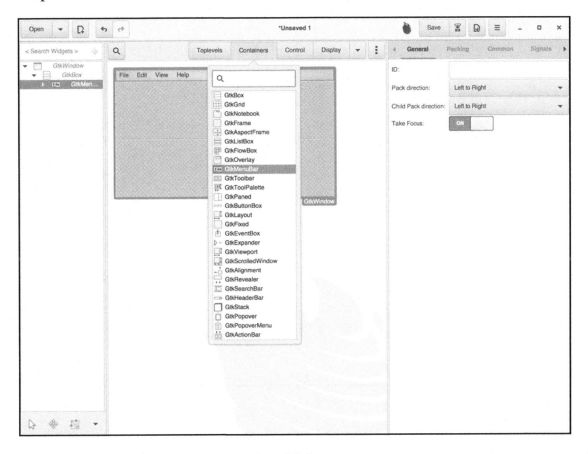

Figure 9

As one can imagine, we can easily design our favorite GUI with the use of Glade. We can import a label with a customized size as shown in *Figure 10*. And there are many more options that we can choose to customize our GUIs.

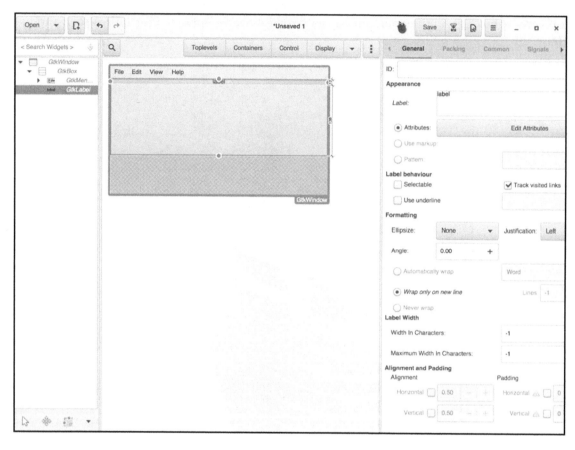

Figure 10

Designing the most effective GUI through Glade is beyond the scope and purview of this book, so we will not go any further into the more advanced options in Glade.

However, we would like to expand on one of the examples that we have worked on previously, and show that it takes just a few lines of code to incorporate a Glade-based GUI into our workflow.

To begin, we will use the class-based polar plot example. First of all, we design the most basic GtkWindow with a size of 400x400 (that's all!) from Glade and save it as a file.

The file is very simple and self-explanatory:

```xml
<?xml version="1.0" encoding="UTF-8"?>
<!-- Generated with glade 3.22.1 -->
<interface>
  <requires lib="gtk+" version="3.22"/>
  <object class="GtkWindow" id="window1">
    <property name="can_focus">False</property>
    <property name="default_width">400</property>
    <property name="default_height">400</property>
    <signal name="destroy" handler="on_window1_destroy" swapped="no"/>
    <child>
      <object class="GtkScrolledWindow" id="scrolledwindow1">
        <property name="visible">True</property>
        <property name="can_focus">True</property>
        <property name="shadow_type">in</property>
        <child>
          <placeholder/>
        </child>
      </object>
    </child>
  </object>
</interface>
```

Readers may understand that we just created a `GtkWindow` with a size of 400x400 plus a child as `GtkScrolledWindow`. This can be completed in a few clicks in Glade.

And what we have to do now is use `Gtk.Builder()` to read the Glade file; everything will be constructed automatically. This actually saves us from defining all the elements of the vertical box!

```python
#Same old, importing Gtk module, we are also importing some other stuff
this time
#such as numpy and the backends of matplotlib
import gi, numpy as np, matplotlib.cm as cm
gi.require_version('Gtk', '3.0')
from gi.repository import Gtk

from matplotlib.figure import Figure
from numpy import arange, pi, random, linspace
import matplotlib.cm as cm
#Possibly this rendering backend is broken currently
from matplotlib.backends.backend_gtk3agg import FigureCanvasGTK3Agg as
FigureCanvas

#New class, here is to invoke Gtk.main_quit() when the window is being
destroyed
```

```
#Necessary to quit the Gtk.main()
class Signals:
    def on_window1_destroy(self, widget):
        Gtk.main_quit()

class MatplotlibEmbed(Gtk.Window):

    #Instantiation, we just need the canvas to store the figure!
    def __init__(self):

        #Readers should find it familiar, as we are creating a matplotlib
figure here with a dpi(resolution) 100
        self.fig = Figure(figsize=(5,5), dpi=100)
        #The axes element, here we indicate we are creating 1x1 grid and
putting the subplot in the only cell
        #Also we are creating a polar plot, therefore we set projection as
'polar
        self.ax = self.fig.add_subplot(111, projection='polar')

        #Here, we borrow one example shown in the matplotlib gtk3 cookbook
        #and show a beautiful bar plot on a circular coordinate system
        self.theta = linspace(0.0, 2 * pi, 30, endpoint=False)
        self.radii = 10 * random.rand(30)
        self.width = pi / 4 * random.rand(30)
        self.bars = self.ax.bar(self.theta, self.radii, width=self.width,
bottom=0.0)

        #Here defines the color of the bar, as well as setting it to be
transparent
        for r, bar in zip(self.radii, self.bars):
            bar.set_facecolor(cm.jet(r / 10.))
            bar.set_alpha(0.5)
        #Here we generate the figure
        self.ax.plot()

        #Creating Canvas which store the matplotlib figure
        self.canvas = FigureCanvas(self.fig)  # a Gtk.DrawingArea

#Here is the magic, we create a GTKBuilder that reads textual description
of a user interface
#and instantiates the described objects
builder = Gtk.Builder()
#We ask the GTKBuilder to read the file and parse the information there
builder.add_objects_from_file('/Users/aldrinyim/Dropbox/Matplotlib for
Developer/Jupyter notebook/ch05/window1_glade.glade', ('window1', '') )
#And we connect the terminating signals with Gtk.main_quit()
builder.connect_signals(Signals())
```

```
#We create the first object window1
window1 = builder.get_object('window1')
#We create the second object scrollwindow
scrolledwindow1 = builder.get_object('scrolledwindow1')

#Instantiate the object and start the drawing!
polar_drawing = MatplotlibEmbed()
#Add the canvas to the scrolledwindow1 object
scrolledwindow1.add(polar_drawing.canvas)

#Show all and keep the Gtk.main() active!
window1.show_all()
Gtk.main()
```

The preceding code demonstrates how we can use Glade to quickly generate a frame and execute it effortlessly.

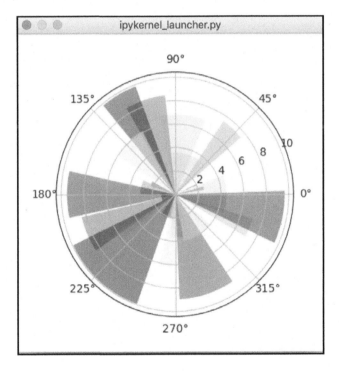

Figure 11

Hopefully, through this example readers would appreciate the power of Glade in enabling programmers to draw a GUI instead of abstracting it in code. This is particularly useful when the GUI gets complicated.

Summary

In this chapter, we have worked through examples on embedding Matplotlib figures inside a simple GTK+3 window, adding the Matplotlib navigation toolbar, plotting data in an interactive framework, and using Glade to design a GUI. We have kept the examples simple to highlight the important parts, but we encourage readers to explore further possibilities. GTK+3 is not the only GUI library that can be used. In the coming chapters, we'll see how to use two other important libraries!

Embedding Matplotlib in Qt 5

6

There are several GUI libraries available, and one widely used library is Qt. In this book, we will be using Qt 5, the latest major version of this library. Unless explicitly mentioned, we are referring to Qt 5 when we simply state Qt throughout the chapter.

We will follow a similar progression to that in `Chapter 5`, *Embedding Matplotlib in GTK+3*, and we will present similar examples but this time written in Qt.

We believe that this method will allow us to directly compare the libraries, and it has the advantage of not leaving the *How would I write something with library X?* question unanswered.

In this chapter, we will learn how to:

- Embed a Matplotlib figure into a Qt widget
- Embed a figure and navigation toolbar into a Qt widget
- Use events to update a Matplotlib plot in real time
- Use QT Designer to draw a GUI and then use it with Matplotlib in a simple Python application

We will begin by giving an introduction to the library.

A brief introduction to Qt 5 and PyQt 5

Qt is a cross-platform application development framework widely used for graphical programs (GUI) and also for non-GUI tools.

Qt was developed by Trolltech (now owned by Nokia), and it's probably best known for being the foundation of the **K Desktop Environment (KDE)** for Linux.

The Qt toolkit is a collection of classes made to simplify the creation of programs. Qt is more than just a GUI toolkit. It includes components for abstractions of network sockets, threads, Unicode, regular expressions, SQL databases, SVG, OpenGL, and XML. It also has a fully functional web browser, help system, multimedia framework, and rich collection of GUI widgets.

Qt is available on several platforms, particularly Unix/Linux, Windows, macOS X, and also some embedded devices. As it uses native APIs of the platform to render the Qt controls, applications developed with Qt have a look and feel that fits the running environment (without looking like something alien in it).

Though written in C++, Qt can also be used in several other programming languages through language bindings available for Ruby, Java, Perl, and also Python with PyQt.

PyQt 5 is available for both Python 2.x and 3.x, but in this book, we will consistently use Python 3 in all our code. PyQt 5 has over 620 classes and 6,000 functions and methods. Before we go into some examples, it is important to know the difference between Qt 4/PyQt 4 and Qt 5/PyQt 5.

Differences between Qt 4 and PyQt 4

PyQt is a comprehensive set of Python bindings for the Qt framework. However, PyQt 5 is not backward compatible with PyQt 4. It is noteworthy that PyQt 5 does not support any part of the Qt API that are marked as deprecated or obsolete in Qt v5.0. However, it is possible that some of these are included accidentally. If included, they *are* considered bugs and will be removed when found.

If you are familiar with Qt 4 or have read the first edition of this book, one thing to note is that the signals and slots of are no longer supported. Therefore, the following are not implemented in PyQt 5:

- QtScript
- QObject.connect()
- QObject.emit()
- SIGNAL()
- SLOT()

Also, there is a modification in `disconnect()` as it no longer takes arguments and will disconnect all connections to the `QObject` instance when invoked.

However, new modules have been introduced, such as the following:

- `QtBluetooth`
- `QtPositioning`
- `Enginio`

Let's start with a very simple example—calling a window. Again for best performance, copy the code, paste it in a file, and run the script on the Terminal. Our codes are optimized for running on a Terminal only:

```
#sys.argv is essential for the instantiation of QApplication!
import sys
#Here we import the PyQt 5 Widgets
from PyQt5.QtWidgets import QApplication, QWidget

#Creating a QApplication object
app = QApplication(sys.argv)
#QWidget is the base class of all user interface objects in PyQt5
w = QWidget()
#Setting the width and height of the window
w.resize(250, 150)
#Move the widget to a position on the screen at x=500, y=500 coordinates
w.move(500, 500)
#Setting the title of the window
w.setWindowTitle('Simple')
#Display the window
w.show()

#app.exec_() is the mainloop of the application
#the sys.exit() is a method to ensure a real exit upon receiving the signal
of exit from the app
sys.exit(app.exec_())
```

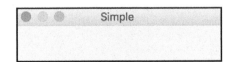

The syntax is very similar to what you see in Chapter 5, *Embedding Matplotlib in GTK+3*. Once you know how to use one particular GUI library fairly well (such as GTK+3), it is very easy to adapt to a new one readily. The code is very similar to that in GTK+3 and the logic follows as well. QApplication manages the GUI application's control flow and main settings. It's the place where the main event loop is executed, processed and dispatched. It is also responsible for application initialization and finalization and handling most of the system-wide and application-wide settings. Since QApplication handles the entire initialization phase, it must be created before any other objects related to the UI are created.

The qApp.exec_() command enters the Qt main event loop. Once exit() or quit() is called, it returns the relevant return code. Until the main loop is started, nothing is displayed on the screen. It's necessary to call this function as the main loop handles all events and signals coming from both the application widgets and the window system; essentially, no user interaction can take place before it is called.

Readers may wonder why there is an underscore in exec_();. The reason is simple: exec() is a reserved word in Python hence the addition of the underscore to the exec() Qt method. Wrapping it inside sys.exit() allows the Python script to exit with the same return code, informing the environment how the application ended (whether successfully or not).

For more experienced readers, you will find something abnormal in the preceding code. While we were instantiating the QApplication class, we were required to parse sys.argv (an empty list in this case) to the constructor of QApplication. At least I found it unexpected when I first used PyQt, but this is required as the instantiation invokes the constructor of the C++ class QApplication, and it uses sys.argv to initialize the Qt application. Parsing sys.argv during QApplication instantiation is a convention in Qt and it is something be aware of. Also every PyQt 5 application must create an application object.

Again, let's try to another one in OOP style:

```
#Described in earlier examples
import sys
from PyQt5.QtWidgets import QWidget, QPushButton, QHBoxLayout, QVBoxLayout,
QApplication

#Here we create a class with the "base" class from QWidget
#We are inheriting the functions of the QWidget from this case
class Qtwindowexample(QWidget):
    #Constructor, will be executed upon instantiation of the object
    def __init__(self):
        #Upon self instantiation, we are calling constructor of the QWidget
```

```
        #to set up the bases of the QWidget's object
        QWidget.__init__(self)
        #Resizing, moving and setting the window
        self.resize(250, 150)
        self.move(300, 300)
        self.setWindowTitle('2 Click buttons!')
        #Here we create the first button - print1button
        #When clicked, it will invoke the printOnce function, and print
    "Hello world" in the terminal
        self.print1button = QPushButton('Print once!', self)
        self.print1button.clicked.connect(self.printOnce)
        #Here we create the second button - print5button
        #When clicked, it will invoke the printFive function, and print
    "**Hello world" 5 times in the terminal
        self.print5button = QPushButton('Print five times!', self)
        self.print5button.clicked.connect(self.printFive)
        #Something very familiar!
        #It is the vertical box in Qt5
        self.vbox=QVBoxLayout()
        #Simply add the two buttons to the vertical box
        self.vbox.addWidget(self.print1button)
        self.vbox.addWidget(self.print5button)
        #Here put the vertical box into the window
        self.setLayout(self.vbox)
        #And now we are all set, show the window!
        self.show()
    #Function that will print Hello world once when invoked
    def printOnce(self):
        print("Hello World!")
    #Function that will print **Hello world five times when invoked
    def printFive(self):
        for i in range(0,5):
            print("**Hello World!")

#Creating the app object, essential for all Qt usage
app = QApplication(sys.argv)
#Create Qtwindowexample(), construct the window and show!
ex = Qtwindowexample()
#app.exec_() is the mainloop of the application
#the sys.exit() is a method to ensure a real exit upon receiving the signal
of exit from the app
sys.exit(app.exec_())
```

The preceding code creates two buttons, and each button will invoke an individual function—print Hello world once or print Hello World five times in the Terminal. Readers should be able to grasp the event handling system from the code easily.

Here is the output:

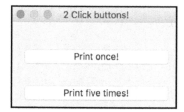

This is another implementation of the two buttons example from Chapter 5, *Embedding Matplotlib in GTK+3,* and the goal of this example is to demonstrate the signal handling approach in PyQt 5 in comparison with GTK+3. Readers should find this fairly similar as we intentionally write it in a way more similar to the example in GTK+3.

Let's try to embed a Matplotlib figure in a Qt window. Be aware that unlike the example in the previous chapter, this figure will be refreshed every second! Therefore, we also use the QtCore.QTimer() function in here and invoke the update_figure() function as an event-action pair:

```
#Importing essential libraries
import sys, os, random, matplotlib, matplotlib.cm as cm
from numpy import arange, sin, pi, random, linspace
#Python Qt5 bindings for GUI objects
from PyQt5 import QtCore, QtWidgets
# import the Qt5Agg FigureCanvas object, that binds Figure to
# Qt5Agg backend.
from matplotlib.backends.backend_qt5agg import FigureCanvasQTAgg as
FigureCanvas
from matplotlib.figure import Figure


#The class DynamicCanvas contains all the functions required to draw and
update the figure
#It contains a canvas that updates itself every second with newly
randomized vecotrs
class DynamicCanvas(FigureCanvas):

    #Invoke upon instantiation, here are the arguments parsing along
    def __init__(self, parent=None, width=5, height=4, dpi=100):
        #Creating a figure with the requested width, height and dpi
        fig = Figure(figsize=(width,height), dpi=dpi)

        #The axes element, here we indicate we are creating 1x1 grid and
putting the subplot in the only cell
        #Also we are creating a polar plot, therefore we set projection as
'polar
```

```
        self.axes = fig.add_subplot(111, projection='polar')
        #Here we invoke the function "compute_initial_figure" to create the
first figure
        self.compute_initial_figure()

        #Creating a FigureCanvas object and putting the figure into it
        FigureCanvas.__init__(self, fig)
        #Setting this figurecanvas parent as None
        self.setParent(parent)

        #Here we are using the Qtimer function
        #As you can imagine, it functions as a timer and will emit a signal
every N milliseconds
        #N is defined by the function QTimer.start(N), in this case - 1000
milliseconds = 1 second
        #For every second, this function will emit a signal and invoke the
update_figure() function defined below
        timer = QtCore.QTimer(self)
        timer.timeout.connect(self.update_figure)
        timer.start(1000)

    #For drawing the first figure
    def compute_initial_figure(self):
        #Here, we borrow one example shown in the matplotlib gtk3 cookbook
        #and show a beautiful bar plot on a circular coordinate system
        self.theta = linspace(0.0, 2 * pi, 30, endpoint=False)
        self.radii = 10 * random.rand(30)
        self.plot_width = pi / 4 * random.rand(30)
        self.bars = self.axes.bar(self.theta, self.radii,
width=self.plot_width, bottom=0.0)

        #Here defines the color of the bar, as well as setting it to be
transparent
        for r, bar in zip(self.radii, self.bars):
            bar.set_facecolor(cm.jet(r / 10.))
            bar.set_alpha(0.5)
        #Here we generate the figure
        self.axes.plot()

    #This function will be invoke every second by the timeout signal from
QTimer
    def update_figure(self):
        #Clear figure and get ready for the new plot
        self.axes.cla()

        #Identical to the code above
        self.theta = linspace(0.0, 2 * pi, 30, endpoint=False)
        self.radii = 10 * random.rand(30)
```

```
        self.plot_width = pi / 4 * random.rand(30)
        self.bars = self.axes.bar(self.theta, self.radii,
width=self.plot_width, bottom=0.0)

        #Here defines the color of the bar, as well as setting it to be
transparent
        for r, bar in zip(self.radii, self.bars):
            bar.set_facecolor(cm.jet(r / 10.))
            bar.set_alpha(0.5)

        #Here we generate the figure
        self.axes.plot()
        self.draw()

#This class will serve as our main application Window
#QMainWindow class provides a framework for us to put window and canvas
class ApplicationWindow(QtWidgets.QMainWindow):

    #Instantiation, initializing and setting up the framework for the
canvas
    def __init__(self):
        #Initializing of Qt MainWindow widget
        QtWidgets.QMainWindow.__init__(self)
        self.setAttribute(QtCore.Qt.WA_DeleteOnClose)
        #Instantiating QWidgets object
        self.main_widget = QtWidgets.QWidget(self)

        #Creating a vertical box!
        vbox = QtWidgets.QVBoxLayout(self.main_widget)
        #Creating the dynamic canvas and this canvas will update itself!
        dc = DynamicCanvas(self.main_widget, width=5, height=4, dpi=100)
        #adding canvas to the vertical box
        vbox.addWidget(dc)

        #This is not necessary, but it is a good practice to setFocus on
your main widget
        self.main_widget.setFocus()
        #This line indicates that main_widget is the main part of the
application
        self.setCentralWidget(self.main_widget)

#Creating the GUI application
qApp = QtWidgets.QApplication(sys.argv)
#Instantiating the ApplicationWindow widget
aw = ApplicationWindow()
#Set the title
aw.setWindowTitle("Dynamic Qt5 visualization")
#Show the widget
```

```
aw.show()
#Start the Qt main loop , and sys.exit() ensure clean exit when closing the
window
sys.exit(qApp.exec_())
```

Again, the figure in this example will randomize the data and update the figure every 1 second through `QTimer`, shown as follows:

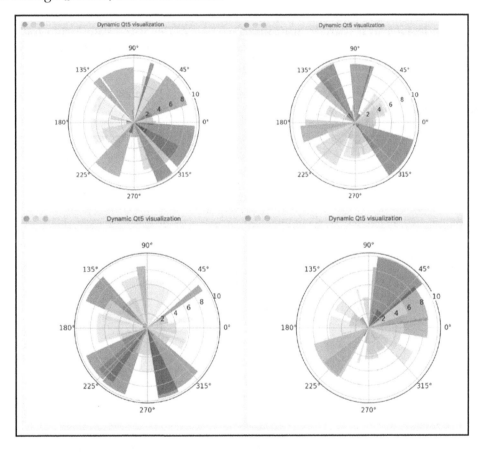

Introducing QT Creator / QT Designer

The four preceding figures are screenshots of the PyQt 5 window, which will refresh itself every second.

For simple examples, designing the GUI in the Python code can be good enough, but for more complex applications, this solution does not scale.

There are some tools to help you design the GUI for Qt, and one of the most commonly used tools was QT Designer. In the first edition of this book, this section was about GUI making with QT Designer. Since the late QT4 development, QT Designer has merged with QT Creator. In the following example, we would learn how to open the secret QT Designer in QT Creator and create a UI file.

Similar to Glade, we can design the user interface part of the application using the on-screen form and drag-and-drop interface. Then we can connect the widgets with the backend code, where we develop the logic of the application.

First of all, let us show you how to open QT Designer in **QT Creator**. When you open **QT Creator**, you will see the following interface:

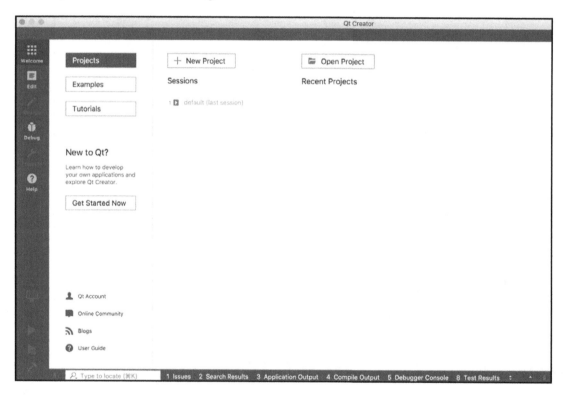

The tricky part is this: Do not create the project by clicking on the **New File or Project** button in the Creator. Instead, create a **New Project**:

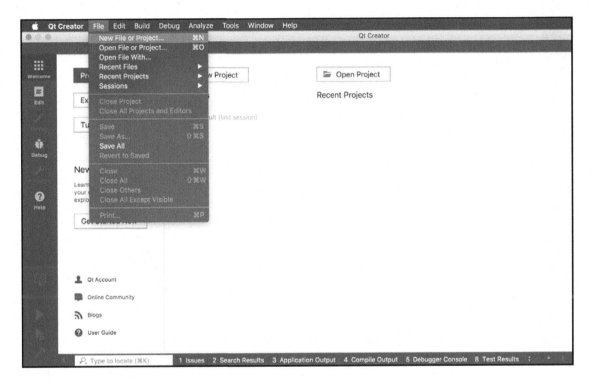

Select **Qt** in **Files and Classes** and **Qt Designer Form** in the middle panel:

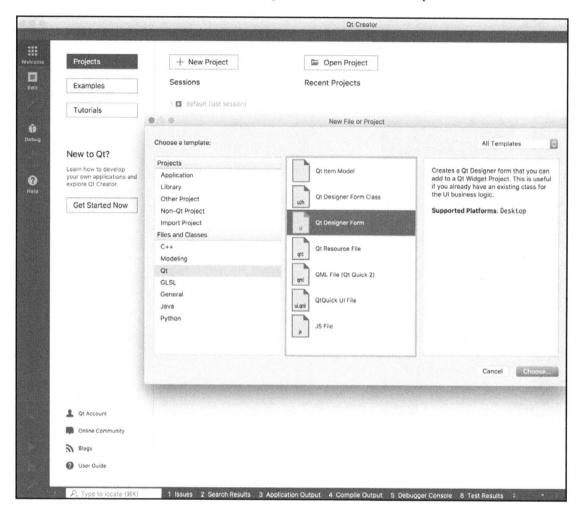

There is a range of template selections, such as **Widget** or **Main Window**. In our case, we pick **Main Window** and simply follow through the remaining steps:

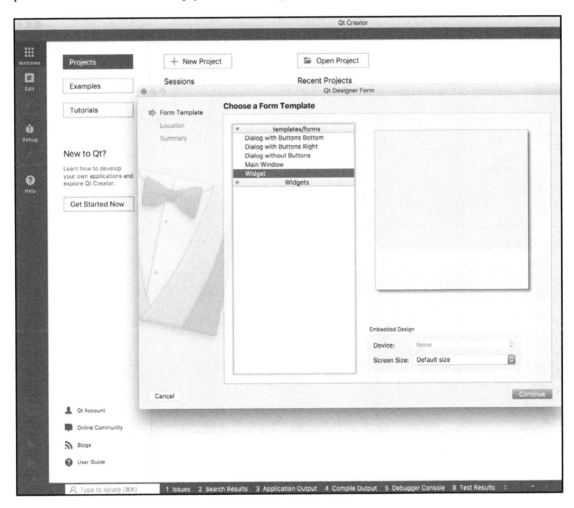

And eventually, we will reach the QT Designer interface. Everything you work on here will be put in your desired folder as a UI file:

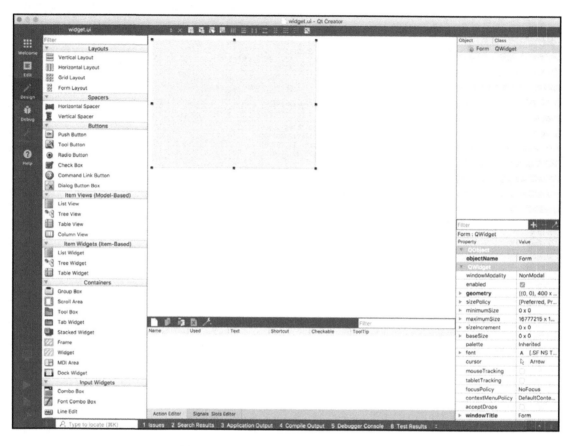

Embedding Matplotlib in a GUI made with QT Creator / QT Designer.

To quickly demonstrate how to embed a Matplotlib figure in Qt 5 using **QT Creator**, let's use the former example and combine it with the scripts generated by **QT Creator**.

First of all, adjust the **Geometry** of the **MainWindow** at the lower right panel; change the **Width** and **Height** to 300x300:

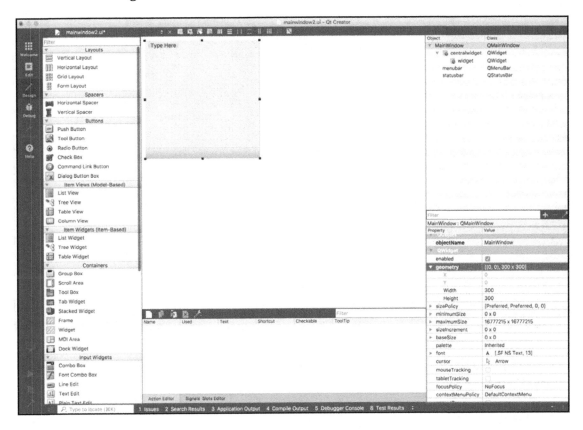

After that, drag a **Widget** from **Container** in the left panel to the **MainWindow** in the middle. Resize it until it fits well in the **MainWindow**:

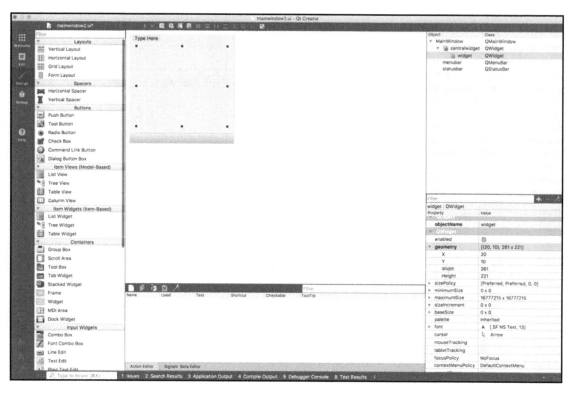

That is it for the basic design! Now save it as a UI file. When you view the UI file, it should display something like this:

```xml
<?xml version="1.0" encoding="UTF-8"?>
<ui version="4.0">
 <class>MainWindow</class>
 <widget class="QMainWindow" name="MainWindow">
  <property name="geometry">
   <rect>
    <x>0</x>
    <y>0</y>
    <width>300</width>
    <height>300</height>
   </rect>
  </property>
  <property name="windowTitle">
```

```
    <string>MainWindow</string>
   </property>
   <widget class="QWidget" name="centralwidget">
    <widget class="QWidget" name="widget" native="true">
     <property name="geometry">
      <rect>
       <x>20</x>
       <y>10</y>
       <width>261</width>
       <height>221</height>
      </rect>
     </property>
    </widget>
   </widget>
   <widget class="QMenuBar" name="menubar">
    <property name="geometry">
     <rect>
      <x>0</x>
      <y>0</y>
      <width>300</width>
      <height>22</height>
     </rect>
    </property>
   </widget>
   <widget class="QStatusBar" name="statusbar"/>
  </widget>
  <resources/>
  <connections/>
 </ui>
```

This file is in XML format, and we need to convert it to a Python file. This can be done simply by using this command:

```
pyuic5 mainwindow.ui > mainwindow.py
```

And now we will have a Python file like this:

```
from PyQt5 import QtCore, QtGui, QtWidgets

class Ui_MainWindow(object):
    def setupUi(self, MainWindow):
        MainWindow.setObjectName("MainWindow")
        MainWindow.resize(300, 300)
        self.centralwidget = QtWidgets.QWidget(MainWindow)
        self.centralwidget.setObjectName("centralwidget")
        self.widget = QtWidgets.QWidget(self.centralwidget)
        self.widget.setGeometry(QtCore.QRect(20, 10, 261, 221))
        self.widget.setObjectName("widget")
```

```
            MainWindow.setCentralWidget(self.centralwidget)
            self.menubar = QtWidgets.QMenuBar(MainWindow)
            self.menubar.setGeometry(QtCore.QRect(0, 0, 300, 22))
            self.menubar.setObjectName("menubar")
            MainWindow.setMenuBar(self.menubar)
            self.statusbar = QtWidgets.QStatusBar(MainWindow)
            self.statusbar.setObjectName("statusbar")
            MainWindow.setStatusBar(self.statusbar)

            self.retranslateUi(MainWindow)
            QtCore.QMetaObject.connectSlotsByName(MainWindow)

        def retranslateUi(self, MainWindow):
            _translate = QtCore.QCoreApplication.translate
            MainWindow.setWindowTitle(_translate("MainWindow", "MainWindow"))
```

Note that this is just the framework for the GUI; we still have to add some things in order to make it work.

We must add `init()` to initialize the `UiMainWindow`, as well as link the `DynamicCanvas` to the widget in the middle of the `MainWindow`. Here it goes:

```
#Replace object to QtWidgets.QMainWindow
class Ui_MainWindow(QtWidgets.QMainWindow):
    #***Instantiation!
    def __init__(self):
        # Initialize and display the user interface
        QtWidgets.QMainWindow.__init__(self)
        self.setupUi(self)
    def setupUi(self, MainWindow):
        MainWindow.setObjectName("MainWindow")
        MainWindow.resize(300, 300)
        self.centralwidget = QtWidgets.QWidget(MainWindow)
        self.centralwidget.setObjectName("centralwidget")
        self.widget = QtWidgets.QWidget(self.centralwidget)
        self.widget.setGeometry(QtCore.QRect(20, 10, 261, 221))
        self.widget.setObjectName("widget")
        MainWindow.setCentralWidget(self.centralwidget)
        self.menubar = QtWidgets.QMenuBar(MainWindow)
        self.menubar.setGeometry(QtCore.QRect(0, 0, 300, 22))
        self.menubar.setObjectName("menubar")
        MainWindow.setMenuBar(self.menubar)
        self.statusbar = QtWidgets.QStatusBar(MainWindow)
        self.statusbar.setObjectName("statusbar")
        MainWindow.setStatusBar(self.statusbar)

        self.retranslateUi(MainWindow)
```

```
    QtCore.QMetaObject.connectSlotsByName(MainWindow)
    #***Putting DynamicCanvas into the widget, and show the window!
    dc = DynamicCanvas(self.widget, width=5, height=4, dpi=100)
    self.show()

def retranslateUi(self, MainWindow):
    _translate = QtCore.QCoreApplication.translate
    MainWindow.setWindowTitle(_translate("MainWindow", "MainWindow"))
```

We have added only five lines of code in here. We can simply replace the class `ApplicationWindow` with this, and here is the outcome:

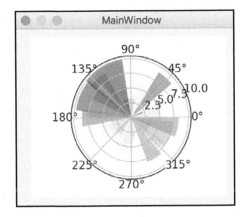

And here is the complete code generating the preceding figure:

```
#Importing essential libraries
import sys, os, random, matplotlib, matplotlib.cm as cm
from numpy import arange, sin, pi, random, linspace
#Python Qt5 bindings for GUI objects
from PyQt5 import QtCore, QtGui, QtWidgets
# import the Qt5Agg FigureCanvas object, that binds Figure to
# Qt5Agg backend.
from matplotlib.backends.backend_qt5agg import FigureCanvasQTAgg as
FigureCanvas
from matplotlib.figure import Figure

#The class DynamicCanvas contains all the functions required to draw and
update the figure
#It contains a canvas that updates itself every second with newly
randomized vecotrs
class DynamicCanvas(FigureCanvas):

    #Invoke upon instantiation, here are the arguments parsing along
```

```
    def __init__(self, parent=None, width=5, height=5, dpi=100):
        #Creating a figure with the requested width, height and dpi
        fig = Figure(figsize=(width,height), dpi=dpi)

        #The axes element, here we indicate we are creating 1x1 grid and
putting the subplot in the only cell
        #Also we are creating a polar plot, therefore we set projection as
'polar
        self.axes = fig.add_subplot(111, projection='polar')
        #Here we invoke the function "compute_initial_figure" to create the
first figure
        self.compute_initial_figure()

        #Creating a FigureCanvas object and putting the figure into it
        FigureCanvas.__init__(self, fig)
        #Setting this figurecanvas parent as None
        self.setParent(parent)

        #Here we are using the Qtimer function
        #As you can imagine, it functions as a timer and will emit a signal
every N milliseconds
        #N is defined by the function QTimer.start(N), in this case - 1000
milliseconds = 1 second
        #For every second, this function will emit a signal and invoke the
update_figure() function defined below
        timer = QtCore.QTimer(self)
        timer.timeout.connect(self.update_figure)
        timer.start(1000)

    #For drawing the first figure
    def compute_initial_figure(self):
        #Here, we borrow one example shown in the matplotlib gtk3 cookbook
        #and show a beautiful bar plot on a circular coordinate system
        self.theta = linspace(0.0, 2 * pi, 30, endpoint=False)
        self.radii = 10 * random.rand(30)
        self.plot_width = pi / 4 * random.rand(30)
        self.bars = self.axes.bar(self.theta, self.radii,
width=self.plot_width, bottom=0.0)

        #Here defines the color of the bar, as well as setting it to be
transparent
        for r, bar in zip(self.radii, self.bars):
            bar.set_facecolor(cm.jet(r / 10.))
            bar.set_alpha(0.5)
        #Here we generate the figure
        self.axes.plot()

    #This function will be invoke every second by the timeout signal from
```

```
QTimer
    def update_figure(self):
        #Clear figure and get ready for the new plot
        self.axes.cla()

        #Identical to the code above
        self.theta = linspace(0.0, 2 * pi, 30, endpoint=False)
        self.radii = 10 * random.rand(30)
        self.plot_width = pi / 4 * random.rand(30)
        self.bars = self.axes.bar(self.theta, self.radii,
width=self.plot_width, bottom=0.0)

        #Here defines the color of the bar, as well as setting it to be
transparent
        for r, bar in zip(self.radii, self.bars):
            bar.set_facecolor(cm.jet(r / 10.))
            bar.set_alpha(0.5)

        #Here we generate the figure
        self.axes.plot()
        self.draw()

#Created by Qt Creator!
class Ui_MainWindow(QtWidgets.QMainWindow):
    def __init__(self):
        # Initialize and display the user interface
        QtWidgets.QMainWindow.__init__(self)
        self.setupUi(self)

    def setupUi(self, MainWindow):
        MainWindow.setObjectName("MainWindow")
        MainWindow.resize(550, 550)
        self.centralwidget = QtWidgets.QWidget(MainWindow)
        self.centralwidget.setObjectName("centralwidget")
        self.widget = QtWidgets.QWidget(self.centralwidget)
        self.widget.setGeometry(QtCore.QRect(20, 10, 800, 800))
        self.widget.setObjectName("widget")
        MainWindow.setCentralWidget(self.centralwidget)
        self.menubar = QtWidgets.QMenuBar(MainWindow)
        self.menubar.setGeometry(QtCore.QRect(0, 0, 300, 22))
        self.menubar.setObjectName("menubar")
        MainWindow.setMenuBar(self.menubar)
        self.statusbar = QtWidgets.QStatusBar(MainWindow)
        self.statusbar.setObjectName("statusbar")
        MainWindow.setStatusBar(self.statusbar)

        self.retranslateUi(MainWindow)
        QtCore.QMetaObject.connectSlotsByName(MainWindow)
```

```
        dc = DynamicCanvas(self.widget, width=5, height=5, dpi=100)
        #self.centralwidget.setFocus()
        #self.setCentralWidget(self.centralwidget)
        self.show()

    def retranslateUi(self, MainWindow):
        _translate = QtCore.QCoreApplication.translate
        MainWindow.setWindowTitle(_translate("MainWindow", "MainWindow"))

#Creating the GUI application
qApp = QtWidgets.QApplication(sys.argv)
#Instantiating the ApplicationWindow widget
aw = Ui_MainWindow()
#Start the Qt main loop , and sys.exit() ensure clean exit when closing the
window
sys.exit(qApp.exec_())
```

Summary

GUI design by using **QT Creator**/ QT Designer has enough material for a book on its own. Therefore, in this chapter, we aimed to show you just a glimpse of GUI design through PyQt 5. Upon finishing this chapter, the readers should now understand how to embed a figure in a QWidget, use the layout manager to pack a figure in a QWidget, create a timer, react to events and update a Matplotlib graph accordingly, and use QT Designer to draw a simple GUI for Matplotlib embedding.

We are now ready to learn another GUI library, wxWidgets.

7
Embedding Matplotlib in wxWidgets Using wxPython

This chapter will explain how we can use Matplotlib in the wxWidgets framework, particularly using wxPython bindings.

The contents of this chapter are as follows:

- A brief introduction to wxWidgets and wxPython
- A simple example of embedding Matplotlib in wxWidgets
- Extending the previous example to include the Matplotlib navigation toolbar
- How to update a Matplotlib plot in real time using the wxWidgets framework
- How to design a GUI with wxGlade and embed a Matplotlib figure in it

Let's start with an overview of the features of wxWidgets and wxPython.

A brief introduction to wxWidgets and wxPython

One of the most important features of wxWidgets is cross-platform portability; it currently supports Windows, macOS X, Linux (with the X11, Motif, and GTK+ libraries), OS/2, and several other operating systems and platforms (including an embedded version that is currently under development).

wxWidgets can best be described as a native mode toolkit because it provides a thin API abstraction layer across platforms and uses platform-native widgets under the hood, as opposed to emulating them. Using native controls gives wxWidgets applications a natural and familiar look and feel. On the other hand, introducing an additional layer can result in a slight performance penalty, although this is unlikely to be noticed in the kind of applications we will commonly develop.

wxWidgets is not restricted to GUI development. It's more than just a graphics toolkit, providing a whole set of additional facilities, such as database libraries, an inter-process communication layer, networking functionalities, and so on. Though it's written in C++, there are several bindings for many commonly used programming languages. Among them is a Python binding provided by wxPython.

wxPython (available at http://www.wxpython.org/) is a Python extension module that provides a set of bindings to the Python language from the wxWidgets library. This extension module allows Python programmers to create instances of wxWidgets classes and to invoke methods of those classes.

It is a great time to introduce wxPython because wxPython 4 was released a year ago. The latest version of wxPython is 4.0.1 to date (April 2018), and it is compatible with both Python 2 and Python 3.

Beginning in 2010, project Phoenix is an effort to clean up the wxPython implementation and to make it compatible with Python 3. As one can imagine, wxPython was entirely rewritten with a focus on performance, maintainability, and extensibility.

Let us walk through the most basic example of using wxPython!

```
#Here imports the wxPython library
import wx
#Every wxPython app is an instance of wx.App
app = wx.App(False)
#Here we create a wx.Frame() and specifying it as a top-level window
#by stating "None" as a parent object
frame = wx.Frame(None, wx.ID_ANY, "Hello World")
#Show the frame!
```

```
frame.Show(True)
#Start the applciation's MainLoop, and ready for events handling
app.MainLoop()
```

Following on from the preceding example, there is one very important thing for beginners.

`wx.Frame` and `wx.Window()` are very different. `wx.Window` in wxWidgets is the base class from which all visual elements are derived, such as buttons and menus; we always refer to a program window as `wx.Frame` in wxWidgets.

The syntax for constructing a `wx.Frame` is `wx.Frame(Parent, ID, Title)`. When specifying `Parent` as `None`, as shown just now, we are essentially saying that the frame is a top-level `window`.

There is also an **ID system** in wxWidgets. Various controls and other parts of wxWidgets need an ID. Sometimes, the ID is provided by users; alternatively, it has a predefined value. However, the value of the ID is unimportant in most cases (such as the preceding example), and we can use `wx.ID_ANY` as the ID of an object, to tell wxWidgets to assign an ID automatically. Remember that all automatically assigned IDs are negative, and user-defined IDs should always be positive to avoid clashing with them.

Now, let us explore an example written in the OOP style that requires event handling—the `Hello world` button example:

```
#Here imports the wxPython library
import wx

#Here is the class for the Frame inheriting from wx.Frame
class MyFrame(wx.Frame):
    #Instantiation based on the constructor defined below
    def __init__(self, parent):
        #creating the frame object and assigning it to self
        wx.Frame.__init__(self, parent, wx.ID_ANY)
        #Create panel
        self.panel = wx.Panel(self)
        #wx.BoxSizer is essentially the vertical box,
```

```
        #and we will add the buttons to the BoxSizer
        self.sizer = wx.BoxSizer(wx.VERTICAL)
        #Creating button 1 that will print Hello World once
        self.button1 = wx.Button(self.panel,label="Hello World!")
        #Create button 2 that will print Hello World twice
        self.button2 = wx.Button(self.panel,label="Hello World 5 times!")
        #There are two ways to bind the button with the event, here is
method 1:
        self.button1.Bind(wx.EVT_BUTTON, self.OnButton1)
        self.button2.Bind(wx.EVT_BUTTON, self.OnButton2)
        #Here is method 2:
        #self.Bind(wx.EVT_BUTTON, self.OnButton1, self.button1)
        #self.Bind(wx.EVT_BUTTON, self.OnButton2, self.button2)
        #Here we add the button to the BoxSizer
        self.sizer.Add(self.button1,0,0,0)
        self.sizer.Add(self.button2,0,0,0)
        #Put sizer into panel
        self.panel.SetSizer(self.sizer)
    #function that will be invoked upon pressing button 1
    def OnButton1(self,event):
        print("Hello world!")
    #function that will be invoked upon pressing button 2
    def OnButton2(self,event):
        for i in range(0,5):
            print("Hello world!")

#Every wxPython app is an instance of wx.App
app = wx.App()
#Here we create a wx.Frame() and specifying it as a top-level window
#by stating "None" as a parent object
frame = MyFrame(None)
#Show the frame!
frame.Show()
#Start the applciation's MainLoop, and ready for events handling
app.MainLoop()
```

The output looks like:

As readers may observe, all three GUI libraries that we have discussed here have a similar syntax. Therefore, getting familiar with just one of them lets you switch easily among them.

The layout managers for wxWidgets are `sizer` widgets: they are the containers for widgets (including other sizers) that will handle the visual arrangement of the widgets' dimensions according to our configuration. `BoxSizer` takes one parameter, its orientation. In this case, we pass the constant `wx.VERTICAL` to have widgets laid out in a column; however, there is also the constant `wx.HORIZONTAL` if we need a row of widgets:

```
self.sizer.Add(self.button1, 1, wx.LEFT | wx.TOP | wx.EXPAND)
```

We are now able to add our `FigureCanvas` object to the `sizer`. The arguments of the `Add()` function are really important:

- The first parameter is a reference to the object to be added.
- Then, we have the second parameter proportion. This is used to express how much of the additional free space should be assigned to this widget. Often, the widgets on a GUI don't take up all the space, so there is some extra space available. This space is redistributed to all the widgets based on the proportion value of each widget with respect to all the widgets present in the GUI. Let's take an example: if we have three widgets respectively with the proportion set to 0, 1, and 2, then the first (with the proportion set to 0) will not change at all. The third (the proportion set to 2) will change twice more than the second (proportion 1). In the book example, we set it to 1, so we declare that the widget should take one slot of the free space available when resizing.
- The third parameter is a combination of flags to further configure widget behavior in the sizer. It controls borders, alignment, separation between widgets, and expansions. Here we declare that the `FigureCanvas` should expand when the window is resized.

Let us try an example to embed a Matplotlib figure (polar plot) into the wxWidgets-powered GUI:

```
#Specifying that we are using WXAgg in matplotlib
import matplotlib
matplotlib.use('WXAgg')
#Here imports the wxPython and other supporting libraries
import wx, sys, os, random, matplotlib, matplotlib.cm as cm,
matplotlib.pyplot as plt
from numpy import arange, sin, pi, random, linspace
from matplotlib.backends.backend_wxagg import FigureCanvasWxAgg as
FigureCanvas
```

```
from matplotlib.backends.backend_wx import NavigationToolbar2Wx
from matplotlib.figure import Figure

class MyFrame(wx.Frame):
    def __init__(self):
        # Initializing the Frame
        wx.Frame.__init__(self, None, -1, title="", size=(600,500))
        #Create panel
        panel = wx.Panel(self)
        #Here we prepare the figure, canvas and axes object for the graph
        self.fig = Figure(figsize=(6,4), dpi=100)
        self.canvas = FigureCanvas(self, -1, self.fig)
        self.ax = self.fig.add_subplot(111, projection='polar')
        #Here, we borrow one example shown in the matplotlib gtk3 cookbook
        #and show a beautiful bar plot on a circular coordinate system
        self.theta = linspace(0.0, 2 * pi, 30, endpoint=False)
        self.radii = 10 * random.rand(30)
        self.plot_width = pi / 4 * random.rand(30)
        self.bars = self.ax.bar(self.theta, self.radii,
width=self.plot_width, bottom=0.0)

        #Here defines the color of the bar, as well as setting it to be
transparent
        for r, bar in zip(self.radii, self.bars):
            bar.set_facecolor(cm.jet(r / 10.))
            bar.set_alpha(0.5)
        #Here we generate the figure
        self.ax.plot()
        #Creating the vertical box of wxPython
        self.vbox = wx.BoxSizer(wx.VERTICAL)
        #Add canvas to the vertical box
        self.vbox.Add(self.canvas, wx.ALIGN_CENTER|wx.ALL, 1)
        #Add vertical box to the panel
        self.SetSizer(self.vbox)
        #Optimizing the size of the elements in vbox
        self.vbox.Fit(self)

#Every wxPython app is an instance of wx.App
app = wx.App()
#Here we create a wx.Frame() and specifying it as a top-level window
#by stating "None" as a parent object
frame = MyFrame()
#Show the frame!
frame.Show()
#Start the applciation's MainLoop, and ready for events handling
app.MainLoop()
```

Output:

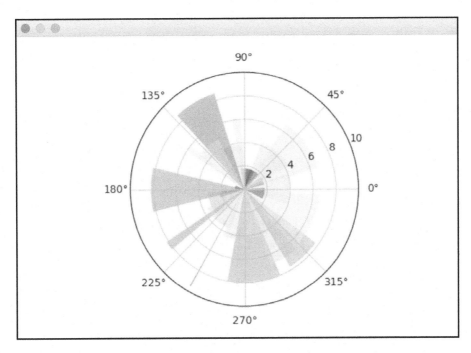

We have shown how to embed a Matplotlib figure into the GUI; however, we have yet to demonstrate the interaction between Matplotlib and wxWidgets. It can be achieved easily by adding a button and a binding (`Bind`) a function to the button. This will update the figure each time the users click on it.

Let's walk through one important example showcasing how to update the plot by clicking a button! Although we are using the same figure, the underlying update methodology is different. Here we will update the figure through a click event instead of an auto-timer as shown in `Chapter 6`, *Embedding Matplotlib in Qt 5*:

```
#Specifying that we are using WXAgg in matplotlib
import matplotlib
matplotlib.use('WXAgg')
#Here imports the wxPython and other supporting libraries
import wx, numpy, matplotlib.cm as cm, matplotlib.pyplot as plt
from numpy import arange, sin, pi, random, linspace
from matplotlib.backends.backend_wxagg import FigureCanvasWxAgg as
FigureCanvas
from matplotlib.backends.backend_wx import NavigationToolbar2Wx
from matplotlib.figure import Figure
```

```
#This figure looks like it is from a radar, so we name the class radar
class Radar(wx.Frame):
    #Instantiation of Radar
    def __init__(self):
        # Initializing the Frame
        wx.Frame.__init__(self, None, -1, title="", size=(600,500))
        # Creating the panel
        panel = wx.Panel(self)
        #Setting up the figure, canvas and axes for drawing
        self.fig = Figure(figsize=(6,4), dpi=100)
        self.canvas = FigureCanvas(self, -1, self.fig)
        self.ax = self.fig.add_subplot(111, projection='polar')
        #Here comes the trick, create the button "Start Radar!"
        self.updateBtn = wx.Button(self, -1, "Start Radar!")
        #Bind the button with the clicking event, and invoke the update_fun
function
        self.Bind(wx.EVT_BUTTON, self.update_fun, self.updateBtn)
        #Create the vertical box of Widgets
        self.vbox = wx.BoxSizer(wx.VERTICAL)
        #Add the canvas to the vertical box
        self.vbox.Add(self.canvas, wx.ALIGN_CENTER|wx.ALL, 1)
        #Add the button to the vertical box
        self.vbox.Add(self.updateBtn)
        #Add the vertical box to the Frame
        self.SetSizer(self.vbox)
        #Make sure the elements in the vertical box fits the figure size
        self.vbox.Fit(self)

    def update_fun(self,event):
        #Make sure we clear the figure each time before redrawing
        self.ax.cla()
        #updating the axes figure
        self.ax = self.fig.add_subplot(111, projection='polar')
        #Here, we borrow one example shown in the matplotlib gtk3 cookbook
        #and show a beautiful bar plot on a circular coordinate system
        self.theta = linspace(0.0, 2 * pi, 30, endpoint=False)
        self.radii = 10 * random.rand(30)
        self.plot_width = pi / 4 * random.rand(30)
        self.bars = self.ax.bar(self.theta, self.radii,
width=self.plot_width, bottom=0.0)

        #Here defines the color of the bar, as well as setting it to be
transparent
        for r, bar in zip(self.radii, self.bars):
            bar.set_facecolor(cm.jet(r / 10.))
            bar.set_alpha(0.5)
        #Here we draw on the canvas!
        self.fig.canvas.draw()
```

```
        #And print on terminal to make sure the function was invoked upon
trigger
        print('Updating figure!')

#Every wxPython app is an instance of wx.App
app = wx.App(False)
#Here we create a wx.Frame() and specifying it as a top-level window
#by stating "None" as a parent object
frame = Radar()
#Show the frame!
frame.Show()
#Start the applciation's MainLoop, and ready for events handling
app.MainLoop()
```

Output:

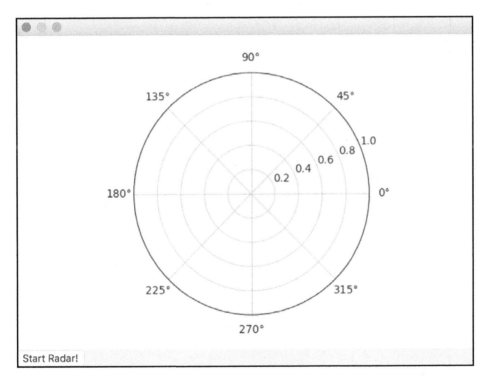

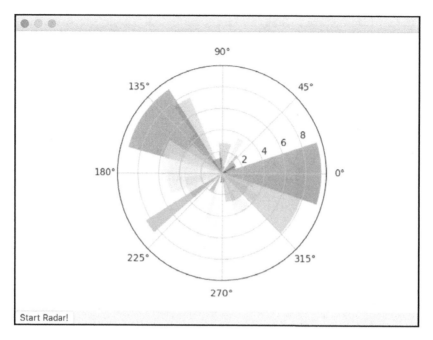

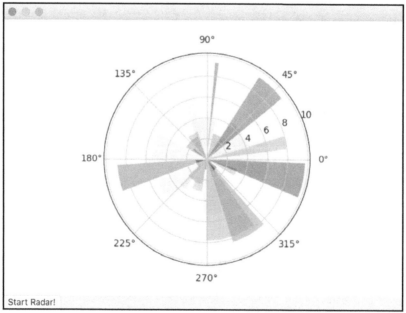

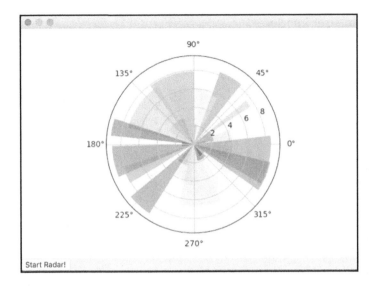

By clicking on the **Start Radar!** button, we invoke the function `update_fun` and redraw a new graph every time.

Embedding Matplotlib in a GUI from wxGlade

For very simple applications with limited GUIs, we can design the interface from inside the application source code. Once the GUI becomes more complex, this solution is not acceptable and we need a tool to support us in the GUI design. One of the most well-known tools for this activity in wxWidgets is wxGlade.

wxGlade is an interface design program written in Python using wxPython, and this allows it to run on all platforms where these two are available.

The philosophy is similar to Glade, the famous GTK+ GUI designer, and the look and feel are very similar as well. wxGlade is a program that helps us to create wxWidgets or wxPython user interfaces, but it is not a full-featured code editor; it's just a designer, and the code it generates does nothing more than display the created widgets.

Although project Phoenix and wxPython 4 are relatively new, they are both supported by wxGlade. wxGlade can be downloaded from sourceforge, and one can easily download the zipped file, unzip it, and run wxGlade with the `python3` command:

```
python3 wxglade.py
```

And here comes the user interface!

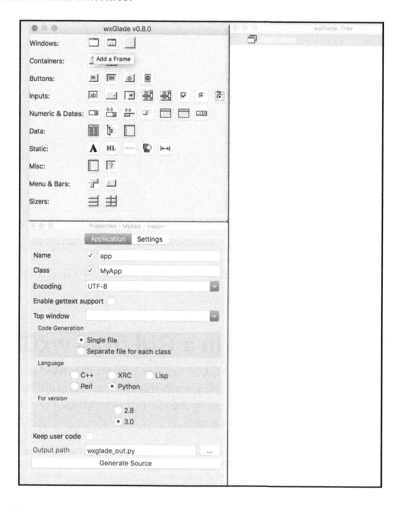

Here is a breakdown of the three main windows in *Figure 5*. The upper left window is the main **Palette** window. The first button of the first row (**Windows**) is the button to create a frame as a basis of everything. The lower left window is the **Properties** window, which lets us display and edit the properties of applications, windows, and controls. The window on the right is the **Tree** window. It enables us to visualize the structure. It allows editing the structure of the project, with its application, windows, sizers, and controls. By choosing an item in the **Tree** window, we can edit its corresponding properties in the **Properties** window.

Let us click on the button to **Add a Frame**. This will be followed by this small window:

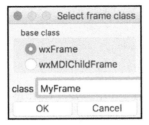

Select the base class as **wxFrame**; and here we will generate a **Design** window as shown in the following screenshot. From here, we can start to click and add buttons and features that we like:

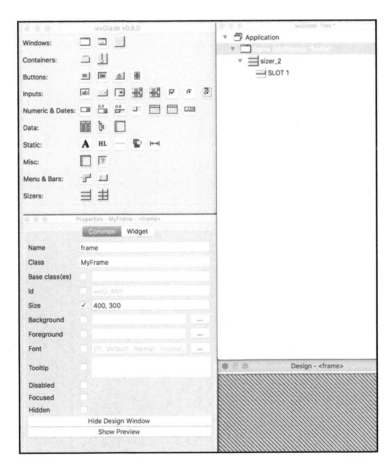

Let us first create a container for the code we have shown previously. Before we click on any buttons, let us revisit the essential elements needed for the preceding GUI:

- Frame
- Vertical box (`wx.BoxSizer`)
- Button

So it's very straightforward; let's click on the sizer button in the **Palette** window and then click on the **Design** window:

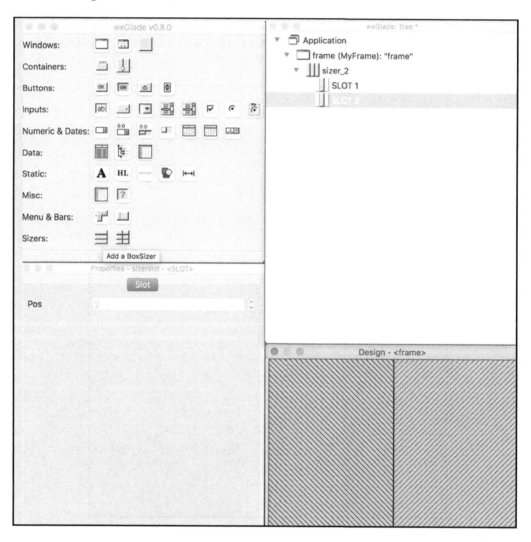

From the **Tree** window, we can see the structure of our GUI. We have a frame containing a sizer of two slots. However, we want a vertical box instead of a horizontal one; this can be modified in the **Properties** window when we click on **sizer_2**:

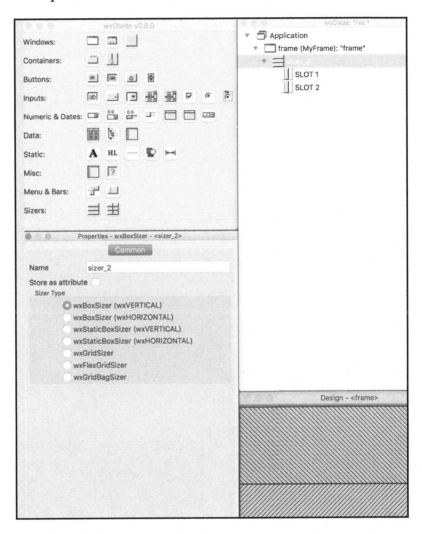

Now let's add a button to slot 2! This can be done by simply clicking on **Button** in the **Palette** window, then clicking on the slot in the lower part of the **Design** window. However, the button doesn't look very nice from there. It's on the left-hand side of the lower panel. This can be altered by selecting **_button1** in the **Tree** window and modifying the alignment details in the **Layout** tab of the **Properties** window.

In here, we have selected **wxEXPAND** and **wxALIGN_CENTER**, which indicate that it has to expand and fill the width of the frame; this also ensures that it aligns at the center of the slot at all times:

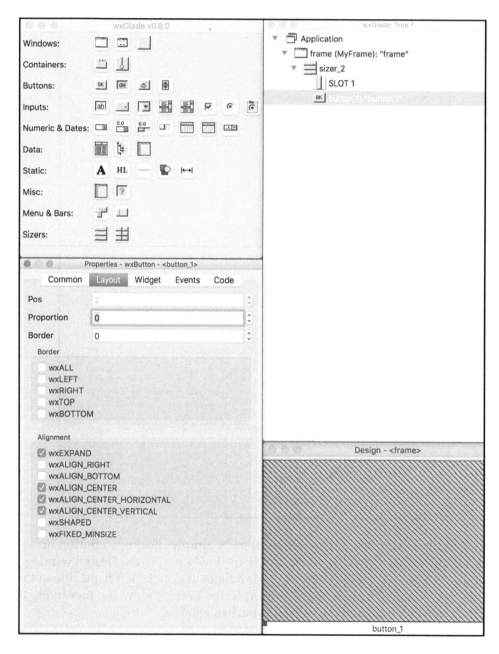

For now, the frame is all set. Let's export the code by choosing **File** and **Generate Code**:

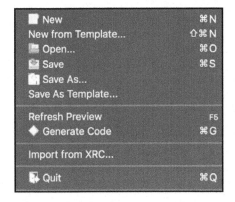

Upon clicking on **Generate Code**, a file will be saved in the desired folder (where the user saved the `wxWidget` file) and here is a code snippet:

```python
#!/usr/bin/env python
# -*- coding: UTF-8 -*-
#
# generated by wxGlade 0.8.0 on Sun Apr  8 20:35:42 2018
#

import wx

# begin wxGlade: dependencies
# end wxGlade

# begin wxGlade: extracode
# end wxGlade


class MyFrame(wx.Frame):
    def __init__(self, *args, **kwds):
        # begin wxGlade: MyFrame.__init__
        kwds["style"] = kwds.get("style", 0) | wx.DEFAULT_FRAME_STYLE
        wx.Frame.__init__(self, *args, **kwds)
        self.SetSize((500, 550))
        self.button_1 = wx.Button(self, wx.ID_ANY, "button_1")

        self.__set_properties()
        self.__do_layout()
        # end wxGlade

    def __set_properties(self):
```

```
        # begin wxGlade: MyFrame.__set_properties
        self.SetTitle("frame")
        # end wxGlade

    def __do_layout(self):
        # begin wxGlade: MyFrame.__do_layout
        sizer_2 = wx.BoxSizer(wx.VERTICAL)
        sizer_2.Add((0, 0), 0, 0, 0)
        sizer_2.Add(self.button_1, 0, wx.ALIGN_CENTER | wx.EXPAND, 0)
        self.SetSizer(sizer_2)
        self.Layout()
        # end wxGlade

# end of class MyFrame

class MyApp(wx.App):
    def OnInit(self):
        self.frame = MyFrame(None, wx.ID_ANY, "")
        self.SetTopWindow(self.frame)
        self.frame.Show()
        return True

# end of class MyApp

if __name__ == "__main__":
    app = MyApp(0)
    app.MainLoop()
```

The preceding code provides the GUI on its own. However, it lacks some key functions to make everything work. Let's quickly expand on that to see how it works:

```
import matplotlib
matplotlib.use('WXAgg')

import wx, numpy, matplotlib.cm as cm, matplotlib.pyplot as plt
from numpy import arange, sin, pi, random, linspace
from matplotlib.backends.backend_wxagg import FigureCanvasWxAgg as
FigureCanvas
from matplotlib.backends.backend_wx import NavigationToolbar2Wx
from matplotlib.figure import Figure

class MyFrame(wx.Frame):
    def __init__(self, *args, **kwds):
        # begin wxGlade: MyFrame.__init__
        kwds["style"] = kwds.get("style", 0) | wx.DEFAULT_FRAME_STYLE
        wx.Frame.__init__(self, *args, **kwds)
        self.SetSize((500, 550))
        self.button_1 = wx.Button(self, wx.ID_ANY, "button_1")
```

```
##Code being added***
        self.Bind(wx.EVT_BUTTON, self.__updat_fun, self.button_1)
        #Setting up the figure, canvas and axes
        self.fig = Figure(figsize=(5,5), dpi=100)
        self.canvas = FigureCanvas(self, -1, self.fig)
        self.ax = self.fig.add_subplot(111, projection='polar')
        ##End of Code being added***self.__set_properties()
        self.__do_layout()
        # end wxGlade

    def __set_properties(self):
        # begin wxGlade: MyFrame.__set_properties
        self.SetTitle("frame")
        # end wxGlade

    def __do_layout(self):
        # begin wxGlade: MyFrame.__do_layout
        sizer_2 = wx.BoxSizer(wx.VERTICAL)
        sizer_2.Add(self.canvas, 0, wx.ALIGN_CENTER|wx.ALL, 1)
        sizer_2.Add(self.button_1, 0, wx.ALIGN_CENTER | wx.EXPAND, 0)
        self.SetSizer(sizer_2)
        self.Layout()
        # end wxGlade
##The udpate_fun that allows the figure to be updated upon clicking
##The __ in front of the update_fun indicates that it is a private function
in Python syntax
    def __updat_fun(self,event):
        self.ax.cla()
        self.ax = self.fig.add_subplot(111, projection='polar')
        #Here, we borrow one example shown in the matplotlib gtk3 cookbook
        #and show a beautiful bar plot on a circular coordinate system
        self.theta = linspace(0.0, 2 * pi, 30, endpoint=False)
        self.radii = 10 * random.rand(30)
        self.plot_width = pi / 4 * random.rand(30)
        self.bars = self.ax.bar(self.theta, self.radii,
width=self.plot_width, bottom=0.0)

        #Here defines the color of the bar, as well as setting it to be
transparent
        for r, bar in zip(self.radii, self.bars):
            bar.set_facecolor(cm.jet(r / 10.))
            bar.set_alpha(0.5)

        self.fig.canvas.draw()
        print('Updating figure!')
# end of class MyFrame
class MyApp(wx.App):
    def OnInit(self):
```

```
        self.frame = MyFrame(None, wx.ID_ANY, "")
        self.SetTopWindow(self.frame)
        self.frame.Show()
        return True

# end of class MyApp

if __name__ == "__main__":
    app = MyApp(0)
    app.MainLoop()
```

Summary

We are now able to develop wxWidgets applications and then embed Matplotlib in them. To be specific, readers should be able to embed a Matplotlib figure in a **wxFrame**, use a sizer to embed both the figure and navigation toolbar in a **wxFrame**, update a plot through interaction, and use wxGlade to design a GUI for Matplotlib embedding.

We are now ready to move further and see how to integrate Matplotlib into the web.

8
Integrating Matplotlib with Web Applications

Web-based applications (web apps) offer multi-level advantages. First, users can enjoy a unified experience across platforms. Second, since an installation process is not required, users can enjoy a simpler workflow. Lastly, from the perspective of developers, the development cycle can be simplified as less platform-specific code has to be maintained. Given these advantages, more and more applications are being developed online.

Owing to the popularity and flexibility of Python, it makes sense for web developers to use Python-based web frameworks such as Django and Flask to develop web applications. In fact, Django and Flask ranked 6th and 13th out of 175 respectively in terms of popularity, according to `http://hotframeworks.com/`. These frameworks are *batteries included*. From user authentication, user administration, and content management to API design, these frameworks have got them all covered. The code base is closely reviewed by the open source community such that sites that were developed using these frameworks are protected against common attacks, such as SQL injection, cross-site request forgery, and cross-site scripting.

In this chapter, we are going to learn how to develop a simple site that displays the price of Bitcoin. Examples based on Django will be covered. We will use Docker 18.03.0-ce, and Django 2.0.4 for demonstration. Let's begin by going through the steps of initializing a Docker-based development environment.

Installing Docker

Docker allows developers to run applications in self-contained and lightweight containers. Since its introduction in 2013, Docker has quickly gained popularity among developers. At the center of its technology, Docker uses the resource isolation methods of the Linux kernel instead of a full-blown virtualization hypervisor to run applications.

This enables easier development, packaging, deployment, and management of code. Therefore, all code development work in this chapter will be conducted using a Docker-based environment.

Docker for Windows users

There are two ways to install Docker on Windows: the aptly named Docker for Windows package, and Docker Toolbox. I recommend stable versions of the Docker Toolbox because Docker for Windows requires Hyper-V support in 64-bit Windows 10 Pro. Meanwhile, Docker for Windows is not supported by older versions of Windows. Detailed installation instructions can be found at `https://docs.docker.com/toolbox/toolbox_install_windows/`, but we will also cover the important steps here.

First, download Docker Toolbox from the following link: `https://github.com/docker/toolbox/releases`. Choose the file with the name `DockerToolbox-xx.xx.x-ce.exe`, where `x` refers to the latest version numbers:

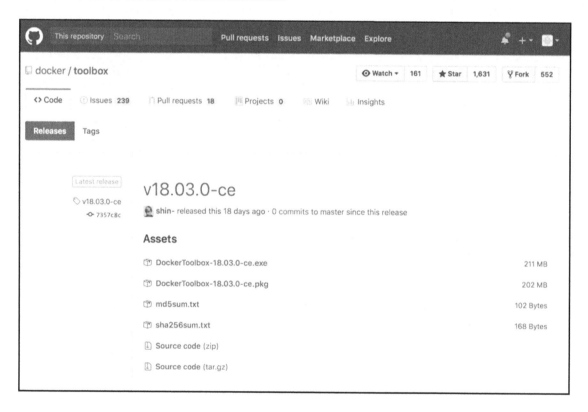

Next, run the downloaded installer. Follow the default instructions of each prompt to install:

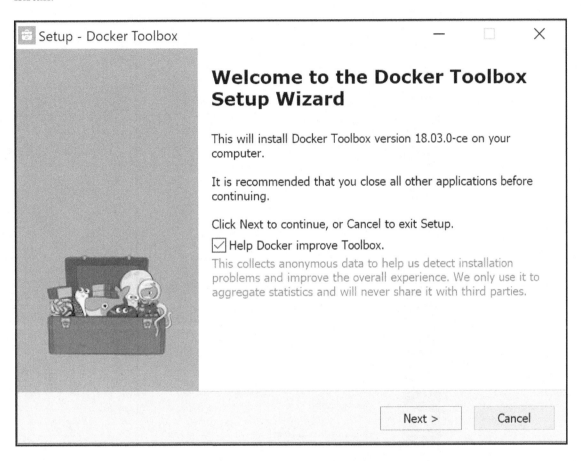

Windows might ask you for permission to make certain changes. It is normal, and make sure you allow the changes to happen.

Finally, once the installation is complete, you should be able to locate **Docker Quickstart Terminal** in the Start menu:

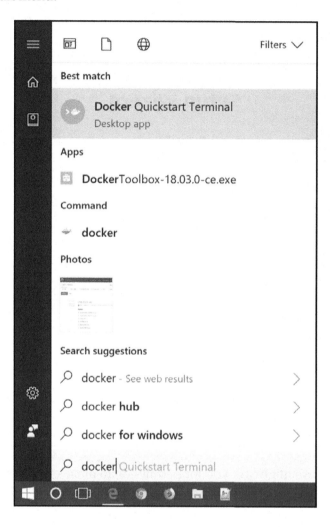

Click on the icon to launch the **Docker Toolbox Terminal**, which begins an initialization process. When the process is complete, the following terminal will be shown:

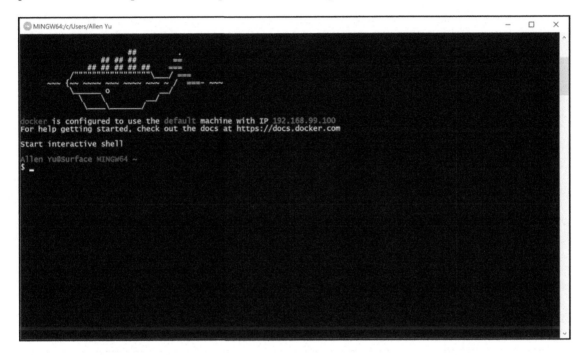

Docker for Mac users

For Mac users, I recommend the Docker CE for Mac (stable) app, which is available at https://store.docker.com/editions/community/docker-ce-desktop-mac. In addition, a full installation guide can be found via the following link: https://docs.docker.com/docker-for-mac/install/.

The installation process of Docker CE for Mac is arguably simpler than for its Windows counterpart. Here are the major steps:

1. First, double-click on the downloaded `Docker.dmg` file to mount the image. When you see the following popup, drag and drop the Docker icon on the left to the **Applications** folder on the right:

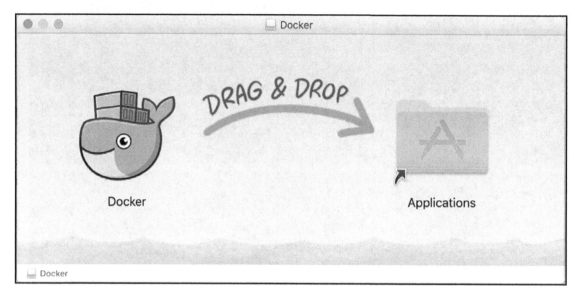

2. Next, in your **Applications** folder or Launchpad, locate and double-click on the Docker app. You should be able to see a whale icon in the top status bar if Docker was successfully launched:

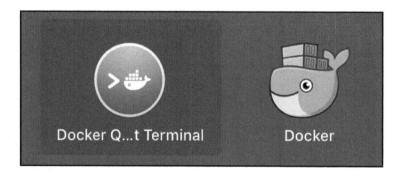

3. Finally, open the Terminal app in the **Applications | Utilities** folder. Type `docker info`, followed by *Enter* to check whether Docker is installed properly:

```
                                   chishingyu — -bash — Solarized Dark ansi — 120×30
Last login: Tue Apr 10 00:38:27 on ttys002
Allen-MBP:~ chishingyu$ docker info
Containers: 2
 Running: 0
 Paused: 0
 Stopped: 2
Images: 37
Server Version: 18.03.0-ce
Storage Driver: aufs
 Root Dir: /var/lib/docker/aufs
 Backing Filesystem: extfs
 Dirs: 87
 Dirperm1 Supported: true
Logging Driver: json-file
Cgroup Driver: cgroupfs
Plugins:
 Volume: local
 Network: bridge host ipvlan macvlan null overlay
 Log: awslogs fluentd gcplogs gelf journald json-file logentries splunk syslog
Swarm: inactive
Runtimes: runc
Default Runtime: runc
Init Binary: docker-init
containerd version: cfd04396dc68220d1cecbe686a6cc3aa5ce3667c
runc version: 4fc53a81fb7c994640722ac585fa9ca548971871
init version: 949e6fa
Security Options:
 seccomp
  Profile: default
Kernel Version: 4.9.87-linuxkit-aufs
```

More about Django

Django is a popular web framework that is designed to simplify the development and deployment of web applications. It includes loads of boilerplate code for everyday tasks, such as database model management, frontend templating, session authentication, and security. Django was built around the **Model-Template-View** (**MTV**) design pattern.

The model is perhaps the most critical component of MTV. It refers to how you represent your data in terms of different tables and attributes. It also abstracts away the nitty-gritty details of different database engines such that the same model can be applied to SQLite, MySQL, and PostgreSQL. Meanwhile, the model layer of Django would expose engine-specific parameters, such as `ArrayField` and `JSONField` in PostgreSQL, for fine-tuning of your data representation.

The template is similar to the role of a view in the canonical MTV framework. It handles the presentation of data to the users. In other words, it doesn't handle the logic of how the data was generated.

The view in Django is responsible for handling a user's request, and the subsequent logic of returning a response. It sits between the model layer and the template layer. A view determines what kind of data should be fetched from the model and how to process the data for the template.

The key selling points of Django are as follows:

- **Development speed**: Loads of key components are provided; this reduces the number of repetitive tasks in a development cycle. For instance, it takes mere minutes to build a simple blog using Django.
- **Security**: Best practices of web security are included in Django. The risks of hacks such as SQL injection, cross-site scripting, cross-site request forgery, and clickjacking are greatly reduced. Its user authentication system uses the PBKDF2 algorithm with a salted SHA256 hash, which is recommended by NIST. Other state-of-the-art hash algorithms, such as Argon2, are also available.
- **Scalability**: The MTV layers of Django use a shared-nothing architecture. If a certain layer is the bottleneck of the web application, just throw more hardware to it; Django will take advantage of the additional hardware for each of the layers.

Django development in Docker containers

To keep things tidy, let's create an empty directory named Django to host all the files. Inside the Django directory, we need to define the content of a container by creating a Dockerfile using our favorite text editor. A Dockerfile defines the base image of a container as well as the commands that are necessary to compile an image.

For more information about Dockerfile, please visit `https://docs.docker.com/engine/reference/builder/`.

We will use Python 3.6.5 as our base image. Please copy the following code to your Dockerfile. A series of additional commands define the working directory and the initiation process:

```
# The official Python 3.6.5 runtime is used as the base image
FROM python:3.6.5-slim
# Disable buffering of output streams
ENV PYTHONUNBUFFERED 1
# Create a working directory within the container
RUN mkdir /app
WORKDIR /app
# Copy files and directories in the current directory to the container
ADD . /app/
# Install Django and other dependencies
RUN pip install -r requirements.txt
```

As you may notice, we also need a text file, `requirements.txt`, to define any package dependencies in our project. Please add the following content to the `requirements.txt` file in the folder where the project is present:

```
Django==2.0.4
Matplotlib==2.2.2
stockstats==0.2.0
seaborn==0.8.1
```

Now, we can run `docker build -t django` in the terminal to build the image. It takes up to several minutes before the process is complete:

Please make sure you are currently located in the same project folder before running the command.

```
●  ●  ●                        Django — -bash — Solarized Dark ansi — 120×37
Allen-MBP:Django chishingyu$ docker build -t django .
Sending build context to Docker daemon  3.072kB
Step 1/6 : FROM python:3.6.5-slim
3.6.5-slim: Pulling from library/python
b0568b191983: Pull complete
2092fcb29521: Pull complete
c78f86fad884: Pull complete
d9888dfa4bc6: Pull complete
4a08cead57f4: Pull complete
Digest: sha256:2eb5910e86479d3e2dc1bb06411b4c039e31f5634bc3046e0ea505e4c8b434f2
Status: Downloaded newer image for python:3.6.5-slim
 ---> e7455bcafa38
Step 2/6 : ENV PYTHONUNBUFFERED 1
 ---> Running in 2fdbe143f820
Removing intermediate container 2fdbe143f820
 ---> 6695432580f9
Step 3/6 : RUN mkdir /app
 ---> Running in 85e5e04d6ab4
Removing intermediate container 85e5e04d6ab4
 ---> acab71d04980
Step 4/6 : WORKDIR /app
Removing intermediate container 9978565a7d83
 ---> 8fecc1b66602
Step 5/6 : ADD . /app/
 ---> 511963892172
Step 6/6 : RUN pip install -r requirements.txt
 ---> Running in d1421595f7f9
Collecting Django==2.0.4 (from -r requirements.txt (line 1))
  Downloading Django-2.0.4-py3-none-any.whl (7.1MB)
Collecting Matplotlib==2.2.2 (from -r requirements.txt (line 2))
  Downloading matplotlib-2.2.2-cp36-cp36m-manylinux1_x86_64.whl (12.6MB)
Collecting stockstats==0.2.0 (from -r requirements.txt (line 3))
  Downloading stockstats-0.2.0-py2.py3-none-any.whl
Collecting seaborn==0.8.1 (from -r requirements.txt (line 4))
  Downloading seaborn-0.8.1.tar.gz (178kB)
Collecting pytz (from Django==2.0.4->-r requirements.txt (line 1))
  Downloading pytz-2018.3-py2.py3-none-any.whl (509kB)
```

The following message will be shown if the building process is complete. The exact hash code at the end of the `Successfully built ...` message could be different:

```
Successfully built 018e75992e59
Successfully tagged django:latest
```

Starting a new Django site

We will now create a new Docker container using the `docker run` command. The `-v "$(pwd)":/app` parameter creates a bind-mount of the current directory to `/app` in the container. Files in the current directory are shared between the host and the guest systems.

The second untagged parameter `django` defines the image that we use for the creation of a container. The rest of the command string is as follows:

```
django django-admin startproject --
template=https://github.com/arocks/edge/archive/master.zip --
extension=py,md,html,env crypto_stats
```

This is passed to the guest container for execution. It creates a new Django project named `crypto_stats` using the edge template by Arun Ravindran (`https://django-edge. readthedocs.io/en/latest/`):

```
docker run -v "$(pwd)":/app django django-admin startproject --
template=https://github.com/arocks/edge/archive/master.zip --
extension=py,md,html,env crypto_stats
```

Upon successful execution, you should be able to see the following files and directories if you go inside the newly created `crypto_stats` folder:

Installation of Django dependencies

The `requirements.txt` file in the `crypto_stats` folder defines the Python package dependencies of our Django project. To install these dependencies, please issue the following `docker run` command.

The -p 8000:8000 parameter exposes port 8000 from the guest to the host machine. The -it parameter creates a pseudo-terminal with stdin support to allow an interactive terminal session.

We are again using the django image, but this time we launch a Bash Terminal shell instead:

```
docker run -v "$(pwd)":/app -p 8000:8000 -it django bash
cd crypto_stats
pip install -r requirements.txt
```

 You should make sure that you are still in your root project folder (that is, Django) when you issue the command.

The chain of commands would produce the following results:

Django environment setup

Sensitive environment variables, such as Django's SECRET_KEY (https://docs.djangoproject.com/en/2.0/ref/settings/#std:setting-SECRET_KEY), should be kept in a private file that is excluded from version control software. For simplicity, we can just use the sample from the project template:

```
cd src
cp crypto_stats/settings/local.sample.env crypto_stats/settings/local.env
```

Next, we can use manage.py to create a default SQLite database and the superuser:

```
python manage.py migrate
python manage.py createsuperuser
```

The migrate command initializes the database models, including user authentication, admin, user profiles, user sessions, content types, and thumbnails.

The createsuperuser command will ask you a series of questions for the creation of a superuser:

Running the development server

Launching the default development server is very simple; in fact, it takes only a single line of code:

```
python manage.py runserver 0.0.0.0:8000
```

The 0.0.0.0:8000 parameter will tell Django to serve the website to all addresses at port 8000.

In your host machine, you can now launch your favorite browser and go to http://localhost:8000 to see your site:

The look of the site is decent, isn't it?

Showing Bitcoin prices using Django and Matplotlib

We have now established a fully fledged website backbone using just a few commands. I hope you will appreciate the simplicity of using Django for web development. Now, I will demonstrate how we can integrate Matplotlib charts into a Django site, which is the key topic of this chapter.

Creating a Django app

An app in the Django ecosystem refers to an application that handles a specific function within a site. For instance, our default project comes with the profile and account apps already. With the terminology clarified, we are set to build an app to display the latest price of bitcoin.

We should keep our development server running in the background. When the server detects any changes to our code base, it will reload automatically to reflect the changes. Therefore, right now, we need to launch a new Terminal and attach to the running server container:

```
docker exec -it 377bfb2f3db4 bash
```

The strange-looking numbers before `bash` refer to the ID of the container. We can find the ID from the terminal that holds the running server:

Alternatively, we can get the IDs of all running containers by issuing the following command:

```
docker ps -a
```

The `docker exec` command helps you go back to the same Bash environment as the development server. We can now start a new app:

```
cd /app/crypto_stats/src
python manage.py startapp bitcoin
```

Inside the host computer's project directory, we should be able to see a new `bitcoin` folder inside `crypto_stats/src/`:

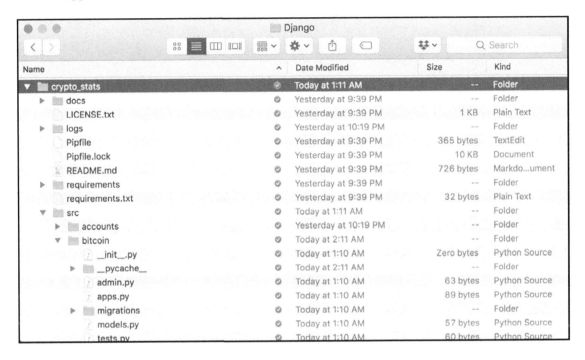

Creating a simple Django view

I will demonstrate the workflow of creating a Django view via a simple line chart.

Inside the newly created bitcoin app folder, you should be able to find `views.py`, which stores all the views within the app. Let's edit it and create a view that outputs a Matplotlib line chart:

```python
from django.shortcuts import render
from django.http import HttpResponse

# Create your views here.
from io import BytesIO
import matplotlib
matplotlib.use('Agg')
import matplotlib.pyplot as plt

def test_view(request):
```

```
# Create a new Matplotlib figure
fig, ax = plt.subplots()

# Prepare a simple line chart
ax.plot([1, 2, 3, 4], [3, 6, 9, 12])

ax.set_title('Matplotlib Chart in Django')
plt.tight_layout()
# Create a bytes buffer for saving image
fig_buffer = BytesIO()
plt.savefig(fig_buffer, dpi=150)
# Save the figure as a HttpResponse
response = HttpResponse(content_type='image/png')
response.write(fig_buffer.getvalue())
fig_buffer.close()
return response
```

Since Tkinter is not available inside our server container, we need to switch the Matplotlib graphical backend from the default TkAgg to Agg by calling `matplotlib.use('Agg')` first.

 `matplotlib.use('Agg')` must be called right after the line `import matplotlib` and before any other function calls of Matplotlib.

The function `test_view`(request) expects a Django `HttpRequest` object (https://docs. djangoproject.com/en/2.0/ref/request-response/#django.http.HttpRequest) as input, and outputs a Django `HttpResponse` object (https://docs.djangoproject.com/en/2.0/ ref/request-response/#django.http.HttpResponse).

To import a Matplotlib plot to the `HttpResponse` object, we need to save the plot to an intermediate `BytesIO` object first, which can be found in the `io` package (https://docs. python.org/3/library/io.html#binary-i-o). The `BytesIO` object acts as a buffer of the binary image file, such that `plt.savefig` can write a PNG file directly into it.

Next, we create a new `HttpResponse()` object with the `content_type` parameter set to `image/png`. The binary content inside the buffer is exported to the `HttpResponse()` object via `response.write(fig_buffer.getvalue())`. Finally, the buffer is closed to free up the temporary memory.

To direct users to this view, we need to create a new file called `urls.py` inside the `{Project_folder}/crypto_stats/src/bitcoin` folder.

```
from django.urls import path

from . import views

app_name = 'bitcoin'
urlpatterns = [
    path('test/', views.test_view),
]
```

The line `path('test/', views.test_view)` states that all URLs with suffix `test/` will be directed to the `test_view`.

We need to add our app's `url` patterns to the global patterns as well. Let's edit `{Project_folder}/crypto_stats/src/crypto_stats/urls.py`, and add the two lines commented as follows:

```
...
import profiles.urls
import accounts.urls
# Import your app's url patterns here
import bitcoin.urls
from . import views


...

urlpatterns = [
    path('', views.HomePage.as_view(), name='home'),
    path('about/', views.AboutPage.as_view(), name='about'),
    path('users/', include(profiles.urls)),
    path('admin/', admin.site.urls),
    # Add your app's url patterns here
    path('bitcoin/', include(bitcoin.urls)),
    path('', include(accounts.urls)),
]
...
```

The line `path('bitcoin/', include(bitcoin.urls))`, states that every URL that begins with `http://<your-domain>/bitcoin` would be directed to the bitcoin app.

Wait for a few seconds until the development server reloads. You can now head to `http://localhost:8000/bitcoin/test/` to see your plot.

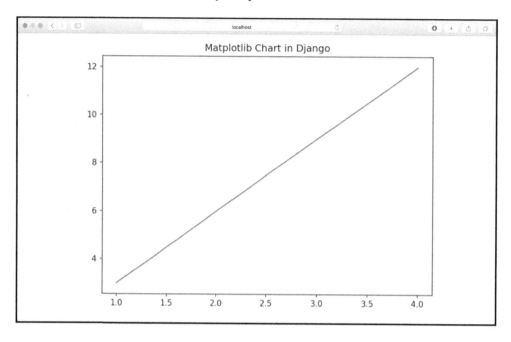

Creating a Bitcoin candlestick view

In this section, we are going to fetch the historical prices of Bitcoin from the Quandl API. Please note that we do not guarantee the accuracy, completeness, or validity of the visualizations presented; nor are we responsible for any errors or omissions that may have occurred. The data, visualizations, and analyses are provided on an *as is* basis for educational purposes only, without any warranties of any kind. Readers are advised to conduct their own independent research into individual cryptocurrencies before making a investment decision.

If you are not familiar with Quandl, it is a financial and economic data warehouse that stores millions of datasets from hundreds of publishers. Before you can use the Quandl API, you would need to register an account on its website (`https://www.quandl.com`). A free API access key can be obtained by following the instructions in this link `https://docs.quandl.com/docs#section-authentication`. I will cover more about Quandl and APIs in the next chapter.

Now, remove the existing `views.py` file from the `crypto_stats/src/bitcoin` folder. Copy `views1.py` from this chapter's code repository to `crypto_stats/src/bitcoin`, and rename it as `views.py`. I will explain each part of `views1.py` accordingly.

The historical bitcoin prices data in the Bitstamp exchange can be found here: `https://www.quandl.com/data/BCHARTS/BITSTAMPUSD-Bitcoin-Markets-bitstampUSD`. The corresponding unique identifier for our target dataset is `BCHARTS/BITSTAMPUSD`. Although an official Python client library is available from Quandl, we are not going to use that for the sake of demonstrating the general procedures of importing JSON data. The function `get_bitcoin_dataset` uses nothing more than `urllib.request.urlopen` and `json.loads` to fetch the JSON data from the API. Finally the data is processed into a pandas DataFrame for our further consumption.

```python
... A bunch of import statements

def get_bitcoin_dataset():
    """Obtain and parse a quandl bitcoin dataset in Pandas DataFrame
format
        Quandl returns dataset in JSON format, where data is stored as a
        list of lists in response['dataset']['data'], and column headers
        stored in response['dataset']['column_names'].

        Returns:
        df: Pandas DataFrame of a Quandl dataset"""

    # Input your own API key here
    api_key = ""

    # Quandl code for Bitcoin historical price in BitStamp exchange
    code = "BCHARTS/BITSTAMPUSD"
    base_url = "https://www.quandl.com/api/v3/datasets/"
    url_suffix = ".json?api_key="

    # We want to get the data within a one-year window only
    time_now = datetime.datetime.now()
    one_year_ago = time_now.replace(year=time_now.year-1)
    start_date = one_year_ago.date().isoformat()
    end_date = time_now.date().isoformat()
    date = "&start_date={}&end_date={}".format(start_date, end_date)
    # Fetch the JSON response
    u = urlopen(base_url + code + url_suffix + api_key + date)
    response = json.loads(u.read().decode('utf-8'))

    # Format the response as Pandas Dataframe
    df = pd.DataFrame(response['dataset']['data'],
columns=response['dataset']['column_names'])
```

```
    # Convert Date column from string to Python datetime object,
    # then to float number that is supported by Matplotlib.
    df["Datetime"] = date2num(pd.to_datetime(df["Date"], format="%Y-%m-
%d").tolist())

    return df
```

Remember to specify your own API key at this line: `api_key = ""`.

The `Date` column in `df` is recorded as a series of Python strings. Although Seaborn can use string-formatted dates in some functions, Matplotlib cannot. To make the dates malleable to data processing and visualizations, we need to convert the values to float numbers that is supported by Matplotlib. Therefore, I have used `matplotlib.dates.date2num` to perform the conversion.

Our data frame contains the opening and closing price, as well as the highest and lowest price per trading day. None of the plots we described thus far are able to describe the trend of all these variables in a single plot.

In the financial world, candlestick plot is almost the default choice for describing price movements of stocks, currencies, and commodities over a time period. Each candlestick consists of the body that describes the opening and closing prices, and extended wicks that illustrate the highest and lowest prices, in one particular trading day. If the closing price is higher than the opening price, the candlestick is often colored black. Conversely, the candlestick would be colored red if the closing is lower. Traders can then infer the opening and closing prices based on the combination of color and the boundary of candlestick body.

In the following example, we are going to prepare a candlestick chart of bitcoin in the last 30 trading days of our data frame. The `candlestick_ohlc` function was adapted from the deprecated `matplotlib.finance` package. It plots the time, open, high, low, and close as a vertical line ranging from low to high. It further uses a series of colored rectangular bars to represent the open-close span.

```
def candlestick_ohlc(ax, quotes, width=0.2, colorup='k', colordown='r',
    alpha=1.0):
    """
    Parameters
    ----------
    ax : `Axes`
    an Axes instance to plot to
```

```
quotes : sequence of (time, open, high, low, close, ...) sequences
As long as the first 5 elements are these values,
the record can be as long as you want (e.g., it may store volume).
time must be in float days format - see date2num
width : float
    fraction of a day for the rectangle width
colorup : color
    the color of the rectangle where close >= open
colordown : color
    the color of the rectangle where close < open
alpha : float
    the rectangle alpha level
Returns
-------
ret : tuple
    returns (lines, patches) where lines is a list of lines
    added and patches is a list of the rectangle patches added
"""
OFFSET = width / 2.0
lines = []
patches = []
for q in quotes:
    t, open, high, low, close = q[:5]
    if close >= open:
        color = colorup
        lower = open
        height = close - open
    else:
        color = colordown
        lower = close
        height = open - close

    vline = Line2D(
                xdata=(t, t), ydata=(low, high),
                color=color,
                linewidth=0.5,
                antialiased=True,
            )
    rect = Rectangle(
                xy=(t - OFFSET, lower),
                width=width,
                height=height,
                facecolor=color,
                edgecolor=color,
            )
    rect.set_alpha(alpha)
    lines.append(vline)
    patches.append(rect)
```

```
        ax.add_line(vline)
        ax.add_patch(rect)
        ax.autoscale_view()

    return lines, patches
```

The `bitcoin_chart` **function handles the actual processing of user requests and the output of** `HttpResponse`.

```
def bitcoin_chart(request):
    # Get a dataframe of bitcoin prices
    bitcoin_df = get_bitcoin_dataset()
    # candlestick_ohlc expects Date (in floating point number), Open, High,
Low, Close columns only
    # So we need to select the useful columns first using DataFrame.loc[].
Extra columns can exist,
    # but they are ignored. Next we get the data for the last 30 trading
only for simplicity of plots.
    candlestick_data = bitcoin_df.loc[:, ["Datetime",
                                          "Open",
                                          "High",
                                          "Low",
                                          "Close",
                                          "Volume (Currency)"]].iloc[:30]

    # Create a new Matplotlib figure
    fig, ax = plt.subplots()

    # Prepare a candlestick plot
    candlestick_ohlc(ax, candlestick_data.values, width=0.6)

    ax.xaxis.set_major_locator(WeekdayLocator(MONDAY)) # major ticks on the
mondays
    ax.xaxis.set_minor_locator(DayLocator()) # minor ticks on the days
    ax.xaxis.set_major_formatter(DateFormatter('%Y-%m-%d'))
    ax.xaxis_date() # treat the x data as dates
    # rotate all ticks to vertical
    plt.setp(ax.get_xticklabels(), rotation=90,
horizontalalignment='right')

    ax.set_ylabel('Price (US $)') # Set y-axis label
    plt.tight_layout()
    # Create a bytes buffer for saving image
    fig_buffer = BytesIO()
    plt.savefig(fig_buffer, dpi=150)
    # Save the figure as a HttpResponse
    response = HttpResponse(content_type='image/png')
```

```
response.write(fig_buffer.getvalue())
fig_buffer.close()
return response
```

 `ax.xaxis.set_major_formatter(DateFormatter('%Y-%m-%d'))` is useful for the conversion of floating point numbers back to dates.

Like the first Django view example, we need to modify our urls.py to direct the URLs to our `bitcoin_chart` view.

```
from django.urls import path

from . import views

app_name = 'bitcoin'
urlpatterns = [
    path('30/', views.bitcoin_chart),
]
```

Voila! You can look at the bitcoin candlestick plot by going to `http://localhost:8000/bitcoin/30/`.

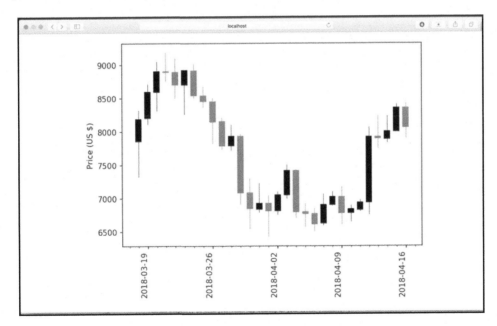

Integrating more pricing indicators

The candlestick plot in the current form is a bit bland. Traders would usually overlay stock indicators such as **average true range (ATR)**, Bollinger band, **commodity channel index (CCI)**, **exponential moving average (EMA)**, **moving average convergence divergence (MACD)**, **relative strength index (RSI)**, and other various stats for technical analysis.

Stockstats (`https://github.com/jealous/stockstats`) is a great package for calculating the preceding indicators/stats and much more. It wraps around pandas DataFrames and generate that stats on the fly when they are accessed.

In this section, we can convert a pandas DataFrame to a stockstats DataFrame via `stockstats.StockDataFrame.retype()`. A plethora of stock indicators can then be accessed by following the pattern `StockDataFrame["variable_timeWindow_indicator"]`. For example, `StockDataFrame['open_2_sma']` would give us 2-day simple moving average on opening price. Shortcuts may be available for some indicators, so please consult the official documentation for more information.

The file `views2.py` in our code repository contains the code to create an extended Bitcoin pricing view. You can copy `views2.py` from this chapter's code repository to `crypto_stats/src/bitcoin`, and rename it as `views.py`.

Here are the important changes to our previous code:

```python
# FuncFormatter to convert tick values to Millions
def millions(x, pos):
    return '%dM' % (x/1e6)
def bitcoin_chart(request):
    # Get a dataframe of bitcoin prices
    bitcoin_df = get_bitcoin_dataset()
    # candlestick_ohlc expects Date (in floating point number), Open, High,
Low, Close columns only
    # So we need to select the useful columns first using DataFrame.loc[].
Extra columns can exist,
    # but they are ignored. Next we get the data for the last 30 trading
only for simplicity of plots.
    candlestick_data = bitcoin_df.loc[:, ["Datetime",
                                          "Open",
                                          "High",
                                          "Low",
                                          "Close",
                                          "Volume (Currency)"]].iloc[:30]
    # Convert to StockDataFrame
    # Need to pass a copy of candlestick_data to StockDataFrame.retype
```

```
    # Otherwise the original candlestick_data will be modified
    stockstats = StockDataFrame.retype(candlestick_data.copy())
    # 5-day exponential moving average on closing price
    ema_5 = stockstats["close_5_ema"]
    # 10-day exponential moving average on closing price
    ema_10 = stockstats["close_10_ema"]
    # 30-day exponential moving average on closing price
    ema_30 = stockstats["close_30_ema"]
    # Upper Bollinger band
    boll_ub = stockstats["boll_ub"]
    # Lower Bollinger band
    boll_lb = stockstats["boll_lb"]
    # 7-day Relative Strength Index
    rsi_7 = stockstats['rsi_7']
    # 14-day Relative Strength Index
    rsi_14 = stockstats['rsi_14']

    # Create 3 subplots spread across three rows, with shared x-axis.
    # The height ratio is specified via gridspec_kw
    fig, axarr = plt.subplots(nrows=3, ncols=1, sharex=True, figsize=(8,8),
                        gridspec_kw={'height_ratios':[3,1,1]})

    # Prepare a candlestick plot in the first axes
    candlestick_ohlc(axarr[0], candlestick_data.values, width=0.6)

    # Overlay stock indicators in the first axes
    axarr[0].plot(candlestick_data["Datetime"], ema_5, lw=1, label='EMA
(5)')
    axarr[0].plot(candlestick_data["Datetime"], ema_10, lw=1, label='EMA
(10)')
    axarr[0].plot(candlestick_data["Datetime"], ema_30, lw=1, label='EMA
(30)')
    axarr[0].plot(candlestick_data["Datetime"], boll_ub, lw=2, linestyle="-
-", label='Bollinger upper')
    axarr[0].plot(candlestick_data["Datetime"], boll_lb, lw=2, linestyle="-
-", label='Bollinger lower')

    # Display RSI in the second axes
    axarr[1].axhline(y=30, lw=2, color = '0.7') # Line for oversold
threshold
    axarr[1].axhline(y=50, lw=2, linestyle="--", color = '0.8') # Neutral
RSI
    axarr[1].axhline(y=70, lw=2, color = '0.7') # Line for overbought
threshold
    axarr[1].plot(candlestick_data["Datetime"], rsi_7, lw=2, label='RSI
(7)')
    axarr[1].plot(candlestick_data["Datetime"], rsi_14, lw=2, label='RSI
(14)')
```

```
    # Display trade volume in the third axes
    axarr[2].bar(candlestick_data["Datetime"], candlestick_data['Volume
(Currency)'])

    # Label the axes
    axarr[0].set_ylabel('Price (US $)')
    axarr[1].set_ylabel('RSI')
    axarr[2].set_ylabel('Volume (US $)')

    axarr[2].xaxis.set_major_locator(WeekdayLocator(MONDAY)) # major ticks
on the mondays
    axarr[2].xaxis.set_minor_locator(DayLocator()) # minor ticks on the
days
    axarr[2].xaxis.set_major_formatter(DateFormatter('%Y-%m-%d'))
    axarr[2].xaxis_date() # treat the x data as dates
    axarr[2].yaxis.set_major_formatter(FuncFormatter(millions)) # Change
the y-axis ticks to millions
    plt.setp(axarr[2].get_xticklabels(), rotation=90,
horizontalalignment='right') # Rotate x-tick labels by 90 degree

    # Limit the x-axis range to the last 30 days
    time_now = datetime.datetime.now()
    datemin = time_now-datetime.timedelta(days=30)
    datemax = time_now
    axarr[2].set_xlim(datemin, datemax)

    # Show figure legend
    axarr[0].legend()
    axarr[1].legend()

    # Show figure title
    axarr[0].set_title("Bitcoin 30-day price trend", loc='left')
    plt.tight_layout()
    # Create a bytes buffer for saving image
    fig_buffer = BytesIO()
    plt.savefig(fig_buffer, dpi=150)
    # Save the figure as a HttpResponse
    response = HttpResponse(content_type='image/png')
    response.write(fig_buffer.getvalue())
    fig_buffer.close()
    return response
```

Again, remember to specify your own API key at the line inside
`get_bitcoin_dataset():   api_key = ""`.

The modified `bitcoin_chart` view would create three subplots that are spread across three rows, with a shared *x* axis. The height ratio between the subplots is specified via `gridspec_kw`.

The first subplot would display a candlestick chart as well as various stock indicators from the `stockstats` package.

The second subplot displays the **relative strength index (RSI)** of bitcoin across the 30-day window.

Finally, the third subplot displays the volume (USD) of Bitcoin. A custom `FuncFormatter` `millions` is used to convert the *y* axis values to millions.

You can now go to the same link at `http://localhost:8000/bitcoin/30/` to view the complete chart.

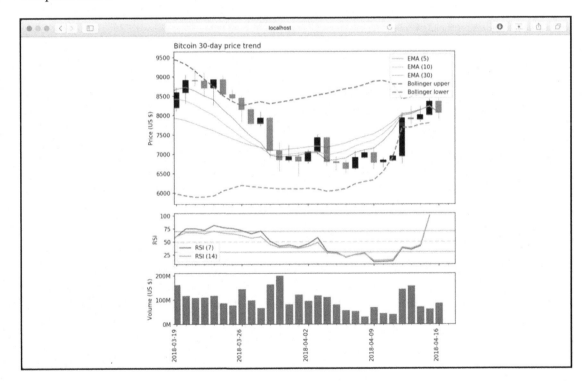

Integrating the image into a Django template

To display the chart in our home page, we can modify the home page template at `{Project_folder}/crypto_stats/src/templates/home.html`.

We would need to modify the lines after the comment sentence `<!-- Benefits of the Django application -->` to the following:

```html
{% block container %}
<!-- Benefits of the Django application -->
<a name="about"></a>

<div class="container">
  <div class="row">
    <div class="col-lg-8">
      <h2>Bitcoin pricing trend</h2>
      <img src="/bitcoin/30/" alt="Bitcoin prices" style="width:100%">
      <p><a class="btn btn-primary" href="#" role="button">View details
&raquo;</a></p>
    </div>
    <div class="col-lg-4">
      <h2>Heading</h2>
      <p>Donec sed odio dui. Cras justo odio, dapibus ac facilisis in,
egestas eget quam. Vestibulum id ligula porta felis euismod semper. Fusce
dapibus, tellus ac cursus commodo, tortor mauris condimentum nibh, ut
fermentum massa.</p>
      <p><a class="btn btn-primary" href="#" role="button">View details
&raquo;</a></p>
    </div>
  </div>
</div>

{% endblock container %}
```

Basically, our `bitcoin_chart` view is loaded as an image through the line `<img src="/bitcoin/30/" alt="Bitcoin prices" style="width:100%">`. I have also reduced the number of columns in the container section from 3 to 2, and adjusted the size of the first column by setting the class to `col-lg-8` instead.

If you go to the home page (that is, `http://localhost:8000`), you will see the following screen when you scroll to the bottom:

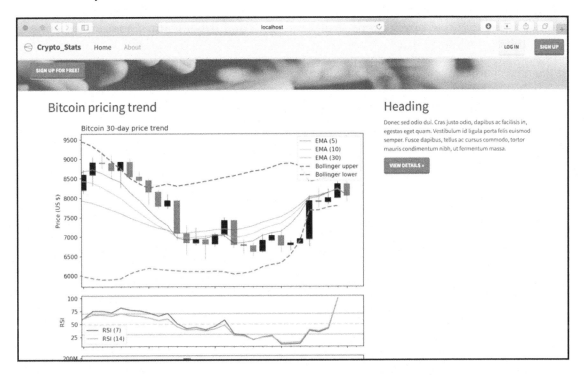

There are a few caveats of this implementation. First, each page visit would incur an API call to Quandl, so your free API quota will be consumed quickly. A better way would be to fetch the prices daily and record the data in a proper database model.

Second, the image output in its current form is not integrated into the app-specific template. This is out of the scope of this Matplotlib-focused book. However, interested readers can refer to the instructions in the online documentation (`https://docs.djangoproject.com/en/2.0/topics/templates/`).

Lastly, the images are static. There are third-party packages such as `mpld3` and Plotly that can turn a Matplotlib chart into an interactive Javascript-based chart. The use of these packages may further enhance the user experience.

Summary

In this chapter, you learned about a popular framework made to simplify the development and deployment of web applications, called Django. You further learned about integrating Matplotlib charts into a Django site.

In the next chapter, we will cover some useful techniques to customize figure aesthetics for effective storytelling.

Matplotlib in the Real World 9

At this point, we hope you are equipped with the techniques of creating and customizing plots using Matplotlib. Let's build on top of the things we have learned so far, and begin our journey of understanding more advanced Matplotlib usage through real-world examples.

First, we will cover how to fetch online data, which is commonly obtained through an **application programming interface (API)** or plain old web scraping techniques. Next, we will explore how to integrate Matplotlib 2.x with other scientific computing packages in Python for visualizations of different data types.

Typical API data formats

Many websites distribute data via their API, which bridges applications via standardized architecture. While we are not going to cover the details of using APIs here, we will cover the most common API data exchange formats, namely CSV and JSON.

 Interested readers can visit site-specific documentations for the use of APIs.

We have briefly covered parsing of CSV files in Chapter 4, *Advanced Matplotlib*. To aid your understanding, we are going to represent the same data using both CSV and JSON.

CSV

Comma-separated values (CSV) is one of the oldest file formats, introduced long before the World Wide Web even existed. However, it is now becoming deprecated as other advanced formats such as JSON and XML are gaining popularity. As the name suggests, data values are separated by commas. The preinstalled `csv` package and the `pandas` package contain classes to read and write data in CSV format. The following CSV example defines a population table with two countries:

```
Country,Time,Sex,Age,Value
United Kingdom,1950,Male,0-4,2238.735
United States of America,1950,Male,0-4,8812.309
```

JSON

JavaScript Object Notation (JSON) is gaining popularity these days due to its efficiency and simplicity. JSON allows the specification of number, string, Boolean, array, and object. Python provides the default `json` package for parsing JSON. Alternatively, the `pandas.read_json` class can be used to import JSON as a pandas DataFrame. The preceding population table can be represented as JSON as follows:

```
{
  "population": [
  {
  "Country": "United Kingdom",
  "Time": 1950,
  "Sex", "Male",
  "Age", "0-4",
  "Value",2238.735
  },{
  "Country": "United States of America",
  "Time": 1950,
  "Sex", "Male",
  "Age", "0-4",
  "Value",8812.309
  },
  ]
}
```

Importing and visualizing data from a JSON API

Now, let's learn how to parse financial data from Quandl's API to create insightful visualizations. Quandl is a financial and economic data warehouse, storing millions of datasets from hundreds of publishers. The best thing about Quandl is that these datasets are delivered via the unified API, without worrying about the procedures to parse the data correctly. Anonymous users can get up to 50 API calls per day, or up to 500 free API calls if registered. Readers can sign up for a free API key at `https://www.quandl.com/?modal=register`.

At Quandl, every dataset is identified by a unique ID, as defined by the Quandl code on each search result web page. For example, the Quandl code `GOOG/NASDAQ_SWTX` defines the historical NASDAQ index data published by Google Finance. Every dataset is available in three different formats—CSV, JSON, and XML.

Although an official Python client library is available from Quandl, we are not going to use that, for the sake of demonstrating the general procedures of importing JSON data from an API. According to Quandl's documentation, we can fetch JSON-formatted data tables through the following API call:

```
GET https://www.quandl.com/api/v3/datasets/{Quandl code}/data.json
```

To begin with, let's try to get the Big Mac index data from Quandl. The Big Mac index was invented by *The Economist* in 1986 as a lighthearted guide to whether currencies are at their **correct** level. It is based on the theory of **purchasing power parity** (PPP), and is considered an informal measure of currency exchange rates at PPP. It measures their value against a similar basket of goods and services, in this case a Big Mac. Differing prices at market exchange rates would imply that one currency is undervalued or overvalued:

```python
from urllib.request import urlopen
import json
import time
import pandas as pd


def get_bigmac_codes():
    """Get a pandas DataFrame of all codes in the Big Mac index dataset

    The first column contains the code, while the second header
    contains the description of the code.
    E.g.
    ECONOMIST/BIGMAC_ARG,Big Mac Index - Argentina
```

```
     ECONOMIST/BIGMAC_AUS,Big Mac Index - Australia
     ECONOMIST/BIGMAC_BRA,Big Mac Index - Brazil
     Returns:
         codes: pandas DataFrame of Quandl dataset codes"""
     codes_url = "https://www.quandl.com/api/v3/databases/ECONOMIST/codes"
     codes = pd.read_csv(codes_url, header=None, names=['Code',
'Description'],
                              compression='zip', encoding='latin_1')
     return codes

def get_quandl_dataset(api_key, code):
    """Obtain and parse a quandl dataset in pandas DataFrame format

    Quandl returns dataset in JSON format, where data is stored as a
    list of lists in response['dataset']['data'], and column headers
    stored in response['dataset']['column_names'].
    E.g. {'dataset': {...,
            'column_names': ['Date',
                             'local_price',
                             'dollar_ex',
                             'dollar_price',
                             'dollar_ppp',
                             'dollar_valuation',
                             'dollar_adj_valuation',
                             'euro_adj_valuation',
                             'sterling_adj_valuation',
                             'yen_adj_valuation',
                             'yuan_adj_valuation'],
              'data': [['2017-01-31',
                        55.0,
                        15.8575,
                        3.4683903515687,
                        10.869565217391,
                        -31.454736135007,
                        6.2671477203176,
                        8.2697553162259,
                        29.626894343348,
                        32.714616745128,
                        13.625825886047],
                       ['2016-07-31',
                        50.0,
                        14.935,
                        3.3478406427854,
                        9.9206349206349,
                        -33.574590420925,
                        2.0726096168216,
                        0.40224795003514,
                        17.56448458418,
```

```
                    19.76377270142,
                    11.643103380531]
                    ],
            'database_code': 'ECONOMIST',
            'dataset_code': 'BIGMAC_ARG',
            ... }}
    A custom column--country is added to denote the 3-letter country code.
    Args:
        api_key: Quandl API key
        code: Quandl dataset code

    Returns:
        df: pandas DataFrame of a Quandl dataset

    """
    base_url = "https://www.quandl.com/api/v3/datasets/"
    url_suffix = ".json?api_key="

    # Fetch the JSON response
    u = urlopen(base_url + code + url_suffix + api_key)
    response = json.loads(u.read().decode('utf-8'))
    # Format the response as pandas Dataframe
    df = pd.DataFrame(response['dataset']['data'],
columns=response['dataset']['column_names'])
    # Label the country code
    df['country'] = code[-3:]
    return df


quandl_dfs = []
codes = get_bigmac_codes()

# Replace this with your own API key
api_key = "INSERT-YOUR-KEY-HERE"

for code in codes.Code:
    # Get the DataFrame of a Quandl dataset
    df = get_quandl_dataset(api_key, code)
    # Store in a list
    quandl_dfs.append(df)
    # Prevents exceeding the API speed limit
    time.sleep(2)
# Concatenate the list of data frames into a single one
bigmac_df = pd.concat(quandl_dfs)
bigmac_df.head()
```

Here comes the expected result, which shows the first five rows of the data frame:

	0	1	2	3	4
Date	31-07-17	31-01-17	31-07-16	31-01-16	31-07-15
local_price	5.9	5.8	5.75	5.3	5.3
dollar_ex	1.303016	1.356668	1.335738	1.415729	1.35126
dollar_price	4.527955	4.27518	4.304737	3.743655	3.922265
dollar_ppp	1.113208	1.146245	1.140873	1.075051	1.106472
dollar_valuation	-14.56689	-15.510277	-14.588542	-24.06379	-18.115553
dollar_adj_valuation	-11.7012	-11.9234	-11.0236	-28.1641	-22.1691
euro_adj_valuation	-13.0262	-10.2636	-12.4796	-22.2864	-18.573
sterling_adj_valuation	2.58422	7.43771	2.48065	-22.293	-23.1926
yen_adj_valuation	19.9417	9.99688	4.39776	-4.0042	6.93893
yuan_adj_valuation	-2.35772	-5.82434	-2.681	-20.6755	-14.1711
country	AUS	AUS	AUS	AUS	AUS

The code for parsing JSON from Quandl API is a bit complicated, and thus requires extra explanation. The first function, `get_bigmac_codes()`, parses the list of all available dataset codes in the Quandl Economist database as a pandas DataFrame. Meanwhile, the second function, `get_quandl_dataset(api_key, code)`, converts the JSON response of a Quandl dataset API query to a pandas DataFrame. All datasets obtained are concatenated into a single data frame using `pandas.concat()`.

 We should bear in mind that the Big Mac index is not directly comparable between countries. Normally, we would expect commodities in poor countries to be cheaper than those in rich ones. To represent a fairer picture of the index, it would be better to show the relationship between Big Mac pricing and **gross domestic product (GDP)** per capita.

To that end, we are going to acquire the GDP dataset from Quandl's **World Bank World Development Indicators (WWDI)** database. Based on the previous code example of acquiring JSON data from Quandl, can you try to adapt it to download the GDP per capita dataset?

For those who are impatient, here is the full code:

```python
import urllib
import json
import pandas as pd
import time
from urllib.request import urlopen

def get_gdp_dataset(api_key, country_code):
    """Obtain and parse a quandl GDP dataset in pandas DataFrame format
    Quandl returns dataset in JSON format, where data is stored as a
    list of lists in response['dataset']['data'], and column headers
    stored in response['dataset']['column_names'].

    Args:
        api_key: Quandl API key
        country_code: Three letter code to represent country

    Returns:
        df: pandas DataFrame of a Quandl dataset
    """
    base_url = "https://www.quandl.com/api/v3/datasets/"
    url_suffix = ".json?api_key="

    # Compose the Quandl API dataset code to get GDP per capita (constant
2000 US$) dataset
    gdp_code = "WWDI/" + country_code + "_NY_GDP_PCAP_KD"

    # Parse the JSON response from Quandl API
    # Some countries might be missing, so we need error handling code
    try:
        u = urlopen(base_url + gdp_code + url_suffix + api_key)
    except urllib.error.URLError as e:
        print(gdp_code, e)
        return None

    response = json.loads(u.read().decode('utf-8'))

    # Format the response as pandas Dataframe
    df = pd.DataFrame(response['dataset']['data'],
columns=response['dataset']['column_names'])

    # Add a new country code column
    df['country'] = country_code

    return df

api_key = "INSERT-YOUR-KEY-HERE" #Change this to your own API key
```

```
quandl_dfs = []

# Loop through all unique country code values in the BigMac index DataFrame
for country_code in bigmac_df.country.unique():
    # Fetch the GDP dataset for the corresponding country
    df = get_gdp_dataset(api_key, country_code)
    # Skip if the response is empty
    if df is None:
        continue
    # Store in a list DataFrames
    quandl_dfs.append(df)
    # Prevents exceeding the API speed limit
    time.sleep(2)
# Concatenate the list of DataFrames into a single one
gdp_df = pd.concat(quandl_dfs)
gdp_df.head()
```

The GDP data of several geographical regions is missing, but this should be handled gracefully by the try...except code block in the get_gdp_dataset function. This is what you are expecting to see after running the preceding code:

```
WWDI/EUR_NY_GDP_PCAP_KD HTTP Error 404: Not Found
WWDI/ROC_NY_GDP_PCAP_KD HTTP Error 404: Not Found
WWDI/SIN_NY_GDP_PCAP_KD HTTP Error 404: Not Found
WWDI/UAE_NY_GDP_PCAP_KD HTTP Error 404: Not Found
```

	Date	Value	country
0	2016-12-31	55478.577294	AUS
1	2015-12-31	54800.366396	AUS
2	2014-12-31	54293.794205	AUS
3	2013-12-31	53732.003969	AUS
4	2012-12-31	53315.029915	AUS

Next, we will merge the two pandas DataFrames that contain Big Mac Index or GDP per capita using pandas.merge(). The most recent record in WWDI's GDP per capita dataset was collected at the end of 2016, so let's pair that up with the closest Big Mac index dataset in January 2017.

For those who are familiar with the SQL language, `pandas.merge()` supports four modes, namely left, right, inner, and outer joins. Since we are interested in rows that have matching countries in both pandas DataFrames only, we are going to choose inner join:

```
merged_df = pd.merge(bigmac_df[(bigmac_df.Date == "2017-01-31")],
    gdp_df[(gdp_df.Date == "2016-12-31")], how='inner', on='country')
merged_df.head()
```

Here is the merged data frame:

	0	1	2	3	4
Date_x	31-01-17	31-01-17	31-01-17	31-01-17	31-01-17
local_price	5.8	16.5	3.09	2450	55
dollar_ex	1.356668	3.22395	0.828775	672.805	15.8575
dollar_price	4.27518	5.117945	3.728394	3.641471	3.46839
dollar_ppp	1.146245	3.26087	0.610672	484.189723	10.869565
dollar_valuation	-15.510277	1.145166	-26.316324	-28.034167	-31.454736
dollar_adj_valuation	-11.9234	67.5509	-18.0208	11.9319	6.26715
euro_adj_valuation	-10.2636	70.7084	-16.4759	14.0413	8.26976
sterling_adj_valuation	7.43771	104.382	0	36.5369	29.6269
yen_adj_valuation	9.99688	109.251	2.38201	39.7892	32.7146
yuan_adj_valuation	-5.82434	79.1533	-12.3439	19.6828	13.6258
Country	AUS	BRA	GBR	CHL	ARG
Date_y	31-12-16	31-12-16	31-12-16	31-12-16	31-12-16
Value	55478.5773	10826.2714	41981.3921	15019.633	10153.99791

Using Seaborn to simplify visualization tasks

The scatter plot is one of the most common plots in the scientific and business worlds. It is particularly useful for displaying the relationship between two variables. While we can simply use `matplotlib.pyplot.scatter` to draw a scatterplot (see Chapter 2, *Getting Started with Matplotlib*, and Chapter 4, *Advanced Matplotlib*, for more details), we can also use Seaborn to build similar plots with more advanced features.

The two functions, `seaborn.regplot()` and `seaborn.lmplot()`, display a linear relationship in the form of a scatter plot, a regression line, and the 95% confidence interval around the regression line. The main difference between the two functions is that `lmplot()` combines `regplot()` with `FacetGrid`, such that we can create color-coded or faceted scatter plots to show the interaction between three or more pairs of variables.

The simplest form of `seaborn.regplot()` supports NumPy arrays, pandas Series, or pandas DataFrames as input. The regression line and the confidence interval can be removed by specifying `fit_reg=False`.

We are going to investigate the hypothesis that Big Macs are cheaper in countries with lower GDP, and vice versa. To that end, we will try to find out whether there is any correlation between the Big Mac index and GDP per capita:

```
import seaborn as sns
import matplotlib.pyplot as plt

# seaborn.regplot() returns a matplotlib.Axes object
ax = sns.regplot(x="Value", y="dollar_price", data=merged_df,
fit_reg=False)
# We can modify the axes labels just like other ordinary
# Matplotlib objects
ax.set_xlabel("GDP per capita (constant 2000 US$)")
ax.set_ylabel("BigMac index (US$)")
plt.show()
```

The code will greet you with a good old scatter plot:

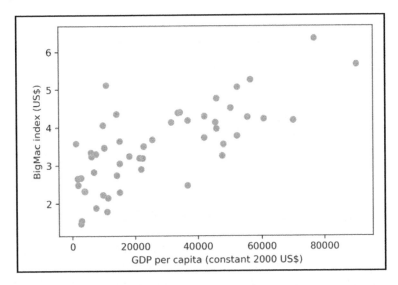

So far so good! It looks like the Big Mac index is positively correlated with GDP per capita. Let's turn the regression line back on and label a few countries that show extreme Big Mac index values (that is, ≥ 5 or ≤ 2). Meanwhile, the default plotting style is a bit plain; we can spice up the graph by running sns.set(style="whitegrid"). There are four other styles to choose from, namely darkgrid, dark, white, and ticks:

```
sns.set(style="whitegrid")
ax = sns.regplot(x="Value", y="dollar_price", data=merged_df)
ax.set_xlabel("GDP per capita (constant 2000 US$)")
ax.set_ylabel("BigMac index (US$)")
# Label the country codes which demonstrate extreme BigMac index
for row in merged_df.itertuples():
    if row.dollar_price >= 5 or row.dollar_price <= 2:
      ax.text(row.Value,row.dollar_price+0.1,row.country)
plt.show()
```

Here is the labeled plot:

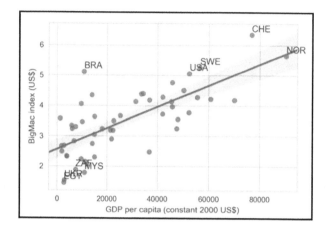

We can see that many countries fall within the confidence interval of the regression line. Given the GDP per capita level for each country, the linear regression model predicts the corresponding Big Mac index. The currency value shows signs of undervaluation or overvaluation if the actual index deviates from the regression model.

By labeling the countries that show extremely high or low values, we can clearly see that the average price of a Big Mac in Brazil and Switzerland were overvalued, while it is undervalued in South Africa, Malaysia, Ukraine, and Egypt.

Since Seaborn is not a package for statistical analysis, we need to use other packages, such as `scipy.stats` or `statsmodels`, to obtain the parameters of a regression model. In the next example, we are going to get the slope and intercept parameters from the regression model, and apply different colors for points that are above or below the regression line:

```
from scipy.stats import linregress

ax = sns.regplot(x="Value", y="dollar_price", data=merged_df)
ax.set_xlabel("GDP per capita (constant 2000 US$)")
ax.set_ylabel("BigMac index (US$)")

# Calculate linear regression parameters
slope, intercept, r_value, p_value, std_err = linregress(merged_df.Value,
merged_df.dollar_price)

colors = []
for row in merged_df.itertuples():
    if row.dollar_price > row.Value * slope + intercept:
        # Color markers as darkred if they are above the regression line
```

```
            color = "darkred"
    else:
        # Color markers as darkblue if they are below the regression line
        color = "darkblue"

    # Label the country code for those who demonstrate extreme BigMac index
    if row.dollar_price >= 5 or row.dollar_price <= 2:
        ax.text(row.Value,row.dollar_price+0.1,row.country)

    # Highlight the marker that corresponds to China
    if row.country == "CHN":
        t = ax.text(row.Value,row.dollar_price+0.1,row.country)
        color = "yellow"

    colors.append(color)

# Overlay another scatter plot on top with marker-specific color
ax.scatter(merged_df.Value, merged_df.dollar_price, c=colors)

# Label the r squared value and p value of the linear regression model.
# transform=ax.transAxes indicates that the coordinates are given relative
to the axes bounding box,
# with 0,0 being the lower left of the axes and 1,1 the upper right.
ax.text(0.1, 0.9, "$r^2={0:.3f}, p={1:.3e}$".format(r_value ** 2, p_value),
transform=ax.transAxes)

plt.show()
```

This screenshot shows the color-labeled plot:

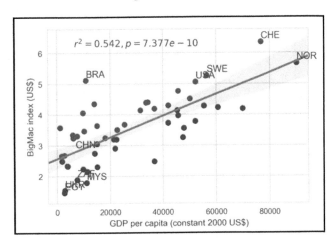

Contrary to popular belief, it looks as if China's currency was not significantly undervalued in 2016, as the value lies within the 95% confidence interval of the regression line.

We can also combine histograms of x and y values with a scatter plot using `seaborn.jointplot`:

> **TIP**
>
> By additionally specifying the `kind` parameter in `jointplot` to any one of `reg`, `resid`, `hex`, or `kde`, we can quickly change the plot type to regression, residual, hex bin, or KDE contour plot, respectively.

```
# seaborn.jointplot() returns a seaborn.JointGrid object
g = sns.jointplot(x="Value", y="dollar_price", data=merged_df)

# Provide custom axes labels through accessing the underlying axes object
# We can get matplotlib.axes.Axes of the scatter plot by calling g.ax_joint
g.ax_joint.set_xlabel("GDP per capita (constant 2000 US$)")
g.ax_joint.set_ylabel("BigMac index (US$)")

# Set the title and adjust the margin
g.fig.suptitle("Relationship between GDP per capita and BigMac Index")
g.fig.subplots_adjust(top=0.9)
plt.show()
```

The `jointplot` is as follows:

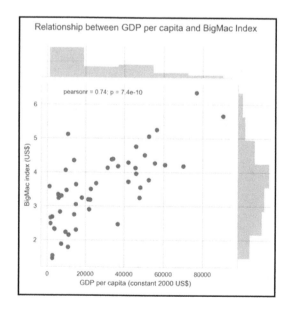

Here is the big disclaimer. With all the data in our hands, it is still too early to make any conclusion about the valuation of currencies! Different business factors such as labor cost, rent, raw material costs, and taxation can all contribute to the pricing model of Big Mac, but this is beyond the scope of this book.

Scraping information from websites

Governments or jurisdictions around the world are increasingly embracing the importance of open data, which aims to increase citizen involvement and informed decision-making, and also aims to make policies more open to public scrutiny. Some examples of open data initiatives around the world include `https://www.data.gov/` (United States of America), `https://data.gov.uk/` (United Kingdom), and `https://data.gov.hk/en/` (Hong Kong).

These data portals often provide an API for programmatic access of data. However, an API is not available for some datasets, hence we need to rely on good old web scraping techniques to extract information from websites.

Beautiful Soup (`https://www.crummy.com/software/BeautifulSoup/`) is an incredibly useful package for scraping information from websites. Basically, everything marked with an HTML tag can be scraped with this wonderful package. Scrapy is also a good package for web scraping, but it is more like a framework for writing powerful web crawlers. So if you just need to fetch a table from the page, Beautiful Soup offers simpler procedures.

We are going to use Beautiful Soup version 4.6 throughout this chapter. To install Beautiful Soup 4, we can once again rely on PyPI:

```
pip install beautifulsoup4
```

The US unemployment rates and earnings by educational attainment data (2017) is available from the following website: `https://www.bls.gov/emp/ep_table_001.htm`. Currently, Beautiful Soup does not handle HTML requests. So we need to use the `urllib.request` or `requests` package to fetch a web page for us. Among the two options, the `requests` package is arguably easier to use due to its higher-level HTTP client interface. If `requests` is not available on your system, we can install that through PyPI:

```
pip install requests
```

Let's take a look at the web page before we write the web scraping code. If we use Google Chrome to visit the Bureau of Labor Statistics website, we can inspect the HTML code corresponding to the table we need:

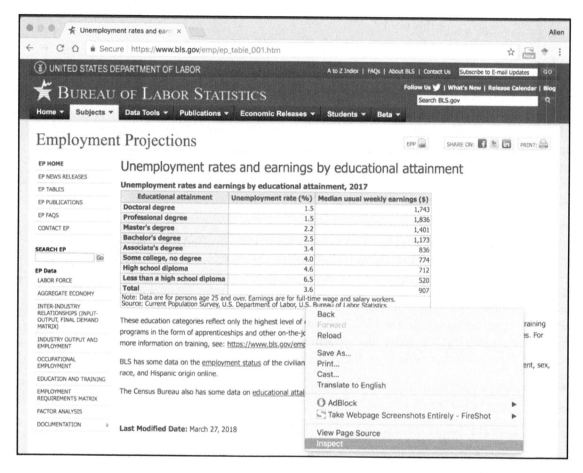

Next, expand `<div id="bodytext" class="verdana md">` until you can see `<table class="regular" cellspacing="0" cellpadding="0" xborder="1">...</table>`. When you put your mouse over the HTML code, the corresponding section on the page will be highlighted:

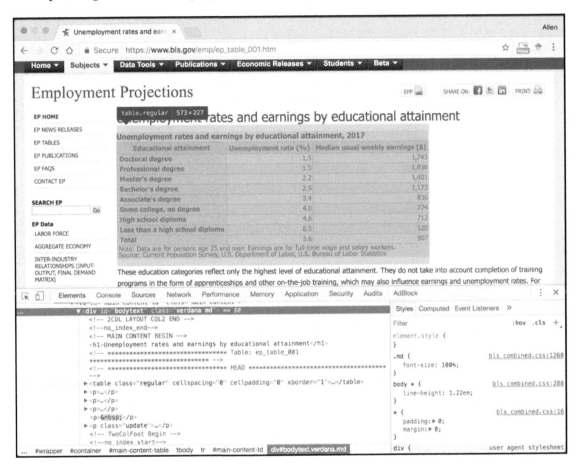

After further expanding the HTML code of the `<table>`, we can see that the column names are defined in the `<thead>...</thead>` section, while the table content is defined in the `<tbody>...</tbody>` section.

In order to instruct Beautiful Soup to scrape the information we need, we need to give clear directions to it. We can right-click on the relevant section in the code inspection window and copy the unique identifier in the format of a CSS selector:

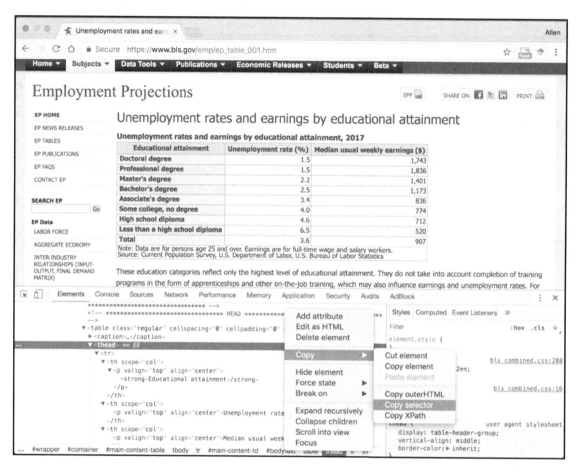

Let's try to get the CSS selectors for `thead` and `tbody`, and use the `BeautifulSoup.select()` method to scrape the respective HTML code:

```
import requests
from bs4 import BeautifulSoup

# Specify the url
url = "https://www.bls.gov/emp/ep_table_001.htm"

# Query the website and get the html response
response = requests.get(url)
```

```
# Parse the returned html using BeautifulSoup
bs = BeautifulSoup(response.text)

# Select the table header by CSS selector
thead = bs.select("#bodytext > table > thead")[0]

# Select the table body by CSS selector
tbody = bs.select("#bodytext > table > tbody")[0]

# Make sure the code works
print(thead)
```

You will be greeted by the HTML code of the table headers:

```
<thead>
<tr>
<th scope="col"><p align="center" valign="top"><strong>Educational
attainment</strong></p></th>
<th scope="col"><p align="center" valign="top">Unemployment rate
(%)</p></th>
<th scope="col"><p align="center" valign="top">Median usual weekly earnings
($)</p></th>
</tr>
</thead>
```

Next, we are going to find all instances of `<th></th>`, which contains the name of each column. We will build a dictionary of lists with headers as keys to hold the data:

```
# Get the column names
headers = []

# Find all header columns in <thead> as specified by <th> html tags
for col in thead.find_all('th'):
    headers.append(col.text.strip())

# Dictionary of lists for storing parsed data
data = {header:[] for header in headers}
```

Finally, we parse the remaining rows of the table and convert the data to a pandas DataFrame:

```
import pandas as pd

# Parse the rows in table body
for row in tbody.find_all('tr'):
    # Find all columns in a row as specified by <th> or <td> html tags
    cols = row.find_all(['th','td'])
```

```
# enumerate() allows us to loop over an iterable,
# and return each item preceded by a counter
for i, col in enumerate(cols):
    # Strip white space around the text
    value = col.text.strip()

    # Try to convert the columns to float, except the first column
    if i > 0:
        value = float(value.replace(',','')) # Remove all commas in string

    # Append the float number to the dict of lists
    data[headers[i]].append(value)

# Create a data frame from the parsed dictionary
df = pd.DataFrame(data)

# Show an excerpt of parsed data
df.head()
```

We should now be able to reproduce the first few rows of the main table:

	Educational attainment	Median usual weekly earnings ($)	Unemployment rate (%)
0	Doctoral degree	1743.0	1.5
1	Professional degree	1836.0	1.5
2	Master's degree	1401.0	2.2
3	Bachelor's degree	1173.0	2.5
4	Associate's degree	836.0	3.4

The main HTML table has been formatted as a structured pandas DataFrame. We can now proceed to visualize the data.

Matplotlib graphical backends

The code for plotting graphs is considered the frontend in Matplotlib's terminology. We first mentioned backends in Chapter 1, *Introduction to Matplotlib*, when we were talking about output formats. In reality, Matplotlib backends have much more differences than just support for graphical formats. Backends handle so many things behind the scenes! And that would determine the support of plotting capabilities. For example, the LaTeX text layout is supported only by Agg, PDF, PGF, and PS backends.

Non-interactive backends

We have been using several non-interactive backends so far, which include Agg, Cairo, GDK, PDF, PGF, PS, and SVG. Most of these backends work without extra dependencies, but Cairo and GDK require the Cairo graphics library or GIMP Drawing Kit, respectively, to work.

Non-interactive backends can be further classified into two groups—vector or raster. Vector graphics describe images in terms of points, paths, and shapes that are calculated using mathematical formulas. A vector graphic will always appear smooth irrespective of the scale, and its size is usually much smaller than the raster counterpart. PDF, PGF, PS, and SVG backends belong to the vector group.

Raster graphics describe images in terms of a finite number of tiny color blocks (pixels). So if we zoom in enough, we start to see an *unsmooth* representation of the image, in other words, pixelation. By increasing the resolution or **dots per inch** (**DPI**) of the image, we are less likely to observe pixelation. Agg, Cairo, and GDK belong to this group of backends. The following table summarizes the key functionalities and differences among the non-interactive backends:

Backend	Vector or raster?	Output formats
Agg	Raster	`.png`
Cairo	Vector/Raster	`.pdf`, `.png`, `.ps`, `.svg`
PDF	Vector	`.pdf`
PGF	Vector	`.pdf`, `.pgf`
PS	Vector	`.ps`
SVG	Vector	`.svg`
GDK*	Raster	`.png`, `.jpg`, `.tiff`

*Deprecated in Matplotlib 2.0.

Normally, we don't need to manually select a backend, as the default choice would work great for most tasks. On the other hand, we can specify a backend through the `matplotlib.use()` method before importing `matplotlib.pyplot` for the **first** time:

```
import matplotlib
matplotlib.use('SVG') # Change to SVG backend
import matplotlib.pyplot as plt
import textwrap # Standard library for text wrapping
```

```
# Create a figure
fig, ax = plt.subplots(figsize=(6,7))

# Create a list of x ticks positions
ind = range(df.shape[0])

# Plot a bar chart of median usual weekly earnings by educational
attainments
rects = ax.barh(ind, df["Median usual weekly earnings ($)"], height=0.5)

# Set the x-axis label
ax.set_xlabel('Median weekly earnings (USD)')

# Label the x ticks
# The tick labels are a bit too long, let's wrap them in 15-char lines
ylabels=[textwrap.fill(label,15) for label in df["Educational attainment"]]
ax.set_yticks(ind)
ax.set_yticklabels(ylabels)

# Give extra margin at the bottom to display the tick labels
fig.subplots_adjust(left=0.3)

# Save the figure in SVG format
plt.savefig("test.svg")
```

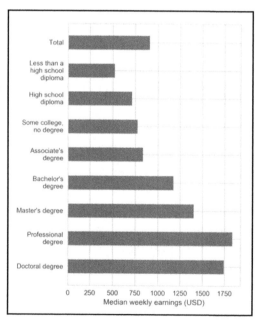

Interactive backends

Matplotlib can build interactive figures that are far more engaging for readers. Sometimes, a plot might be overwhelmed with graphical elements, making it hard to discern individual data points. On other occasions, some data points may appear so similar, in which it could be hard to spot the differences with our naked eyes. An interactive plot can address these two scenarios by allowing us to zoom in, zoom out, pan, and explore the plot in the way we want.

Through the use of interactive backends, plots in Matplotlib can be embedded in **graphical user interfaces (GUI)** applications. By default, Matplotlib supports the pairing of the Agg raster graphics renderer with a wide variety of GUI toolkits, including wxWidgets (Wx), GIMP Toolkit (GTK+), Qt and TkInter (Tk). As Tkinter is the de facto standard GUI for Python, which is built on top of Tcl/Tk, we can create an interactive plot with nothing more than calling `plt.show()` in a standalone Python script. Let's try to copy the following code to a separate text file and name it `interactive.py`. After that, type `python interactive.py` in your Terminal (Mac/Linux) or Command Prompt (Windows). If you are unsure about how to open a Terminal or Command Prompt, please refer to `Chapter 1`, *Introduction to Matplotlib*, for more details:

```python
import matplotlib
import matplotlib.pyplot as plt
import textwrap
import requests
import pandas as pd
from bs4 import BeautifulSoup
# Import Matplotlib radio button widget
from matplotlib.widgets import RadioButtons


url = "https://www.bls.gov/emp/ep_table_001.htm"
response = requests.get(url)
bs = BeautifulSoup(response.text)
thead = bs.select("#bodytext > table > thead")[0]
tbody = bs.select("#bodytext > table > tbody")[0]

headers = []
for col in thead.find_all('th'):
    headers.append(col.text.strip())

data = {header:[] for header in headers}
for row in tbody.find_all('tr'):
    cols = row.find_all(['th','td'])
    for i, col in enumerate(cols):
        value = col.text.strip()
```

```
        if i > 0:
            value = float(value.replace(',',''))
        data[headers[i]].append(value)

df = pd.DataFrame(data)

fig, ax = plt.subplots(figsize=(6,7))
ind = range(df.shape[0])
rects = ax.barh(ind, df["Median usual weekly earnings ($)"], height=0.5)
ax.set_xlabel('Median weekly earnings (USD)')
ylabels=[textwrap.fill(label,15) for label in df["Educational attainment"]]
ax.set_yticks(ind)
ax.set_yticklabels(ylabels)
fig.subplots_adjust(left=0.3)

# Create axes for holding the radio selectors.
# supply [left, bottom, width, height] in normalized (0, 1) units
bax = plt.axes([0.3, 0.9, 0.4, 0.1])
radio = RadioButtons(bax, ('Weekly earnings', 'Unemployment rate'))

# Define the function for updating the displayed values
# when the radio button is clicked
def radiofunc(label):
  # Select columns from dataframe depending on label
  if label == 'Weekly earnings':
    data = df["Median usual weekly earnings ($)"]
    ax.set_xlabel('Median weekly earnings (USD)')
  elif label == 'Unemployment rate':
    data = df["Unemployment rate (%)"]
    ax.set_xlabel('Unemployment rate (%)')
  # Update the bar heights
  for i, rect in enumerate(rects):
    rect.set_width(data[i])

  # Rescale the x-axis range
  ax.set_xlim(xmin=0, xmax=data.max()*1.1)
  # Redraw the figure
  plt.draw()
radio.on_clicked(radiofunc)

plt.show()
```

We shall see a pop-up window similar to the following one. We can pan, zoom to selection, configure subplot margins, save, and go back and forth between different views by clicking on the buttons on the bottom toolbar. If we put our mouse over the plot, we can also observe the exact coordinates in the lower-right corner. This feature is extremely useful for dissecting data points that are close to each other:

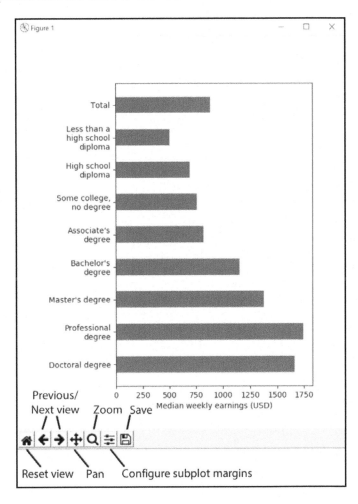

Next, we are going to extend the application by adding a radio button widget on top of the figure, such that we can switch between the display of weekly earnings or unemployment rates. The radio button can be found in `matplotlib.widgets`, and we are going to attach a data updating function to the `.on_clicked()` event of the button. You can paste the following code right before the `plt.show()` line to the previous code example (`interactive.py`). Let's see how it works:

```
# Import Matplotlib radio button widget
from matplotlib.widgets import RadioButtons

# Create axes for holding the radio selectors.
# supply [left, bottom, width, height] in normalized (0, 1) units
bax = plt.axes([0.3, 0.9, 0.4, 0.1])
radio = RadioButtons(bax, ('Weekly earnings', 'Unemployment rate'))

# Define the function for updating the displayed values
# when the radio button is clicked
def radiofunc(label):
    # Select columns from dataframe, and change axis label depending on
selection
    if label == 'Weekly earnings':
        data = df["Median usual weekly earnings ($)"]
        ax.set_xlabel('Median weekly earnings (USD)')
    elif label == 'Unemployment rate':
        data = df["Unemployment rate (%)"]
        ax.set_xlabel('Unemployment rate (%)')

    # Update the bar heights
    for i, rect in enumerate(rects):
        rect.set_width(data[i])

    # Rescale the x-axis range
    ax.set_xlim(xmin=0, xmax=data.max()*1.1)

    # Redraw the figure
    plt.draw()

# Attach radiofunc to the on_clicked event of the radio button
radio.on_clicked(radiofunc)
```

You will be welcomed by a new radio selector box on top of the plot. Try switching between the two states and see if the figure would be updated accordingly. The complete code is also available in the code bundle:

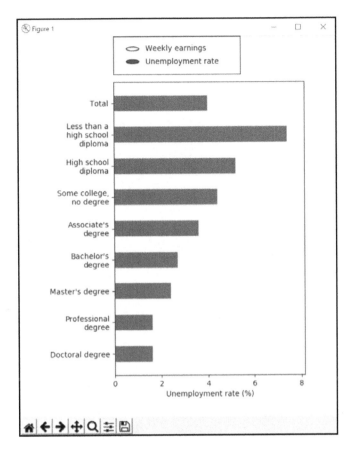

Before we conclude this section, we are going to introduce one more interactive backend that is rarely covered by books. Starting with Matplotlib 1.4, there is an interactive backend specifically designed for Jupyter Notebook. To invoke that, we simply need to paste `%matplotlib notebook` at the start of your notebook. We are going to adapt one of the earlier examples in this chapter to use this backend:

```
# Import the interactive backend for Jupyter Notebook
%matplotlib notebook
import matplotlib
import matplotlib.pyplot as plt
import textwrap

fig, ax = plt.subplots(figsize=(6,7))
ind = range(df.shape[0])
rects = ax.barh(ind, df["Median usual weekly earnings ($)"], height=0.5)
ax.set_xlabel('Median weekly earnings (USD)')
ylabels=[textwrap.fill(label,15) for label in df["Educational attainment"]]
```

```
ax.set_yticks(ind)
ax.set_yticklabels(ylabels)
fig.subplots_adjust(left=0.3)

# Show the figure using interactive notebook backend
plt.show()
```

The following interactive plot will be embedded right into your Jupyter Notebook:

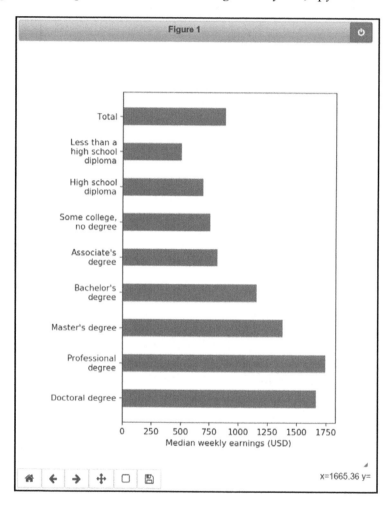

Creating animated plot

Matplotlib was not designed as an animation package from the get-go, and thus it would appear sluggish in some advanced usages. For animation-centric applications, PyGame is a very good alternative (`https://www.pygame.org`) which supports OpenGL- and Direct3D-accelerated graphics for the ultimate speed in animating objects. Nevertheless, Matplotlib has acceptable performance most of the time, and we will guide you through the steps to create animations that are more engaging than static plots.

Before we start making animations, we need to install either FFmpeg, avconv, mencoder, or ImageMagick on our system. These additional dependencies are not bundled with Matplotlib, and thus we need to install them separately. We are going to walk you through the steps of installing FFmpeg.

For Debian-based Linux users, FFmpeg can be installed by simply issuing the following command in Terminal.

```
sudo apt-get install ffmpeg
```

For Mac users, Homebrew (`https://brew.sh/`) is the simplest way to search and install `ffmpeg` package. If you don't have Homebrew, you can paste the following code into your Terminal to install it.

```
/usr/bin/ruby -e "$(curl -fsSL
https://raw.githubusercontent.com/Homebrew/install/master/install)"
```

After that, we can install FFmpeg by issuing the following command in the Terminal:

```
brew install ffmpeg
```

Alternatively, you may install FFmpeg by copying the binaries (`https://evermeet.cx/ffmpeg/`) to the system path (for example, `/usr/local/bin`).

The installation for Windows users is quite a bit more involved, but luckily there is a detailed guide on wikiHow (`https://www.wikihow.com/Install-FFmpeg-on-Windows`).

Matplotlib provides two main interfaces for creating animations: `TimedAnimation` and `FuncAnimation`. `TimedAnimation` is useful for creating time-based animation, while `FuncAnimation` can be used to create animation according to a custom-defined function. Given by the much higher level of flexibility offered by `FuncAnimation`, we will only explore the use of `FuncAnimation` in this section. Interested readers can refer to the official documentation (`https://matplotlib.org/api/animation_api.html`) for more information about `TimedAnimation`.

In the following example, we simulated the change in median weekly earnings by assuming a 5% annual increase. We are going to create a custom function—animate, which returns Matplotlib `Artist` objects that are changed in each frame. This function will be supplied to `animation.FuncAnimation()` together with a few more extra parameters:

```
import textwrap
import matplotlib.pyplot as plt
import random
# Matplotlib animation module
from matplotlib import animation
# Used for generating HTML video embed code
from IPython.display import HTML

# Adapted from previous example, codes that are modified are commented
fig, ax = plt.subplots(figsize=(6,7))
ind = range(df.shape[0])
rects = ax.barh(ind, df["Median usual weekly earnings ($)"], height=0.5)
ax.set_xlabel('Median weekly earnings (USD)')
ylabels=[textwrap.fill(label,15) for label in df["Educational attainment"]]
ax.set_yticks(ind)
ax.set_yticklabels(ylabels)
fig.subplots_adjust(left=0.3)

# Change the x-axis range
ax.set_xlim(0,7600)

# Add a text annotation to show the current year
title = ax.text(0.5,1.05, "Median weekly earnings (USD) in 2017",
 bbox={'facecolor':'w', 'alpha':0.5, 'pad':5},
 transform=ax.transAxes, ha="center")

# Animation related stuff
n=30 #Number of frames

def animate(frame):
    # Simulate 5% annual pay rise
    data = df["Median usual weekly earnings ($)"] * (1.05 ** frame)
```

```
# Update the bar heights
for i, rect in enumerate(rects):
    rect.set_width(data[i])

# Update the title
title.set_text("Median weekly earnings (USD) in {}".format(2016+frame))

return rects, title

# Call the animator. Re-draw only the changed parts when blit=True.
# Redraw all elements when blit=False
anim=animation.FuncAnimation(fig, animate, blit=False, frames=n)

# Save the animation in MPEG-4 format
anim.save('test.mp4')

# OR--Embed the video in Jupyter Notebook
HTML(anim.to_html5_video())
```

Here is the resultant video:

https://github.com/PacktPublishing/Matplotlib-for-Python-Developers-Second-Edition/blob/master/extra_ch9/ch09_animation.mp4

In the preceding example, we output animation in the form of MPEG-4 encoded videos. The video can also be embedded in Jupyter Notebook in the form of H.264 encoded video. All you need to do is to call the `Animation.to_html5_video()` method, and supply the returned object to `IPython.display.HTML`. Video encoding and HTML5 code generation will happen automagically behind the scenes.

Starting from version 2.2.0, Matplotlib supports the creation of animated GIF writing via the Pillow imaging library and ImageMagick. As the WWW is never tired of GIFs, let's learn how to create one!

Before we are able to create animated GIFs, we need to install ImageMagick first. The download links and the installation instructions for all major platforms can be found here: https://www.imagemagick.org/script/download.php.

Once the package is installed, we can generate animated GIFs by changing the line `anim.save('test.mp4')` to `anim.save('test.gif', writer='imagemagick', fps=10)`. The `fps` parameter denotes the frame rate of the animation.

Here is the resultant animated GIF:

```
https://github.com/PacktPublishing/Matplotlib-for-Python-Developers-Second-
Edition/blob/master/extra_ch9/ch%2009_GIF.gif
```

Summary

In this chapter, you learned how to parse online data in CSV or JSON formats using the versatile pandas package. You further learned how to filter, subset, merge, and process data into insights. Finally, you learned how to scrape information directly from websites. You have now equipped yourself with the knowledge to visualize time series, univariate, and bivariate data. The chapter concluded with a number of useful techniques to customize figure aesthetics for effective storytelling.

Phew! We have just completed a long chapter, so go grab a burger, have a break, and relax.

Integrating Data Visualization into the Workflow

10

We have now come to the concluding chapter of this book. Throughout the course of this book, you have mastered the techniques to create and customize static and animated plots using real-world data in different formats scraped from the web. To wrap up, we will start a mini-project in this chapter to combine the skills of data analytics with the visualization techniques you've learned. We will demonstrate how to integrate visualization techniques in your current workflow.

In the era of big data, machine learning becomes fundamental to ease analytic work by replacing huge amounts of manual curation with automatic prediction. Yet, before we enter model building, **Exploratory Data Analysis (EDA)** is always essential to get a good grasp of what the data is like. Constant review during the optimization process also helps improve our training strategy and results.

High-dimensional data typically requires special processing techniques to be visualized intuitively. Statistical methods such as **Principle Component Analysis (PCA)** and **t-Distributed Stochastic Neighbor Embedding** (t-SNE) are important skills in reducing the dimension of data for effective visualization.

As a showcase, we will demonstrate the use of various visualization techniques in a workflow involving recognizing handwritten digits using a **Convolutional Neural Network (CNN)**.

One important note is that we do not intend to illustrate all the mathematics and machine learning approaches in detail in this chapter. Our goal is to visualize some of the processes in between. Hopefully, readers will appreciate the importance of exploring processes such as the `loss` function when training a CNN, or visualizing the dimension reduction results with different parameters.

Getting started

Recall the MNIST dataset we briefly touched upon in `Chapter 04`, *Advanced Matplotlib*. It contains 70,000 images of handwritten digits, often used in data mining tutorials as *Machine Learning 101*. We will continue using a similar image dataset of handwritten digits for our project in this chapter.

We are almost certain that you had already heard about the popular keywords—deep learning or machine learning in general—before starting with this course. That's why we are choosing it as our showcase. As detailed concepts in machine learning, such as **hyperparameter tuning** to optimize performance, are beyond the scope of this book, we will not go into them. But we will cover the model training part in a cookbook style. We will focus on how visualization helps our workflow. For those of you interested in the details of machine learning, we recommend exploring further resources that are largely available online.

Visualizing sample images from the dataset

Data cleaning and EDA are indispensable components of data science. Before we begin analyzing our data, it is important to understand some basic properties of what we have input. The dataset we are using comprises standardized images with regular shapes and normalized pixel values. The features are simple, thin lines. Our goal is straightforward as well, to recognize digits from images. Yet, in many cases of real-world practice, the problems can be more complicated; the data we collect is going to be raw and often much more heterogeneous. Before tackling the problem, it is usually worth the time to sample a small amount of input data for inspection. Imagine training a model to recognize Ramen just to get you drooling ;). You will probably take a look at some images to decide what features make a good input sample to exemplify the presence of the bowl. Besides the initial preparatory phase, during model building taking out some of the mislabeled samples to examine may also help us devise strategies for optimization.

In case you wonder where the Ramen idea comes from, a data scientist named Kenji Doi created a model to recognize in which restaurant branch a bowl of Ramen was made. You may read more on the Google Cloud Big Data and Machine Learning Blog post on `https://cloud.google.com/blog/big-data/2018/03/automl-vision-in-action-from-ramen-to-branded-goods`.

Importing the UCI ML handwritten digits dataset

While we will be using the MNIST dataset as in `Chapter 04`, *Advanced Matplotlib* (since we will be demonstrating visualization along with model building in machine learning), we will take a shortcut to speed up the training process. Instead of using the 60,000 images with 28x28 pixels each, we will import another similar dataset of 8x8-pixel images from the scikit-learn package.

This dataset is obtained from the University of California, Irvine Machine Learning Repository, found at `http://archive.ics.uci.edu/ml/datasets/Optical+Recognition+of+Handwritten+Digits`. It is a preprocessed version of images of digits written by 43 people, with 30 and 13 contributing to the training and testing set respectively. The preprocessing method is described in M. D. Garris, J. L. Blue, G. T. Candela, D. L. Dimmick, J. Geist, P. J. Grother, S. A. Janet, and C. L. Wilson, NIST Form-Based Handprint Recognition System, NISTIR 5469, 1994.

The code to import the dataset is as follows:

```
from sklearn.datasets import load_digits
```

To begin, let's store our dataset into a variable. We will call it `digits` and reuse it throughout the chapter:

```
digits = load_digits()
```

Let's see what is loaded by the `load_digits()` function by printing out the variable `digits`:

```
print(type(digits))
print(digits)
```

The type of `digits` is `<class 'sklearn.utils.Bunch'>`, which is specific to loading sample dataset.

As the output for `print(digits)` is somewhat long, we will show its beginning and end in two screenshots:

```
print(digits)

{'data': array([[ 0.,  0.,  5., ...,  0.,  0.,  0.],
       [ 0.,  0.,  0., ..., 10.,  0.,  0.],
       [ 0.,  0.,  0., ..., 16.,  9.,  0.],
       ...,
       [ 0.,  0.,  1., ...,  6.,  0.,  0.],
       [ 0.,  0.,  2., ..., 12.,  0.,  0.],
       [ 0.,  0., 10., ..., 12.,  1.,  0.]]), 'target': array([0, 1, 2, ..., 8,
9, 8]), 'target_names': array([0, 1, 2, 3, 4, 5, 6, 7, 8, 9]), 'images': array
([[[ 0.,  0.,  5., ...,  1.,  0.,  0.],
       [ 0.,  0., 13., ..., 15.,  5.,  0.],
       [ 0.,  3., 15., ..., 11.,  8.,  0.],
       ...,
       [ 0.,  4., 11., ..., 12.,  7.,  0.],
       [ 0.,  2., 14., ..., 12.,  0.,  0.],
       [ 0.,  0.,  6., ...,  0.,  0.,  0.]],

      [[ 0.,  0.,  0., ...,  5.,  0.,  0.],
       [ 0.,  0.,  0., ...,  9.,  0.,  0.],
       [ 0.,  0.,  3., ...,  6.,  0.,  0.],
       ...,
       [ 0.,  0.,  1., ...,  6.,  0.,  0.],
       [ 0.,  0.,  1., ...,  6.,  0.,  0.],
       [ 0.,  0.,  0., ..., 10.,  0.,  0.]],
```

The following screenshot shows the tail of the output:

```
       ...,
       [ 0.,  4., 16., ..., 16.,  6.,  0.],
       [ 0.,  8., 16., ..., 16.,  8.,  0.],
       [ 0.,  1.,  8., ..., 12.,  1.,  0.]]]), 'DESCR': "Optical Recognition of
Handwritten Digits Data Set\n=====================================================
\n\nNotes\n-----\nData Set Characteristics:\n    :Number of Instances: 5620\n
:Number of Attributes: 64\n    :Attribute Information: 8x8 image of integer pixel
s in the range 0..16.\n    :Missing Attribute Values: None\n    :Creator: E. Alpa
ydin (alpaydin '@' boun.edu.tr)\n    :Date: July; 1998\n\nThis is a copy of the t
est set of the UCI ML hand-written digits datasets\nhttp://archive.ics.uci.edu/m
l/datasets/Optical+Recognition+of+Handwritten+Digits\n\nThe data set contains ima
ges of hand-written digits: 10 classes where\neach class refers to a digit.\n\nPr
eprocessing programs made available by NIST were used to extract\nnormalized bitm
aps of handwritten digits from a preprinted form. From a\ntotal of 43 people, 30
contributed to the training set and different 13\nto the test set. 32x32 bitmaps
are divided into nonoverlapping blocks of\n4x4 and the number of on pixels are co
unted in each block. This generates\nan input matrix of 8x8 where each element is
an integer in the range\n0..16. This reduces dimensionality and gives invariance
to small\ndistortions.\n\nFor info on NIST preprocessing routines, see M. D. Garr
is, J. L. Blue, G.\nT. Candela, D. L. Dimmick, J. Geist, P. J. Grother, S. A. Jan
et, and C.\nL. Wilson, NIST Form-Based Handprint Recognition System, NISTIR 546
9,\n1994.\n\nReferences\n----------\n  - C. Kaynak (1995) Methods of Combining Mu
ltiple Classifiers and Their\n    Applications to Handwritten Digit Recognition,
MSc Thesis, Institute of\n    Graduate Studies in Science and Engineering, Bogazi
ci University.\n  - E. Alpaydin, C. Kaynak (1998) Cascading Classifiers, Kybernet
ika.\n  - Ken Tang and Ponnuthurai N. Suganthan and Xi Yao and A. Kai Qin.\n    L
inear dimensionalityreduction using relevance weighted LDA. School of\n    Electr
ical and Electronic Engineering Nanyang Technological University.\n    2005.\n  -
Claudio Gentile. A New Approximate Maximal Margin Classification\n    Algorithm.
NIPS. 2000.\n"}
```

We can see that there are five members within the class `digits`:

- `'data'`: Pixel values flattened into 1D NumPy arrays
- `'target'`: A NumPy array of identity labels of each element in the dataset
- `'target_names'`: A list of unique labels existing in the dataset—integers 0-9 in this case
- `'images'`: Pixel values reshaped into 2D NumPy arrays in the dimension of images
- `'DESCR'`: Description of the dataset

Besides having smaller image dimensions than MNIST, this dataset also has far fewer images. So, how many are there in total? We get the dimensions of a NumPy array in a tuple of dimensions by `nd.shape`, where `nd` is the array. Hence, to inquire about the shape of `digits.image`, we call:

```
print(digits.images.shape)
```

We get `(1797, 8, 8)` as result.

You may wonder why the number is so peculiar. If you have particularly sharp eyes, you might have seen that there are 5,620 instances in the description. In fact, the description is retrieved from the archive web page. The data we have loaded is actually the testing portion of the full dataset. You may also download the plain text equivalent from http://archive.ics.uci.edu/ml/machine-learning-databases/optdigits/optdigits.tes.

If you are interested in getting the full MNIST dataset, scikit-learn also offers an API to fetch it:
```
from sklearn.datasets import fetch_mldata
mnist = fetch_mldata('MNIST original',
data_home=custom_data_home)
```

Plotting sample images

Now that we know more about the background of our input data, let's plot out some sample images.

Extracting one sample each of digits 0-9

To get a feel for what the images look like, we want to extract one image of each digit for inspection. For this, we need to find out where the digits are. We can do so by tracking down the right indices (the data labels) with `digits.target` then we write a few lines of code to call 10 images:

```
indices = []
for i in range(10):
    for j in digits.target:
        if i==j:
            indices.append(j)
            break
print(indices)
```

Interestingly, `[0, 1, 2, 3, 4, 5, 6, 7, 8, 9]` is returned as output, which means the first 10 samples happen to be in numerical order. Is it by chance or is the data ordered? We need to check as the sample distribution can impact our training performance.

Examining the randomness of the dataset

Because showing all 1,797 data points will make the plot too dense for any meaningful interpretation, we will plot the first 200 data points to check:

```
import matplotlib.pyplot as plt
plt.scatter(list(range(200)),digits.target[:200])
plt.show()
```

Here we get a scatter plot of the sample distribution. Not quite random, is it? The 0-9 digits are ordered and repeated three times. We also see a repetition of patterns from around the 125th sample. The structure of the data hints at randomization before our training of machine learning model later. For now, we will first take it as-is and continue with our image inspection:

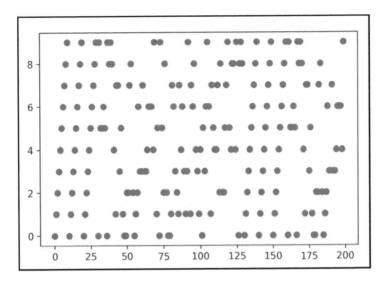

Plotting the 10 digits in subplots

We will align the images in a grid of two rows and five columns. We first set the rectangular canvas by `plt.figure()`. For each sample image of a digit, we define the axes with the `plt.subplot()` function, and then call `imshow()` to show the arrays of color values as images. Recall that the colormap `'gray_r'` plots values in grayscale from white to black with values from zero to maximum. As there is no need for *x* and *y* tick labels to show the scales, we will remove them by passing an empty list to `plt.xticks()` and `plt.yticks()` to remove the clutter. Here is the code snippet to do so:

```
import matplotlib.pyplot as plt

nrows, ncols = 2, 5
plt.figure(figsize=(6,3))

for i in range(ncols * nrows):
    ax = plt.subplot(nrows, ncols, i + 1)
    ax.imshow(digits.images[i], cmap='gray_r')
    plt.xticks([])
    plt.yticks([])
    plt.title(digits.target[i])
```

As you can see from the following figure, the images are a bit blurry to human eyes. But, believe it or not, there are enough details for the algorithm to extract features and differentiate between each digit. We will observe this together along with our workflow:

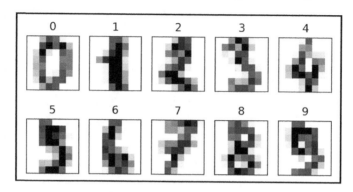

Exploring the data nature by the t-SNE method

After visualizing a few images and glimpsing of how the samples are distributed, we will go deeper into our EDA.

Each pixel comes with an intensity value, which makes 64 variables for each 8x8 image. The human brain is not good at intuitively perceiving dimensions higher than three. For high-dimensional data, we need more effective visual aids.

Dimensionality reduction methods, such as the commonly used PCA and t-SNE, reduce the number of input variables under consideration, while retaining most of the useful information. As a result, the visualization of data becomes more intuitive.

In the following section, we will focus our discussion on the t-SNE method by using the scikit-learn library in Python.

Understanding t-Distributed stochastic neighbor embedding

The t-SNE method was proposed by van der Maaten and Hinton in 2008 in the publication *Visualizing Data using t-SNE*. It is a nonlinear dimension reduction method that aims to effectively visualize high-dimensional data. t-SNE is based on probability distributions with random walk on neighborhood graphs to find the structure within the data. The mathematical details of t-SNE are beyond the scope of this book, and readers are advised to read the paper for more details.

In short, t-SNE is a way to capture non-linear relationships in a high-dimensional data. This is particularly useful when we are trying to extract features from a high-dimensional matrix such as image processing, biological data, and network information. It enables us to reduce high-dimensional data to two or three dimensions; one interesting feature of t-SNE is that it is stochastic, indicating that the final results it shows each time will be different, but still they are all equally correct. Therefore, in order to get the best performance in t-SNE dimension reduction, it is advisable to first perform PCA dimension reduction on the big dataset, and then incorporate the PCA dimensions into t-SNE for subsequent dimension reduction. Thus, you get more consistent and replicable results.

Importing the t-SNE method from scikit-learn

We will implement the t-SNE method by loading the TSNE function from scikit-learn, as follows:

```
from sklearn.manifold import TSNE
```

There are a few hypervariables that the user has to set upon running t-SNE, which include:

- `'init'` : Initialization of embedding
- `'method'`: barnes_hut or exact
- `'perplexity'`: Default 30
- `'n_iter'`: Default 1000
- `'n_components'`: Default 2

Going into the mathematical details of individual hypervariables would be a chapter on its own, but we do have suggestions on what the parameters should be in general. For `init`, it is recommended to use `'pca'` with the reason given before. For method, `barnes_hut` will be faster and gives very similar results if the provided dataset is not highly similar intrinsically. For perplexity, it reflects on the focus in teasing out local and global substructures of the data. `n_iter` indicates the number of iterations that you will run through the algorithm, and `n_components = 2` indicates that the final outcome is a two-dimensional space.

To track the time use for rounds of experiments, we can use the cell magic `%%timeit` in the Jupyter notebook to track the time needed for a cell to run.

Drawing a t-SNE plot for our data

Let's first reorder the data points according to the handwritten numbers:

```
import numpy as np
X = np.vstack([digits.data[digits.target==i]for i in range(10)])
y = np.hstack([digits.target[digits.target==i] for i in range(10)])
```

`y` will become `array([0, 0, 0, ..., 9, 9, 9])`.

Note that the t-SNE transformation can take minutes to compute on a regular laptop, and the `tSNE` command can be simply run as follows. We will first try running t-SNE with `250` iterations:

```
#Here we run tSNE with 250 iterations and time it
%%timeit
tsne_iter_250 =
TSNE(init='pca',method='exact',n_components=2,n_iter=250).fit_transform(X)
```

Let's draw a scatter plot to see how the data cluster:

```
#We import the pandas and matplotlib libraries
import pandas as pd
import matplotlib
matplotlib.style.use('seaborn')
#Here we plot the tSNE results in a reduced two-dimensional space
df = pd.DataFrame(tsne_iter_250)
plt.scatter(df[0],df[1],c=y,cmap=matplotlib.cm.get_cmap('tab10'))
plt.show()
```

We can see that the clusters are not well separated at 250 iterations:

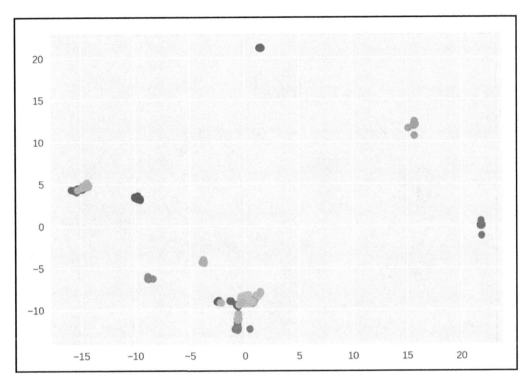

Let's now try running with 2000 iterations:

```
#Here we run tSNE for 2000 iteractions
tsne_iter_2000 =
TSNE(init='pca',method='exact',n_components=2,n_iter=2000).fit_transform(X)
#Here we plot the figure
df2 = pd.DataFrame(tsne_iter_2000)
plt.scatter(df2[0],df2[1],c=y,cmap=matplotlib.cm.get_cmap('tab10'))
plt.show()
```

As seen from the following screenshot, the samples appear as 10 distinct blots of clusters. By running 2000 iterations, we have obtained far more satisfying results:

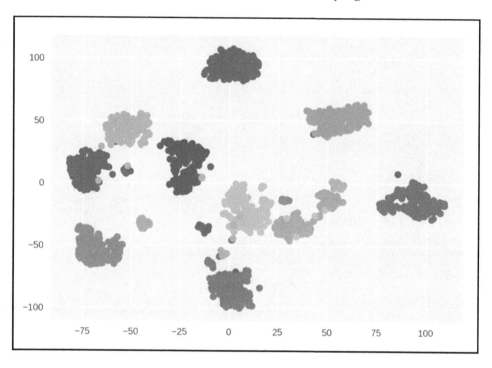

Creating a CNN to recognize digits

In the following section, we will use Keras. Keras is a Python library for neural networks and provides a high-level interface to TensorFlow libraries. We do not intend to give a complete tutorial on Keras or CNN, but we want to show how we can use Matplotlib to visualize the loss function, accuracy, and outliers of the results.

Readers who are not familiar with machine learning should be able to go through the logic of the remaining chapter and hopefully understand why visualizing the loss function, accuracy, and outliers of the results is important in fine-tuning the CNN model.

Here is a snippet of code for the CNN; the most important part is the evaluation section after this!

```
# Import sklearn models for preprocessing input data
from sklearn.model_selection import train_test_split
```

```
from sklearn.preprocessing import LabelBinarizer

# Import the necessary Keras libraries
from keras.models import Sequential
from keras.layers import Dense, Dropout, Flatten
from keras.layers.convolutional import Convolution2D, MaxPooling2D
from keras import backend as K
from keras.callbacks import History

# Randomize and split data into training dataset with right format to feed
to Keras
lb = LabelBinarizer()
X = np.expand_dims(digits.images.T, axis=0).T
y = lb.fit_transform(digits.target)
X_train, X_test, y_train, y_test = train_test_split(X, y, test_size=0.2,
random_state=100)

# Start a Keras sequential model
model = Sequential()

# Set input format shape as (batch, height, width, channels)
K.set_image_data_format('channels_last') # inputs with shape (batch,
height, width, channels)

model.add(Convolution2D(filters=4,kernel_size=(3,3),padding='same',input_sh
ape=(8,8,1),activation='relu'))
model.add(MaxPooling2D(pool_size=(2,2)))

# Drop out 5% of training data in each batch
model.add(Flatten())
model.add(Dropout(0.05))
model.add(Dense(10, activation= 'softmax'))

# Set variable 'history' to store callbacks to track the validation loss
history = History()

# Compile the model
model.compile(loss='categorical_crossentropy', optimizer='adam',
metrics=['accuracy'])

# Fit the model and save the callbacks of validation loss and accuracy to
'history'
model.fit(X_train,y_train, epochs=100, batch_size= 128,
callbacks=[history])
```

Evaluating prediction results with visualizations

We have specified the callbacks that store the loss and accuracy information for each epoch to be saved as the variable `history`. We can retrieve this data from the dictionary `history.history`. Let's check out the dictionary `keys`:

```
print(history.history.keys())
```

This will output `dict_keys(['loss', 'acc'])`.

Next, we will plot out the `loss` function and `accuracy` along epochs in line graphs:

```
import pandas as pd
import matplotlib
matplotlib.style.use('seaborn')

# Here plots the loss function graph along Epochs
pd.DataFrame(history.history['loss']).plot()
plt.legend([])
plt.xlabel('Epoch')
plt.ylabel('Loss')
plt.title('Validation loss across 100
epochs',fontsize=20,fontweight='bold')
plt.show()

# Here plots the percentage of accuracy along Epochs
pd.DataFrame(history.history['acc']).plot()
plt.legend([])
plt.xlabel('Epoch')
plt.ylabel('Accuracy')
plt.title('Accuracy loss across 100 epochs',fontsize=20,fontweight='bold')
plt.show()
```

Upon training, we can say the `loss` function is decreasing, accompanied by an increase in accuracy, which is something we are delighted to see. Here is the first graph showing the `loss` function:

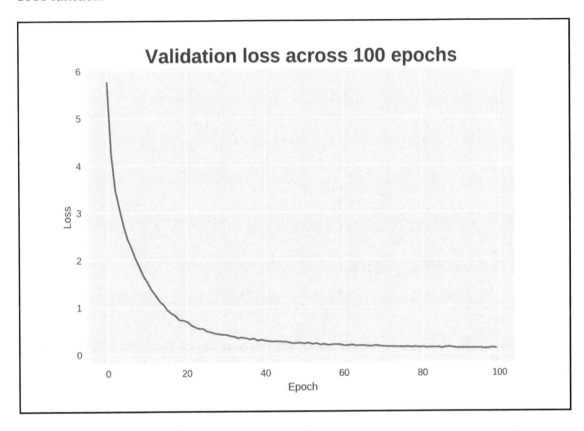

The next graph shows the changes in **Accuracy** across **Epoch**:

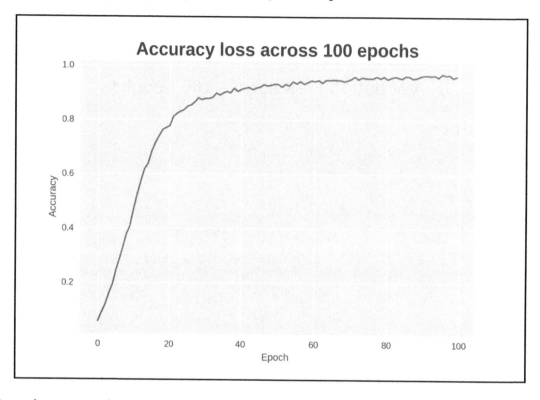

From these screenshots, we can observe a general trend for decreasing loss and increasing accuracy with each epoch along the training process, with alternating ups and downs. We can observe whether the final accuracy or the learning rate is desirable and optimize the model where necessary.

Examining the prediction performance for each digit

We first revert the labels from one-hot format back to lists of integers:

```
y_test1 = model.predict(X_test)
y_test1 = lb.fit_transform(np.round(y_test1))
y_test1 = np.argmax(y_test1, axis=1)
y_test = np.argmax(y_test, axis=1)
```

We will extract the indices of mislabeled images, and use them to retrieve the corresponding true and predicted labels:

```
import numpy as np
mislabeled_indices = np.arange(len(y_test))[y_test!=y_test1]
true_labels = np.asarray([y_test[i] for i in mislabeled_indices])
predicted_labels = np.asarray([y_test1[i] for i in mislabeled_indices])
print(mislabeled_indices)
print(true_labels)
print(predicted_labels)
```

The output is as follows, with NumPy arrays of the indices, true and predicted labels of the array of mislabeled images:

```
[  1   8  56  97 117 186 188 192 198 202 230 260 291 294 323 335 337]
[9 7 8 2 4 4 2 4 8 9 6 9 7 6 8 8 1]
[3 9 5 0 9 1 1 9 1 3 0 3 8 8 1 3 2]
```

Let's count how many samples are mislabeled for each digit. We will store the counts into a list:

```
mislabeled_digit_counts = [len(true_labels[true_labels==i]) for i in
range(10)]
```

Now, we will plot a bar chart of the ratio of mislabeled samples for each digit:

```
# Calculate the ratio of mislabeled samples
total_digit_counts = [len(y_test[y_test==i]) for i in range(10)]
mislabeled_ratio = [mislabeled_digit_counts[i]/total_digit_counts[i] for i
in range(10)]

pd.DataFrame(mislabeled_ratio).plot(kind='bar')
plt.xticks(rotation=0)
plt.xlabel('Digit')
plt.ylabel('Mislabeled ratio')
plt.legend([])
plt.show()
```

This code creates a bar chart showing the ratio of each digit mislabeled by our model:

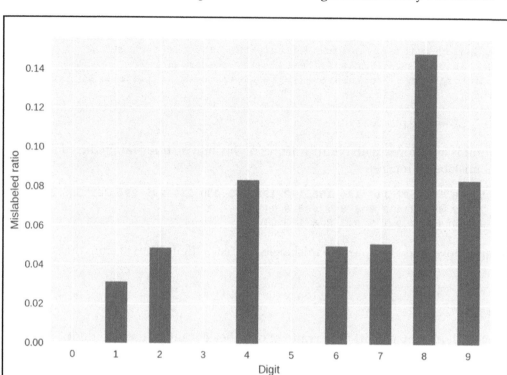

From the preceding figure, we see that the digit 8 is the most easily mis-recognized digit by our model. Let's find out why.

Extracting falsely predicted images

Similar to what we did at the beginning of this chapter, we will draw the digit images out. This time, we pick out the mislabeled ones because they are the ones we're concerned about. We will again pick 10 images and put them in a grid of subplots. We write the true label in green at the bottom as `xlabel` and the false label predicted in `red` as the `title` at the top for each image in a subplot:

```
import matplotlib.pyplot as plt
nrows, ncols = 2, 5
plt.figure(figsize=(6,3))
for i in range(ncols * nrows):
    j = mislabeled_indices[i]
```

```
    ax = plt.subplot(nrows, ncols, i + 1)
    ax.imshow(X_test[j].reshape(8,8),cmap='gray_r')
    plt.xticks([])
    plt.yticks([])
    plt.title(y_test1[j],color='red')
    plt.xlabel(y_test[j],color='green')
plt.show()
```

Let's see how the images look. Does the handwriting look more like the true or falsely predicted label to you?

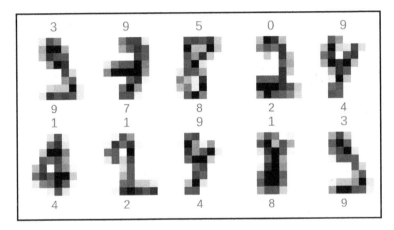

We can observe that, for some images, it is quite difficult to identify the true label at the 8x8 resolution even with the naked eye, such as the number **4** in the middle of the bottom row. However, the leftmost number **4** on the same row should be legible enough for humans to recognize. From here, we can estimate the maximum possible improvement in accuracy by additional training and optimizing the model. This will guide our decision on whether it is worth while to expend further effort to improve our model, or what kind of training data to get or generate next to obtain better results.

Meanwhile, notice that the training and testing datasets generally contain samples from different distributions. It is left for an exercise for you to repeat the process by downloading the actual training dataset from UCI ML, using the larger MNIST dataset (by downloading it via Keras, or even scraping or creating your own).

Summary

Congratulations! You have now completed this chapter as well as the whole book. In this chapter, we integrated various data visualization techniques along with an analytic project workflow, from the initial inspection and exploratory analysis of data, to model building and evaluation. Give yourself a huge round of applause, and get ready to leap forward into the journey of data science!

Index

Made in the USA
Columbia, SC
05 February 2019